MANY PEOPLE, ONE NATION

I

Magnet and Filings

Amerigo Vespucci, shown in this woodcut, deemed the newly discovered lands to be not a part of Asia, but a New World. America was thus named for him, rather than for Columbus. *(Rare Book Room, New York Public Library)*

The American Heritage Library

MANY PEOPLE, ONE NATION

By Bernard A. Weisberger

Houghton Mifflin Company • Boston • 1987

Library of Congress Cataloging-in-Publication Data

Weisberger, Bernard A., date.
  Many people, one nation.

  (The American Heritage library)
  Includes index.
  1. Immigrants—United States—History. 2. Ethnology—
United States. 3. United States—Emigration and immigra-
tion. 4. United States—Civilization. 5. United States—
Ethnic relations. I. Title. II. Series.
E184.A1W354   1987   973′.04   87-3776
ISBN 0-8281-1200-2

Printed in the United States of America

S 10 9 8 7 6 5 4 3 2 1

Western Star by Stephen Vincent Benét. Holt, Rinehart and
Winston, Inc. Copyright © 1943 by Rosemary Carr Benét.
The excerpt is reprinted by permission of Brandt & Brandt.

Table of Conten

merica," says the title of a poem by Archibald Mac-Leish, "was promises." It has been so in every generation of the national history. "America" is imprecise as a descriptive geographical term, standing neither for a particular country nor for a clearly delimited land mass. But it perfectly defines a state of expectation. It has appeared in sundry forms over the centuries and to many pairs of eyes: as a free farm in the dark interior wilderness to a German or Norwegian peasant; as a place without official restrictions on mobility to a Jew in a czarist village; as so many dollars a day for steady work in the mills, on the railroad, or in the garment center to a hungry Irish, Greek, or Puerto Rican immigrant; as the theater of fulfillment of God's word to a Scottish Presbyterian. It is more than milk and honey; it is, in F. Scott Fitzgerald's words, "the green light, the orgiastic future that year by year recedes before us." The green light winked to Columbus to come over the sea's edge, where others feared to go. It has been signaling ever since. It has brought the scattered American people together on their portion of a continent to act out their common destiny.

Tradition has created a dividing moment in time when the word for a new American changes, and associations change with it. Those who came to the New World before 1776 were "colonists," and later arrivals "immigrants." But, as Marcus Lee Hansen, a distinguished twentieth-century historian of immigration, wrote, "in every practical respect the settlers, old and new, were much the same. The Puritan who landed in Massachusetts Bay with his blunderbuss and Bible was an immigrant. The peasant from Eastern Europe who twenty years ago passed through Ellis Island with a pack upon his back was a colonist. They were all colonists, all immigrants. And all were engaged in providing America with ancestors."

The heart of the matter is that with one tragic exception—kidnapped Africans—the history of American settlement from the beginning was the record of people in search of castles in air. The seekers were always led on by tales, both true and misleading, of extraordinary New World gifts for the taking. These allurements sounded with special magic in the ears of Europeans beset by hardship, frustration, discontent, or the rages of ambition. They came westward to their Promised Land. Always they

7

found it occupied by earlier arrivals. And always they and these predecessor Americans have then learned, in one way or another, to live and die in one another's presence and awareness, both groups being transformed in the process. That is the theme on which all else is variation. There is no special period of "immigration," somehow separate from the basic weave of American history.

One begins at the beginning, then, with the early image of America presented in travelers' tales that found their way into currency in a variety of ways—printed books, ballads and broadsides, dockside yarns, and word-of-mouth repetition of solemn reports made by sea captains to interested royal officials and directors of trading companies. Some were fundamentally factual. Some (possibly the majority) were Indian fantasies, further distorted in the imaginations of explorers often half mad with exhaustion and fever. Some were the calculated exaggerations of advertisement, set in motion by colonial promoters looking for settlers. But some were true. The astonishing thing is that in the long run the truth in the best reports outweighed the lies in the worst.

Companions of the Norse adventurer Leif Ericson, who came ashore somewhere on the New England seacoast around A.D. 1000, probably deserve the honor of being the first Europeans to catalogue America's enticements. A saga quotes them as describing a half-frozen Scandinavian's paradise with "bigger salmon than they had seen before . . . conditions . . . so favorable that the cattle would need no fodder there in the wintertime . . . no winter frosts; the grass only withered a little, and day and night were more evenly divided there than in Greenland or Iceland." But the Norsemen did not stay long enough to fertilize their discovery, and America sank into obscurity for another five hundred years. When it reemerged in Western Europe's consciousness, Renaissance man was in full swagger, alive with carnal appetites and avid for gold.

Treasure madness inflames the reports of America that appear from 1500 onward—which is not surprising when the original goal of exploration, a shortcut to the wealth of the Orient, is considered. Gold hunger was fed and increased alike by the reality of what Cortés and Pizarro took in plunder from the Aztecs in Mexico and the Incas in Peru. Thereafter, Spanish (as well as English, French, and Dutch) visions built glittering mountains

8

of spoil whenever Indians gesticulated vaguely toward the horizon. There were broken communications; the Indian gift for metaphor, taken literally by interpreters (and probably the Indian discovery that troublesome whites might move out of a village if told of wealth farther onward), led to wild chases after golden geese. Some Indians paid dearly for the white man's disappointment. Many were tortured and slain for their inability to produce hoards that existed only in the European captains' fancies.

A Spanish history of the "Indies," read with eager curiosity (and later paraphrased) by the English entrepreneur Sir Walter Raleigh, told of the court splendors of a supposed ancestor of the "emperor of Guiana." "All the vessels of his house, table and kitchin," it was said, were of gold and silver. The royal "wardrobe" included "hollow statues of gold which seemed giants, and the figures in proportion and bignesse of all the beasts, birds, trees, and hearbes, that the earth bringeth foorth." Beside this New World pleasure dome there was an imperial garden "which had all kinde of garden-hearbs, flowers and trees of golde and silver," as if the copper-colored sovereign, Guaynacapa, were some Midas who had run his fingers over the vegetation while on a refreshing stroll through his palace grounds. Alvar Núñez Cabeza de Vaca was shipwrecked in the Gulf of Mexico in 1528, taken prisoner by Indians, and led by them on an incredible odyssey throughout the Southwest. When he finally reached Spanish territory in 1536, he spoke excitedly of the "South Sea" (the Pacific) as being only a short journey to the west of what is now Texas; and, he continued, the Indians swore to him that on the blue coasts of that sea were "pearls and great riches, and the best and all the most opulent countries are near there."

Fired in part by such promises, Francisco Vásquez de Coronado led an expedition out from Mexico in 1540, searching in present-day Kansas and eastern Colorado for seven cities of gold—the empire of wishful legend, called Cibola. Seas of grass and herds of buffalo were awesome sights, but the jeweled palaces of the quest turned out to be a few scattered tepees. Still, when Coronado became discouraged, he could listen to the reassurances of a captured Pawnee known as "the Turk," who had met white men before. The Turk told him of some genuine wonders—"a river in the level country which was two leagues wide" (the Platte) in which there were "fishes big as horses" (catfish, perhaps, not as big as horses but impressive and some of them man-sized)—and also of things that Shakespeare might have found usable in *Antony and Cleopatra*: ". . . large numbers of big canoes with more than twenty rowers on a side, . . . they carried sails, . . . their lords sat on the poop under awnings, and on the prow they had a great golden eagle. He said also that the lord of that country took his afternoon nap under a great tree on which were hung a number of little gold bells, which put him to sleep as they swung in the air. He said also that everyone had their ordinary dishes of wrought plate, and the jugs and bowls were made of gold."

So America appears in its earliest depiction a golden land. (Almost four hundred years after de Vaca and Coronado, Yiddish-speaking Eastern European immigrants were to use that precise phrase, *ah goldeneh Land,* to describe their adopted United States, unaware of the dissonance of the images that they and the conquistadors invoked—or the similarities.) By the end of the sixteenth and the beginning of the seventeenth century, however, new ideas were beginning to emerge. Even the visionary Spanish temperament divined by then that the virgin continent had greater prospects than just those measurable in fine ounces of bullion. In 1598, for example, Juan de Oñate undertook a colonizing venture in New Mexico. Expectedly, he reported to the viceroy of New Spain on "the great wealth which the mines have begun to reveal" and on the possible traffic, still dreamed of then, with ports that might be established on the American shore of the South Sea. But he also noted "the wealth of the wool and hides of buffalo" and, "judging from the general nature of the land, the certainty of wines and oils." Buffalo hides, wine, and oil came closer to what the Southwest could actually deliver than the far-from-golden Seven Cities of Cibola.

Foundations of the United States would in a few years begin to be built on the eastern coast as well, by the English in Virginia. Elizabethan merchants and ministers were second to none in their lively concern for treasure, but the real success of Great Britain as a colonizing power was eventually to rest in its ability to sustain permanent, large-scale, self-supporting "plantations" in North America. To that end, farm-hunting settlers were indispensable; and to stir their interest, there were accounts of Virginia like that from the pen of young George Percy, one of 120 men who came in three ships to "plant" Jamestown (now Jamestown Island), in May 1607.

Percy and his companions were not plowmen. They were interested in mines, trade, and possibly the cultivation of such exotic products as silkworms. But the lushness of the New World seems to have distracted them somewhat and was transmitted in undiminished force in Percy's descriptions of the first springtime weeks of the first white Virginians.

At an initial stop in the West Indies, the founders saw fowl flying "over our heads as thick as drops of hail." They sailed on northward to enter "Chesipioc" Bay and on April 26, 1607, landed amidst "fair meadows and goodly tall trees, with such fresh waters running through the woods as I was almost ravished at the first sight thereof." More than just fresh waters ran through the woods, however, and that night a party of Indians crept into Percy's encampment and wounded two men with their arrows before the newcomers drove them off. A short march brought Percy's men to a spot where "good store of mussels" lay on the ground "as thick as stones." Onward they went, passing over ground strewn not only with wild flowers but with "fine and beautiful strawberries, four times bigger and better than ours in England."

As they progressed up the James River, they passed "pleasant springs which issued from the mountains" and "the goodliest cornfields . . . ever were seen in any country." Abundance rioted in an unexploited Virginia Maytime. Everyone marveled at "store of vines in bigness of a man's thigh, running up to the tops of the trees in great abundance" and at "many squirrels, conies, blackbirds with crimson wings," and birds with crimson, blue, green, and yellow feathers. There were flowers "as though it had been in any garden or orchard in England," and fragrance from cedar and cypress and other trees, out of which issued "sweet gum like to balsam." Percy's lyricism was, of course, retrospective, and may not have reflected the sentiments of his men, burdened and hot with their armor, weapons, and coarse linen clothing. "We kept on our way in this paradise," he was to write, having perhaps dreamed of going naked in it and being sustained, like Adam in the first Paradise, without toil. After all, there was fruit in abundance, "great plenty of fish," and the meadows would furnish excellent pasture for cattle. There was also "great store of deer . . . bears, foxes, otters, beavers, musk-rats, and wild beasts unknown." (The fur trade would corrupt Paradise soon enough; Europe was turning to fur garments as tokens of affluence, and there was wealth to be trapped in the woods and rivers—especially in Canada, where, just a year after Percy's excursion in Eden, Samuel de Champlain was to found the city of Quebec.)

America in the seventeenth century was not merely the mines of Montezuma; it was fat and fertile soil. "A remarkably beautiful country," wrote Governor Johan Printz of New Sweden (Delaware) in 1643; and the beauty he extolled was like that of an Old Testament bride, not only pleasing to the eye but with a teeming womb. At about the same time, David De Vries wrote a similar description, calculated to bring fresh settlers to the Dutch West India Company's colony of New Netherland, which he described as a fat Hollander's Utopia: maize stalks "as high as a man can reach, and higher," together with pumpkins, water-melons, hazelnuts, chestnuts, wild grapes, elk, hares, foxes, wildcats, squirrels, minks, otters, polecats, bears, and "many kinds of fur-bearing animals which I cannot name or think of." The soil, De Vries rhapsodized, enabled "our Netherlanders" to raise good wheat, rye, barley, oats, and peas and "brew as good beer here as in our Fatherland." Forty-pound turkeys struggled through the air and fell, exhausted by their own weight, into the hands of pursuers. According to De Vries, fifteen-pound geese flew by in the thousands and were decimated for holiday tables. Meadow hens, herons, turtledoves, and the ubiquitous black-birds darkened the sky; the waters virtually foamed with runs of pike, perch, roach, haddock, and herring, while flounder and sole carpeted the mud bottoms. The very crabs on the beach, said De Vries, had claws "the color of the flag of our Prince [of the Netherlands], orange, white, and blue, so that [they] show sufficiently that we ought to people the country, and that it belongs to us."

Thus the changing portraiture of a promised land: in one century, emperors in feathered robes drinking from golden vessels; in another, fish and grain choking smokehouses and barns, pel-try piling higher and higher at the trading posts. Whatever the terms of the description, America was the opportune moment waiting to be seized. So the first settlers, the first immigrants,

This allegory by a French artist captures the prevailing myth of the New World as the Promised Land. The native, pictured as a Noble Savage with light skin and rosy cheeks, strikes an almost classical pose. Adorned with gold, surrounded by game, and exuding an air of tranquil pride, he lives in a world of lush abundance and open space, a paradise whose promise would draw Europe's oppressed and impoverished. *(Library of Congress)*

English, Dutch, French, Swedish, Spanish, came to seize it—and to confront trials beyond belief. For the gold, the grain, and the fur, it turned out, had to be struggled for after all. The settlers braced for and endured the arrow that flew by noonday and the pestilence that walked in darkness. They outlasted the heartbreak of slain wives, husbands, and children, the torments of thirst, insects, heat, and hunger, and the frustrations of false leads, crops burned out by Indian attack, packs of furs lost as canoes overturned in white water. Later generations of newcomers would know other, different trials. But always hope could only be deferred, not destroyed. America was goodness to come. The stouthearted hung on, for the prize was bound to be there somewhere. That faith would be a dominant note in all of American history.

The faith was sustained for the newcomers not only by the promises ahead but by the horrors left behind, across the Atlantic. Actually, the seventeenth-century impetus to colonization was part of a general tidal shifting of human groups, running deep into a biological past when nomadic cavemen roved over the continents, tied to the migration patterns of the game they pursued. But Europe, from 1600 onward, offered special motives for swarming. The century that began in that year saw England almost constantly writhing in civil disturbance, and those convulsions underlay the great exodus to the colonies responsible for determining the basically English pattern of American life.

The Continent, too, was in ferment. In a sense, the seventeenth century saw the emergence of those institutions that, in the late twentieth, are characteristic of the modern world: centralized and wholly sovereign nation-states; capitalism; individualism, secularism, and heroic grandeur in the arts; the triumphant growth of modern science with its relentless reduction of divine mysteries to a precalculated interplay of forces and effects; and European mastery of the rest of the world—America being one of the first outposts of modern imperialism to be created and one of the first to escape. For the historians of the United States, the seventeenth century is when momentum becomes measurable. Prior to 1600 few settlements were made within modern national boundaries—a Spanish salient in New Mexico and toehold in Florida; two abortive French Huguenot and English ventures in the Carolinas—these were all.

It was the post-Renaissance era that, in a sense, created "America," and that was only one of its achievements. The dynastic splendor of emergent monarchs like France's Louis XIV were reflected in Baroque palaces. The wealth of the merchant princes who founded such mighty trading companies as England's Hamburg Company (1611) or the Netherlands' Dutch East India Company (1602) was embodied in their homes and costumes and captured in expensive portraiture. It was an age of intellectual as well as terrestrial conquest, with a dazzling constellation of great names—Spinoza, Leibniz, Locke, Descartes, and Hobbes in philosophy; Rubens, Rembrandt, Velásquez in painting; Cervantes, Molière, and Milton in literature; Newton, Harvey, Kepler, and Galileo in science.

Yet there was a macabre reverse to the medallion. Royal splendor was attained at the expense of the clergy, the nobility, and the provincial towns. A crop of younger sons and hard-taxed merchants sought to replenish family fortunes under alien skies. And as usual, the pressure fell hardest on the sweated commoners at the bottom of the social ladder. Posterity may gape admiringly at the swank of an era when a single nobleman, the Duke of Lerma, could meet his future bride with 34,000 ducats' worth of jewels on his person and another 72,000 in value carried along behind him. But such opulence was made possible only by levying the most burdensome of taxes on land, crops, houses, and livestock. In 1648 a French writer registered this complaint: "The country has been ruined, the peasants reduced to sleeping on straw, after their furniture has been sold to pay taxes which they cannot raise—to maintain the luxury of Paris, millions of innocent souls are forced to live on bread, bran and oats, and cannot hope for any protection except their impotence. [That is to say, their incapacity to yield up more than the absolute limit.] These unfortunates do not possess anything but their souls, and them only because they cannot be auctioned off."

What was more, warfare, both civil and international, erupted epidemically from massive dislocations of power. France, Spain, England, and the Netherlands were almost continually in combat. The century opened with the Dutch still struggling to free themselves of Spain and ended on the threshold of a general European conflict over the succession to the Spanish throne. The Catalans and Portuguese revolted against Madrid in 1640, the latter successfully. Another revolt, in 1647 in Naples, was put down by the Spanish. Between 1648 and 1653 a civil war in which religious overtones were mingled, known as the War of the Fronde, seethed in France. The Austrians intrigued over and intervened in the German states to the north and the Italian principalities to the south, while to the east they fended off the Turks, who were still pounding at the gates of Vienna as late as 1683.

Seventeenth-century wars did not wreak destruction on a modern scale. The relatively primitive weapons of the time were too crude for that. But the bands of soldiers who marched back and forth over the countryside routinely commandeered wagons, animals, and foodstuffs, set houses and barns afire, tortured and murdered men suspected of hiding either money or goods, committed rape at will, and left starvation and disease to mop up behind them. The brutality of such warfare was magnified when religious zeal kindled the fighting. In the twentieth century, governments arouse men and women to accept the unthinkable by proclaiming rigorous political ideologies. Warring princes sought the same end three centuries earlier by enlisting God on their side. Sometimes the heretics were merely expelled. Sometimes they were massacred, becoming "slaughtered saints" in the vocabulary of their fellow worshipers.

The worst intertwining of religious and dynastic warfare was in the states of Central Europe. From 1618 to 1648 the Thirty Years' War raged, involving not only German principalities but present-day Scandinavia, Bohemia, and Poland. It ended with each prince in the miscellaneous aggregation of political splinters free to determine religious practice in his realm—and with gutted communities. In Sweden, as a later historian was to put it, "hundreds of once-fertile fields lay for years uncultivated and covered with weeds." In Württemberg the number of men capable of bearing arms dropped from 65,400 in 1623 to 14,800 in 1652, and 318 castles as well as 36,100 urban dwellings were destroyed. In a county in Thuringia, half the families disappeared. In another in Brandenburg, only 630 peasants of an estimated 1,900 remained at the war's end. In Munich the number of weavers was halved.

"These days are days of shaking . . . ," observed an English preacher in 1643, "and this shaking is universal. . . ." But even when the earth did not shake under horses' hoofs and the lumbering wheels of cannon, the age was brutal enough. As one historian of the Thirty Years' War, Cicely V. Wedgwood, has noted:

Bloodshed, rape, robbery, torture and famine were less revolting to a people whose ordinary life was encompassed by them in milder forms. Robbery with violence was common enough in peace-time, torture was inflicted at most criminal trials, horrible and prolonged executions were performed before great audiences; plague and famine effected their repeated and indiscriminate devastations.

The outlook even of the educated was harsh. Underneath a veneer of courtesy, manners were primitive; drunkenness and cruelty were common in all classes, judges were more often severe than just, civil authority more often brutal than effective, and charity came limping far behind the needs of the people. Discomfort was too natural to provoke comment; winter's cold and summer's heat found European man lamentably unprepared, his houses too damp and draughty for the one, too airless for the other. Prince and beggar were alike inured to the stink of decaying offal in the streets, of foul drainage about the houses, to the sight of carrion birds picking over public refuse dumps or rotting bodies swinging on the gibbets. On the road from Dresden to Prague a traveller counted "above seven score gallowses and wheels, where thieves were hanged, some fresh and some half rotten, and the carcases of murderers broken limb after limb on the wheels."

The twentieth-century reader must weigh against this *Totentanz* background New World images of dusky parents flinging golden bracelets to their children for trinkets, of skies and rivers swarming with food, of clear air, smiling suns, nodding flowers. In plague-stricken cities, amid offal-choked alleys, and on burned-out farms, in chapels where the Word was preached furtively, with sentinels at the door, Europeans received such tidings as they would rain in the desert.

A theme was thus established. The New World was hope and promise. The Old, though it had the energy, wealth, courage, and yearning to unfold the New, was haunted by a bitter past from which the restless wished to fly. That, too, was a theme that would last.

The first "immigrants," like those who followed, found guardians of the Promised Land waiting for them, but with this difference: later newcomers would hold themselves—and be treated as—inferior to established "Americans" and would struggle to replace their "alien" ways with new patterns; but the first

This plan of New Amsterdam, a miniature
Dutch trading city located on Manhattan Island,
was drawn in 1661. Its meticulous design called
for neatly laid out streets, houses constructed in
almost regimented lines, and a walled-in fort at
the foot of the island for defense against the
Indians. The wide street that runs parallel to the
Hudson River was called the Broad Way, the
forerunner of the avenue that bisects Manhattan
today. *(Rare Book Room, New York Public
Library)*

European settlers found the possessors of the land to be "savages"and immediately set out to impose civilization upon them. Yet in the beginning the transaction worked the other way. The fresh arrivals *did* learn from their untutored hosts. Willynilly, they were dependent on them. The Indians were the first and indispensable reception committee in America. No history of the American people—a title to which, after all, the Indians have the most legitimate claim—can omit the red men and women's role. They held the keys to survival. They knew the land as worshipers know divinity and lovers know each other, taking what they needed without exhausting the supply. They knew where the furs were (and the gold if there *was* gold); they knew how to track game and take fish with tools made of bone, sinew, bark, twig, and vine. They knew what strange flesh was fit to eat, which berries poisoned—and which ones cured.

They were also, as it happened, a test of the embryonic American conscience. That all but a few whites failed the moral examination was tragic but almost inevitable, given the circumstances. The assumptions of European culture virtually dictated that redskin and paleface should be enemies, only temporarily and intermittently allied for trade and profit. Newcomers from the world of the Escorial, the Armada, the Papacy, Parliament, the money markets of Amsterdam, and the gardens of Versailles were bound to regard simple people as much less than equals. (They made no distinction among nonwhites, in fact, tending to regard Indians, Chinese, Africans, and Malays as uniformly backward. For the most part they did not even make useful evaluations among classes and tribes within African or Asian kingdoms, confounding everything and everybody in tableaux of primitivism. This destructive ignorance has not yet worked its full mischief.)

Simplicity was non-European and therefore suspect. Columbus touchingly reported that the Indians of Bahama swam out to his ships with parrots, brightly colored threads, and other gifts. These were the offerings of children, the Spaniards thought, and in return gave childish things: "red caps and glass beads to put round their necks." Later, the faith in Indian innocence was shaken (though it kept reemerging in noble-savage stereotypes), and what replaced it was an enduring caricature of the redskins as naked men, paint-smeared, cunning, fickle, cruel, lazy, destructive—children turned into monsters.

These first Americans, however, were not a single entity but many peoples. Some—perhaps most—were far from the Stone Age barbarism of popular belief. The Indians were themselves migrants to the New World (over a prehistoric land bridge from Asia) and had developed for centuries before they were discovered. The sophistication of the Mexican and Andean Indian empires is well known, but the North American tribesmen were not far behind them. Those who dwelt in the eastern United States (from the Atlantic to the Mississippi, from the Great Lakes and the St. Lawrence to the Carolinas) clustered in hundreds of tribal units whose names, still on the map, are the first and most mellifluous Indian contribution to American life—the Penobscots, Passamaquoddys, Narragansets, and Mohegans of New England; the Delawares, Oneidas, Eries, Pamlicos, Powhatans, Nanticokes, and Susquehannocks of the Middle Atlantic region; the Potawatomis, Ojibwas (Chippewas), Ottawas, Menominees, Sauks and Foxes, Winnebagos, Kaskaskias, and Peorias of the Midwest. The rustle of wilderness is in the syllables, even though they represent only partly successful struggles of Europeans to pronounce the names as the Indians spoke them.

"Primitives" these first Americans were, but the term is relative. About four thousand years before Columbus, the people of the Laurentian Culture, situated in eastern New York, the St. Lawrence Valley, and New England, carved animal bone into gouges, adzes, and harpoons and ground slate points and knives. About a thousand years later the Old Copper Culture in the Great Lakes region made birchbark containers (possibly including canoes) and domesticated the dog. Mound-building cultures such as the Adena placed their dead reverently on hills, surrounded by ornaments of stone, copper, and shell.

Even before Europe hung suspended between the collapse of Roman Imperial order and the emergence of feudalism, in the so-called Dark Ages, some North American Indians had developed what anthropologists call the Hopewellian Culture. They lived in villages, worshiped in ceremonial centers, cultivated corn, squash, beans, and tobacco, and adorned their dead with objects brought to them through a sophisticated trade network: grizzly-bear teeth and obsidian from the Rockies, curly conch shells from the Gulf Coast, mica from the Appalachians, copper and lead from the Great Lakes region and the upper Mississippi Valley. Their beaded jewelry, their tools, and their pottery were decorated with floral and animal figures in intricate interwoven designs. Led by priests bedecked in gorgeous beads and shells, they danced to the music of rattles, pipes, and drums. Their crafts people were true specialists, and hereditary ranks were attached to different specialties.

Not long before the whites came, the intricacies of some Indian clan relationships matched the quarterings and bloodlines of European nobility. Ritual and magic in Indian religious life was not altogether unlike the Latin chants of the Roman priesthood, and the exorcisms of medicine men were not so far from the incantatory curses upon imps and devils that Europeans pronounced during the witchcraft crazes that still swept over Europe long after 1492. (America's own Salem witch trials took place in the 1690s.) The use of shells both as money (wampum) and, strung together on belts, as a device for conveying messages and ideas indicated a growing social sophistication. Elaborate political arrangements were embodied in such a structure as the Iroquois League—a delicately balanced confederation that linked clans, families, and tribes in an unbreakable network, vested much authority in women, and rested decision-making powers in representative councils. These policies argue a developing Indian life far removed from howling animalism.

The Europeans swung to extremes in judging Indian life. At first they called the chiefs they met by names both familiar and curious—princes, emperors, caciques, and werowances. Then they changed, and professed to see mere posturing wildlife in any Indians who claimed authority. In either case the end was the same. The thrust of white culture, with its demand for furs and land, and its trade bait of iron tools and pots, blankets, firearms, and the fatal whisky, broke down the self-sufficiency of the Indian world. The sad course of near-extermination ran its melancholy length.

The Indian's development was overwhelmed in the tragedy of invasion, but the record stands: the Indian was the initial American. It is not necessary to be sentimental. As Bernard DeVoto said, the romantic image of "the squash blossom in the hair" becomes a mask of falsehood in itself, disguising realities of torture and filth. But neither should it be overlooked that the Indians, functionally tied to the continent, eased the white Europeans' first perilous entry into it. They taught them the use of snowshoes, moccasins, canoes, toboggans, and other artifacts (and arts) of wilderness survival. In possessing them, these new arrivals became themselves American. In 1893 Frederick Jackson Turner announced a theory of national history that asserted that American democracy was born in the leveling atmosphere of the frontier. He pointed out that one of the first signs of adaptation to the new environment on a European's part was to strip off the garments of civilization, with their class and social connotations, and wear the undifferentiated skin garments of the Indian (without the decorations, he failed to add, by which some Indians announced their own ranks and titles).

The Indian did more than communicate forest skills, however. As Alvin M. Josephy, Jr., has noted, Indians also introduced almost half the crops that make up the world's total food supply today. Corn and potatoes were their gift, and more than eighty other domesticated plants, according to one historian, "including peanuts, squashes, peppers, tomatoes, pumpkins, pineapples, avocados, cacao [and] chicle . . . and at least fifty-nine drugs as well, including coca (for cocaine and novocaine), curare (a muscle relaxant), cinchona bark (the source of quinine), cascara sagrada (a laxative), datura (a pain reliever), and ephedra (a nasal remedy)."

Finally, of course, there was what Jacques Cartier described in the year 1535 as "a certain kind of herb, whereof in summer they make great provision for all the year . . . first they cause it to be dried in the sun . . . they make powder of it and then put it in one of the ends of the said cornet or pipe and lay in a coal of fire upon it, at the other end suck so long, that they fill their bodies full of smoke, till that it comes out of their mouth and nostrils. . . ."

It can even be argued that the Indian contribution does not end there, but that the New World gold, which swelled the Spanish treasury for two centuries and more after Cortés, was an involuntary Indian gift to European development. But the point need not be labored. The Indian past is vital tissue in the social organism known as the American people. If nothing else bore witness, the evidence could be found in a language enriched by such words as succotash, tobacco, chipmunk, squash, skunk, toboggan, opossum, moose, mackinaw, hickory, pecan, raccoon, cougar, woodchuck, hominy, and hundreds of others. The Indians gave. They set a model of welcome to "immigrants" not always

22

emulated later. George Percy related that in 1607 some Indians "murmured at our planting in the country, whereupon this Werowance [Powhatan] made answer again very wisely of a savage. Why should you be offended with them as long as they hurt you not, nor take anything away by force? They take but a little waste ground, which doth you nor any of us any good."

Centuries afterward, other, white "old stock" Americans could well have used such generous attitudes instead of the restrictive ones they actually displayed. It is a pity that Powhatan's estimate of white needs was altogether too ingenuous.

The story began, then, with interaction among the continent's new and old inhabitants—the Indian "garrison" and the colonizing immigrants. The process that developed in the course of settlement was twofold: it Americanized the settler and Europeanized the land. Its results are still visible and can be seen with special clarity across the vista of more than three centuries if we examine two European settlements almost a continent apart. They are those of the Spaniards in New Mexico and the Dutch in New Netherland, now New York State. Each stamped the design and texture of an Old World way of life on an American region and a pattern on the lives of the succeeding generations who would dwell there.

The Spaniards came first. Today there is a growing Hispanic strain among the American people. It is felt in the impact of minority groups—the Cubans of Florida, the Puerto Ricans of New York, and the Mexicans of Texas and southern California. Latin modes and accents work their way into national habits through the tortuous channels of ethnic and racial participation in politics, sports, entertainment—and in the statistics of the city ghetto. But it is a useful perspective device to see how Spaniards shaped a piece of America to their liking almost four centuries ago, when they were masters of the situation.

As the sixteenth century waned, Hispanic explorers were moving northward from Mexico, hoping to find new sources of wealth. The momentum of Spanish expansion in the East was running down. The little post at St. Augustine, Florida, remained static—an undeveloped hand reaching feebly for the fur trade, merely an appendage to Madrid's Caribbean holdings. But two thousand miles westward there was action. In 1581 Fray Agustín Rodríguez, two other friars, nine soldiers, and about sixteen Indian servants traveled the barren way from Santa Barbara, in Chihuahua, to the Rio Grande. They then continued up that river to the pueblo country around Socorro, modern New Mexico. As the expedition made its way back to Mexico to report the findings, one of the fathers was killed by Indians. Still, the news that got through inspired plans to make the Pueblo Indians colonials. These were not wretched nomads but tribes who had "well-built houses of four and five stories, with corridors and rooms twenty-four feet long and thirteen feet wide, white-washed and painted," with "very good plazas, and . . . streets along which they pass in good order." To colonialize such well-organized natives was a practical and laudable goal.

In 1598 Juan de Oñate's expedition moved into New Mexico, attempting to reenact the great scenario of Cortés and freely killing Indians in the process. But Oñate looked in vain for gold and jewels amid the cactus and the sharp mountain peaks. There were only hungry Hopis and Zuñis. On subsequent quests he probed for a route to the South Sea, and finally found it in the impassable Colorado. It was a dispiriting finale to the treasure hunts. In 1606 a royal edict to the viceroy in Mexico banned further explorations for bonanzas—they had become too costly in lost expeditions, starving men, massacre, torture, and restlessness among the Indians. Spain would now try the less glamorous road to empire, that of plantation. But Oñate's expedition was not wasted. It set up a permanent Spanish lodgment in New Mexico. In 1610, with appropriate ceremony, the capital of the colony was established at Santa Fe.

The Spanish busied themselves with impressing their culture upon New Mexico. They sent their cattle, sheep, horses, and goats to graze in the haciendas—the great unfenced areas granted to them—and the pattern of American ranching was born. They learned to irrigate the desert as is done to this day and to plant life-giving wheat, oats, barley, chilies, onions, peas, beans, and melons. The Indians taught them such tricks as fishing with long nets of yucca fiber. Under Governors Peralta, Eulate, de Rosas, Mendizabel, and Bertugo, the New Mexican colonists of the 1600s prospered and pined for home. The soldiers amused themselves with traditional garrison occupations. Now and then, after finding some outlying settlements in ruins, with corpses bearing evidence of horrible torture, they enjoyed a lively foray into the countryside against marauding Apaches. There would

Peter Stuyvesant was the last Dutch governor
on Manhattan, ruling New Amsterdam for
some seventeen years. The testy and belligerent
Stuyvesant was so violently disliked that in
1664, when an English fleet captured the city,
his own officials eagerly surrendered, leaving
the one-legged governor unable to defend his
domain. *(The New-York Historical Society)*

be battles. Some Indians would hang, as salutary examples. Then back to town, the girls, the wine. They took squaws, sired children, waited for promotion and better duty, went on horseback hunting trips in mountains like those they had known at home, and behaved themselves very much as American soldiers in exactly the same circumstances and locality would do two and a half centuries later.

The friars, meantime, took on the work of converting the Indians. There was an essential similarity among the fifty churches they built in New Mexico before 1625. The chief of the mission was "architect, engineer, carpenter, mason, foreman, building master to apprentices who themselves were masters of a building style," as Paul Horgan has noted in his magnificent book *Great River.* The Spaniard adopted the obvious virtues of the native Indian buildings—simple, rectangular, earth-hugging, and made of such common materials as clay and rock. He undertook the manufacture of adobes, earthen bricks as heavy as sixty pounds each, out of which rose the walls of storehouses and chapels. Scarce wood, for doorframes and beams to support roofs of branches and packed earth, was laboriously hewn and shaped by axes, adzes, saws, chisels, augers, and planes. Locks, nails, hinges, ironware of any sort, was rare and costly. The rich grillwork of Moorish-Iberian churches had to yield to something simpler. What came of it all was an American Southwestern style: stuccoed exterior, low and straight lines, and whitewashed walls (often decorated with Indian symbols), sometimes with attached walled cemeteries that filled with pink reflections and blue shadows in the hot afternoons.

The Spanish friars brought silver chalices, brocaded vestments, and golden crucifixes and candlesticks. The Indians joined to these riches the passion of their own faith (which did not scorn to break through the barriers of consciousness by the use of drugs, sleeplessness, and self-inflicted pain) and the intricate arts that expressed it. The converts needed no instruction in reverence for the spirit-informing life. They had only to transform their native mysticism into loyalty to tangible figures of Saviour, saints, and Madonna. They learned to sing hymns, to pray, even to participate in the Mass, and to hold their new beliefs in a grip that survived the vicissitudes of many years of battle between white warriors and red. And they taught the fathers themselves new lessons in evangelism.

26

By 1679 a valley culture of corn and oil, adobe and silver, Christ and earthen gods, was emerging. Santa Fe was laid out then much as it is today. Mountains on the north overlooked a plaza surrounded on three sides by houses. And on the northern side of that plaza stood a Palace of the Governors, long, low, and containing offices, chapel, living quarters, prison, fortress, and stables—the entire apparatus of rule. Cultivated fields stretched out on all sides. To the west were barracks. On the east was the church of St. Francis; to the south stood the chapel of St. Michael.

It was Indian in one sense; in another, Spanish—but not quite either of them. It was ultimately American. It was also vulnerable. In 1680 an Indian, Popé, outraged by the Spaniards, led an insurrection that swept them from the valley, leaving behind pillars of smoke and circling buzzards.

The Spaniards came back after a time, profoundly to affect the Southwest anew with their style—so appropriate to the stark land—of iron pride, of harshness, of self-tormenting loyalty to honor and other abstractions, of worship, and of deep dignity. The bloodshed, heartbreak, tortured acolytes, and flayed settlers were simply part of the price of migration.

The Dutch, nearly two thousand miles away, were different. (Dutch and Spanish differences, in fact, had bathed the Netherlands in blood for years when the Low Countries were a province of Spain.) The Dutch in North America were a colonial power for a relatively brief period of some fifty years. Yet they showed the variety inherent in the process of transplanting European modes of life to America. There were, the record shows, many ways of populating and characterizing a new land.

The spirit of seventeenth-century Holland was relentlessly dominated by the quest for profit. (That in itself may have been a legacy to later American life, but it came from other sources as well as from the Dutch.) In their pursuit of guilders, the Netherlanders looked unperturbed on the entire catalogue of explorers' hazards: tempests, pirates, disease, and massacre. Their energy was frightening. Throughout the century, from Hudson's Bay to Cape Horn, they were daring and busy. Despite almost constant wars at home, they set up posts in India in 1616, on Java in 1619, in Brazil in 1623, on Ceylon in 1638, and on the Cape of Good Hope in 1652. Yet their accounts of these deeds were never touched with the eager pleasure of a John Smith savoring the wonders of Virginia, or with the half-greedy, half-ecstatic aura surrounding some Spaniard's vision of gold piled in heaps around the feet of men in cuirasses. Step by step they built an empire, but never celebrated the feat in verse or paint. The empire was an investment. Art and philosophy and science—Dutch intellectual strong points—were not concerned with investments.

In creating New Netherland in 1621, however (basing their claim on Henry Hudson's 1609 explorations of the river named for him), the Dutch called on (or rather submitted to) the services of two men who stand at the head of a long line of American promoters: William Usselinx and Peter Minuit. Usselinx, the father of the Dutch West India Company, was an Antwerper who seethed with the commercial aspirations of Northern Europe and with hostility toward the Spaniards who still occupied Belgium. With a successful career in business behind him, he got the ear of Netherlands officials and besought them to form a West India trading company to furnish a Caribbean base from which to harry the Spanish. In 1621 the States-General did charter such a corporation, but by then Usselinx was disgruntled over insufficient Dutch appreciation of his genius. He traveled to several northern cities, singing commercial rhapsodies. One of his auditors was King Gustavus Adolphus of Sweden, who was so impressed that he asked Usselinx to create a Swedish company to trade with Asia, Africa, America, and "Magellanica." Usselinx' glowing dream of ships full of pepper, ivory, camphor, jewels, silks, coffee, tea, gold, and spices unloading (at an immense profit) in the Baltic never was realized. Capital for the company did not materialize from the Swedes, hard pressed by war. But his blandishments probably helped to stir up Swedish interest in a small fur-trading colony that they planted on the lower Delaware River in 1638.

Meanwhile, Usselinx' brainchild, the Dutch West India Company, had set up posts at Fort Orange (Albany) in 1624, and in New Amsterdam (New York City) the next year. A year later, the original governor was replaced by Peter Minuit. Minuit, too, is an early example of Americanization. Like Samuel de Champlain or John Smith, he was a European whose own country filled no special place in his heart and who could therefore become totally attached to the promise of the New World. For seven years Minuit sweated to make New Netherland a profitable fur-trading and farming center, but he managed to accomplish little more than to enter American history books as the purchaser of Manhattan Island for an estimated twenty-four dollars' worth of trinkets.

Replaced, he returned home but could not remain downcast for long while any American prospects were in the offing. He had bought some land in the Delaware Valley, along with Samuel Blommaert, a copper and brass merchant from Amsterdam, always interested in colonial markets for his wares. After an unsuccessful attempt to get the Dutch to plant a new settlement on the Delaware, he traveled to Sweden, exercised his persuasive talents, and was hired to start *Sweden's* colony. After getting it organized, he started back to Europe for fresh recruiting and fund raising. Stopping in the West Indian harbor of St. Christopher, he went aboard a Rotterdam vessel lying at anchor for a visit. A storm arose, blew the ship out to sea, and he disappeared forever. Thus did Minuit leave his bones in the New World and his spirit to generations of land speculators and salesmen of railroad, oil, and mining stocks who came after him in American history.

Technically the Dutch settlements in the future United States were a failure. They were established on territory claimed by England at a time when Holland was not in a strong position to contest matters. The Dutch spread themselves too thin, and in arrangements bound to provoke disputes that they would lose. Wouter Van Twiller, the governor of New Netherland who took over in 1633, established a fort at Hartford just before the English founded a number of settlements in the Connecticut Valley. Willem Kieft, who ruled from 1637 to 1647, provoked cruel and needless battles with the Indians. Peter Stuyvesant, the last Dutch governor on Manhattan, who held the position from 1647 to 1664, rashly squandered funds in overthrowing and capturing the Swedish settlement on the Delaware in 1655, though the Netherlanders themselves could not afford to take it over. All the governors quarreled bitterly with their own people in New Amsterdam—Stuyvesant so violently that when an English fleet finally appeared in the Narrows in 1664, claiming the city for the Duke of York, the splenetic one-legged governor was deserted by his own burghers. They insisted on—and obtained—surrender, when he wanted to fight.

Despite the political weaknesses of the Dutch, they set an impress on the life of Americans yet unborn. Of all the early immigrants, they made their style felt most vigorously. Although the initial settlement around Fort Orange remained tiny, a new policy in 1629 allowed colonizers to carve out great estates, known as patroonships, from choice lands along the Hudson, provided they brought (or sent) numbers of emigrants to populate them. Under that dispensation, the Dutch began to fulfill the Dutch West India Company's charter obligation of "the peopling of those fruitful and unsettled parts." The 270-odd settlers of 1628 grew in number until, by the time of New Amsterdam's capture, much of the Hudson Valley was Dutch in appearance. From as far north as Rensselaerswyck (near the present-day Troy), sloops loaded the produce of good Dutch farmsteads—beef, pork, butter, cheese, turnips, and carrots—and carried them to Manhattan markets.

The Hollanders pushed out into New Jersey, Long Island, and Connecticut like twentieth-century New York commuters. Michael Paauw bought land in New Jersey and Staten Island that he named Pavonia. It is not as well known today as Breuckelen (transformed into Brooklyn) or the Bronx (named for the tract of land once owned by Jonas Bronck) or Yonkers, an Anglicization of the Dutch *Jonker,* an estate holder. Dutch names persist everywhere in New York State (and New Jersey) like baggy-trousered, wide-hatted ghosts of Dutchmen, now gone, who once looked with satisfaction on their American lands.

New Amsterdam itself became a model Dutch town. Gabled houses turned narrow fronts to the street. Tradesmen went home, entered through brick-faced doorways and ascended to cozy rooms where, under tiled roofs, windows with tiny panes illuminated polished delftware. Tulips danced in back yards. Housewives proudly set out their *crullers* and *cookies. Scows* plied the rivers. On snowy winter days, one got around by *sleigh,* and when December arrived, children excitedly dreamed of the visit of *Santa Claus.*

But New Amsterdam was more than simply a Dutch exclave in America. The Hollanders' tolerance of dissent spread from old to New Amsterdam. True, the Dutch Reformed Church was the official, and Calvinistic, propagator of the colony's religious outlook. And the profits of the settlement were meant for Dutch bank accounts and no others. Yet from the start, New

Netherland recruited from all nationalities, perhaps because the hearth-loving Dutch themselves emigrated reluctantly. The first boatload of settlers shipped to New Amsterdam were French-speaking Walloons. French Huguenots, Danes, Italians, and Spaniards soon were included in the populace. The first Jews in the area of the future United States came from Brazil to New Amsterdam in 1654 and were allowed the free exercise of their faith. (They were, however, put under certain civic restrictions; they could not, for example, serve in the town's defense forces, a deprivation of which they soon complained.)

Observers were quick to comment on the polyglot nature of the settlement. It has been claimed, perhaps improbably, that as early as 1629 some fourteen languages were spoken in the streets of the tiny village. In 1643 the French missionary Isaac Jogues reported hearing eighteen. By the time of the settlement's fall to the English, it was a lively port city. Indians, sailors, and African slaves (the latter brought in for domestic service by the imperturbable and busy Dutch "blackbirders") jostled one another in the lanes; and despite the Dutch Reformed Church's strictures, the town was known for the presence, in Peter Stuyvesant's words, of many "rumshops and houses where nothing can be had but beer and tobacco."

In 1809 the young Washington Irving wrote his playful *History of New York . . . by Diedrich Knickerbocker*. This portrait of the outpost as a community of fat, guzzling, pipe-smoking Dutchmen is a comic distortion, but it suggests the kind of easygoing, cosmopolitan spirit that made New Amsterdam unique among early American towns, and a worthy predecessor of an internationally oriented New York City over three hundred years later.

Thus, when the century of the Baroque ended, a beginning had been made in North America. Uprooted Europeans had adventured into the void of unmapped lands, looking for the realization of their various hopes. They had planted themselves and their national customs at several points in the unknown. They had outlasted grim challenges—and clung on. European flags flew over their settlements. European laws, institutions, and customs structured their lives, their beliefs, their tongues, and their decorative arts. Yet these transplanted Europeans were already demonstrating what it was like to become Americans.

II

The English Imprint

By claiming all English discoveries in America as sovereign, King James I extorted a share of the profits made in Jamestown, Virginia, his namesake colony. *(National Portrait Gallery, London)*

As the nineteenth century entered its last years, some euphoric Americans liked nothing better than to expound on the dazzling future of what they called "the Anglo-Saxon peoples." It was a time when the spirit of Darwin hovered above the intellectual deeps, and when certain patriots marched to the cadence of a social theory that pressed biology into the service of chauvinism. The outlines of this theory were simple: the degree of a nation's success was determined by the supposed racial inheritance of its populace. The world's two most "successful" nations—those that most happily combined self-government, wealth, command of technology—were Great Britain and the United States. It was clear that this was no mere accident but a scientifically comprehensible and inevitable development. Bloodlines were the basis. England was America's "mother country." It was England's law, letters, and social patterns that had been transplanted to the colonies that became a nation. And England itself had been settled, in dark antiquity, by invading Saxons and Danes and other tribes of vaguely Teutonic origin, who mingled with the native Britons and later received strains of Norman blood to produce the final Anglo-Saxon amalgam.

It was a little murky. At one point a leading American proponent of the Anglo-Saxon gospel, the Congregational clergyman Josiah Strong, referred to the chosen race as one of "the branches of the great German family," and only a few paragraphs farther on was counting one hundred and twenty million Anglo-Saxons by using "the term somewhat broadly to include all English-speaking peoples." (It was wavering of this sort that led the Irish-American humorist Finley Peter Dunne to have his fictional bartender-philosopher, Mr. Dooley, remark that "an Anglo-Saxon . . . is a German that's forgot who was his parents.") But there was no ambiguity in the record of Anglo-Saxon triumph or in the promise of future Anglo-Saxon glory, especially for that larger portion of the postulated race that lived in the United States. "Here, also," wrote the Reverend Mr. Strong, "has been evolved the form of government consistent with the largest possible civil liberty. Furthermore, it is significant that the marked characteristics of this race are being here emphasized most." Those characteristics included "money-making power," plus "an instinct or genius for colonizing," as well as "intense and persistent energy," perhaps "the most forceful and tremendous energy in the world." It was clear to Strong that "God, with infinite wisdom and skill," was "training the Anglo-Saxon race" for an apotheosis that, as representative of "the largest liberty, the purest Christianity, the highest civilization," and other attributes, would spread itself over the earth. Earlier in the same work, he had quoted Darwin to the effect that there was "much truth in the belief that the wonderful progress of the United States, as well as the character of the people, are the results of natural selection." In this way Strong neatly enlisted both religion *and* evolution in the service of his prophecies, making them almost irresistible to the popular mind of his day.

This glorification of the Anglo-American connection made for a striking discontinuity in the narrative of American settlement. It assumed, in effect, two classes of migrants. Those settlers who did not speak English were truly strangers in the land, but those from Britain's fast-anchored isle were unconscious agents of destiny. Born to become Americans, they merely crossed the Atlantic to reach a foreordained home. It was in this version of history that the distinction between "colonists" and "immigrants" took shape, and it is significant that the line was drawn at a turn-of-the-century hour of anxiety among "old stock" Americans over the rising tide of Southern and Eastern European newcomers to the United States.

The trouble with the Anglo-Saxon formulation was that it retroactively cheated thousands of seventeenth-century English out of their humanity. It made historical puppets of suffering people who had lived out the pains of their conscious choices like all other self-uprooted wanderers. The basic mold of the thirteen American colonies *was* English, certainly. The great initial plantings were England's and its imprint on the land was the most distinctive, the most visible, the most determinative of things to come. But the English settlers who dared the Atlantic crossing and the added perils of the wilderness were themselves products of a Western European civilization. Their migration came at a particular moment in their own national history. The cultural and institutional baggage they brought was not packed by divine, invisible hands but by the immediate circumstances of their time: their birth, their nurture, their problems of livelihood and family rearing, no less than abstract desires for political and religious liberty.

They too were immigrants, fleeing to find opportunity abroad. They changed the land they found and were in turn changed by it, like millions who followed them. In the words of Stephen Vincent Benét:

> . . . those that came were resolved to be Englishmen,
> Gone to the world's end, but English every one,
> And they ate the white corn-kernels, parched in the sun,
> And they knew it not, but they'd not be English again.

The "immigrant experience," in short, was also an English experience. And it began as it did for all the footloose of the earth, with trouble in the national family.

It was under the Tudors that England first sent explorers to the New World—the Cabots, Hawkins, Frobisher, Drake, Gilbert, and the rest. But the actual planting of English settlements was accomplished almost entirely under the reign of the star-crossed Stuarts. James I came to the throne in 1603. Four years later Jamestown was planted, the seed from which Virginia grew. In 1681 Pennsylvania joined the family of English colonies in North America—the last save for latecoming Georgia (1732). In 1688, Parliament engineered the ouster of James II (a grandson of James I) from the kingship and the country itself, ending once and for all the Stuart claim to rule by divine right instead of by national consent through a representative body.

Between the accession of James I and the deposition of James II, the pressures that sent Englishmen swarming abroad built up relentlessly. James I, a burlesque of intelligent royalty, spent his reign in clumsy destruction of an equilibrium carefully created by Elizabeth and her ministers. True, her era had known its conflicts. The Church of England, for example, though firmly established, did not command the loyalties of great Catholic families on the one hand, or, on the other, of the Puritans who hoped to purge it of "Romish idolatry." Country squires and local officials were jealous of the powers of the nobility gathered at court in London. Lords and Commons quarreled with each other in Parliament, and both quarreled with the throne. In particular, the merchants and middling landowners represented in the Commons were eager for the right to discuss and criticize the royal ambitions and techniques for raising large revenues through taxes.

But the great queen had astutely balanced these antiphonal zealotries and united the nation in support of her own person and the English achievements in war and trade. James started with this reservoir of goodwill and with the asset of being King of Scotland as well, thus terminating the traditional border conflicts. But he soon squandered these resources. He bestowed on favored friends monopolies in certain trades and industries, thus alienating important segments of the mercantile and artisan classes. He denied Puritan clergymen official status within the Church of England and further outraged them by enforcing rigid adherence to some of its detested ritual prescriptions. He rode hard on the law courts, traditional moderators of royal power, insisting that his prerogative enabled him to overrule their decisions. When, in 1616, James removed the Lord Chief Justice, Edward Coke, for insisting that the king's edicts were valid only when they added force to—and did not replace—existing law, sober Englishmen began to fear that they had to choose between two certainties that should have been harmonious, the royal will *and* the law's majesty. Finally, to compound his woes, James lavished wealth and power on certain associates like the Duke of Buckingham, and raised money through such ignoble expedients as the sale of offices and honors. When Parliament objected to such steps, the Stuart wrath thundered over Westminster. At the close of one session, James with his own hands seized the Parliamentary journal in which a "protestation" against his acts had been recorded and tore out the offending pages.

James died in 1625, but his son Charles I continued his disastrous policies. After many clashes with Parliament, he dissolved that body and tried to rule without it. But this course compelled him to resort to ever more abrasive forced loans and grants in order to sustain the cost of wars that never seemed to come to satisfactory resolutions—with the Spanish, the French, the Irish, even the Scots. Finally, after resistance to royal exactions had led to innumerable arrests, protests, angry sermons, and state trials, open fighting broke out between Parliamentary forces and those loyal to Charles. That was in 1642. By 1646 the "New Model Army," led by the fiercely Puritan country gentleman Oliver Cromwell, had defeated the king. Parliament was not of one mind about what to do with its victory; its own ranks included every shade of religious and political opinion from high-church royalists whose quarrel was with Charles, not the monarchy, to ultrademocratic groups like the Levellers, who held that "every man that is to live under a government ought first by his own consent to put himself under that government." But Charles's obstinacy and Cromwell's seizure of power finally combined to produce the unthinkable: regicide. On January 30, 1649, before a great multitude at Whitehall, Charles I of England and Scotland was beheaded.

For eleven years, England was kingless. At first the "rump" Parliament ruled the Commonwealth, as it was by then called, but the real power lay with the army, and as almost always happens, that army's commander became dictator. Cromwell, established as Lord Protector, held together the country's discordant elements until his death in 1658. Then in 1660, recognizing that only around the magnetic symbols of royalty could the particles of society cohere, Parliament welcomed back the exiled older son of the murdered sovereign, as King Charles II.

For almost a full generation thereafter, England groped toward its eighteenth-century system—a Parliament with ultimate power, and a king whose great influence and prestige made him more than a puppet but less than an absolute ruler. The road was difficult, and was made more so by the second Charles, whose attachment to the Catholic Louis XIV of France aroused deep fears of a royal drive against Protestantism at home. When Charles died without legitimate issue in 1685 and was succeeded by his brother, James II, matters came quickly to a head. James was openly Catholic and refused to renounce his allegiance to the Pope, in spite of a Test Act requiring such renunciation of all officials. The nation had to choose between a legitimate Catholic monarch (and the possibility of endlessly continuing religious strife) and a Protestant ruler who was far down in the line of succession but acceptable to the great majority of Englishmen. Parliament made its decision and offered joint possession of the throne to Mary, Protestant daughter of James II, and to her Dutch husband, William of Orange, provided they could oust James II from the country. The thing was done, and the "Glorious Revolution" of 1688 was entered into the history books. A series of acts provided that Parliament must remain free from royal dissolution or harassment, that the judiciary must remain independent, and the religious dissenters must be granted freedom of worship.

Even in such sketchy outline, the course of British history in the seventeenth century demonstrates its solid impact on the future of America. Especially after 1688, colonial legislatures considered themselves to be little parliaments, and the royal governors to be surrogate kings—properly kept in line on approved Whig principles. (The Whigs were the pro-Parliamentary party in English politics.) Moreover, the leaders of the American resistance to Britain after 1760 long insisted that they were claiming no more than the rights of English citizens, established by the Glorious Revolution. Only the obduracy of London forced them finally to change that tune and demand the liberties of Americans. American constitutional democracy owes much of its form to the fact of English transatlantic migration at the very time that English democracy was assuming its own patterns. To that extent the Anglo-Saxon mythmakers were correct, except that they insisted on calling a series of historically connected events a fulfillment of divine or scientific law. They also overlooked the many contributions of European thinkers to English libertarian theory.

But there is more. The riven England of Puritanism, Parliamentary obstinacy, civil war, and regicide was the political matrix of America, and its anguish furnished the final cutting edge that severed thousands of its people from their home roots. The war itself was short. But for decades before and after, the land was in flux. The center of authority shifted erratically. A landholder, a clergyman, a scholar, a member of a guild, borough, or corporation, an "adventurer" (as an investor was called) went through years of uncertainty. Sometimes he was a friend to the party in power, and sometimes a quick turn of the wheel threatened him with expropriation, arrest, even death. The patronage of a nobleman could be a risk as well as an asset, depending on what side he took and who won. Even the justices, those guardians of stability, danced a tortured quickstep between conscience and fear of reprisal. With chronic misgivings about the future, no wonder that some men were tempted by the prospects of secure estates and freedom from harassment across what seemed an infinity of ocean.

Moreover, these conflicts took place against a background of

The Great Plague of London, which struck in
1664–65, claimed 70,000 lives from a total population of 460,000. Although it killed indiscrim-
inately, the Black Death seemed to turn more
cruelly on the city's poor, heaping loss and grief
onto their lot of starvation and hopelessness.
Escape from indigence and illness increasingly
took the form of emigration to the New World.
(Pepipian Library, Cambridge)

economic revolution. Late in the sixteenth century, landowners began to react to rising prices for raw wool by "enclosing" their estates. This meant turning plowed fields into sheep meadows and driving off tenants, who thereupon became part of a mass of "idlers" flocking to the cities. There they could not be absorbed into the labor force readily because of guild restrictions, and there thousands of them languished as burdens on public charity, as potential criminals, and as the prey of the press gangs that rounded up unwilling soldiers and sailors for the wars. The conviction that the country suffered from overpopulation was inescapable, and the cry of a country gentleman, John Winthrop, in 1629 was widely echoed: ". . . this lande growes wearye of her Inhabitantes, so as man which is the most pretious of all the Creatures is here more vile and base, then the earthe they treade upon: so as children, neighbours, and freindes (especially if they be poore) are rated the greatest burdens, which if things were right, would be the cheifest earthly blessings."

In an earlier, more pungent image, one clergyman had preached that "the people, blessed be God, do swarm in the land, as young bees in a hive. . . . The mightier, like old strong bees, thrust the weaker . . . out of their hives." The beehive was constantly shaken by depressions. From the opening of the century until 1603 times were hard, and again in the periods from 1619 to 1624, from 1629 to 1631, and from 1637 to 1640. In 1622 a preacher (and preachers were the most frequent public commentators on the state of the realm in that age of no journals and many pulpits) noted that the almshouses were full, that multitudes got their livelihood by begging, and what was most poignant, that "neither come these straits upon men, alwaies through intemperancy, ill husbandry, indiscretion, etc., as some thinke, but even the most wise, sober and discreet men goe often to the wall, when they have done their best. . . ."

Huddled into the cities, the poor were helpless before the plagues that swept devastatingly into their slums and then undiscriminatingly went on to lay low the proud and wealthy as well. Between 1603 and 1605 the provincial cities of Norwich, York, and Bristol each suffered about 3,000 deaths by plague (presumably the dread bubonic plague), exclusive of those who died of smallpox and other scourges. London suffered incredibly from the plague's visitations. Almost 35,000 succumbed in 1603 and a like number in 1625. In the latter year, 5,205 Londoners and another 4,000 in the suburbs of Westminster and Stepney died in a single week.

Imperiled by pestilence and starvation, many of the able-bodied men among the poor might have looked to impressment as an opportunity at least to eat and to be clothed. But they were disabused of any such notions by the facts of life as reported in the words of veterans. Typhus, scurvy, and other diseases incident to filth and improper diet ravaged the ranks as badly as enemy bullets. Of eight thousand troops sent on one expedition (to the Île de Ré in 1627), only three thousand sickly men returned. Small wonder that even "rogues" went to ghastly lengths to avoid service. In one group of impressed men, one hanged himself, another threw himself into the Thames, a third cut off the fingers of one hand, and another "put out his owne eyes with salt."

For thousands, then, life was as Thomas Hobbes had said it was for early man in his *Leviathan*, published in 1651: "nasty, brutish, and short." And those who endured it on such terms found nothing to encourage any fantasies of escape through a change in their social status. English ranks and degrees were firmly set. Each class had its particular style, and while each might have its discontents, none expected much alteration in its condition within England itself. The great landed families had little outward need for a change in their condition. They had built themselves stately mansions, where they maintained a tradition of hospitality which required that no guest of a true aristocrat should leave until the spirit moved him. Travelers accompanied by large retinues might linger for months, eating, drinking, womanizing, gaming, gossiping, and pelting over privately owned hill and dale in pursuit of the flying deer. The host himself sometimes escaped these obligations only by going on a journey of his own, and this of course required not only a coach and outriders but also suitable expensive clothing for himself and in particular for his wife and daughters. It was all very picturesque—and its cost was staggering. (A suit for an exquisite blue-blood might cost $1,000 in modern money.) Debt gnawed all too often at the most richly endowed landowner. His position rested, in many cases, on nothing more solid than title, style, manners, and insolvency. And nothing short of a spectacular piece of luck or royal preferment seemed likely to improve the situation. In a striking and fateful line of historical development, this pattern was to be faithfully and consciously emulated—down to and including the debts—two centuries later by plantation owners in Virginia and elsewhere in the southern United States.

The country gentleman (one to whom the Heralds' College, in view of his property, had granted the right to "gentility") lived in a fashion less socially constrained than that of his titled neighbors and superiors. His home was full of the evidences of an active outdoor life, and he could, if so inclined, take a hand in the haying or harvesting of his own fields and orchards without loss of status. At worst, he might be a boorish Squire Western; at best, an Allworthy, dutifully serving as judge, social-service administrator, lay church leader, and moral pacesetter for the community. (Although *Tom Jones* was written in the mid-eighteenth century, country ways had not then changed much from Stuart times.) But the country squire, too, might be hard pressed. His religious views might bring him into trouble, and any combination of high taxes and falling agricultural prices could score his face with anxiety lines. If at such times he did not think of emigrating, his sons might well do so.

For the younger sons of country gentlemen and noblemen alike, who saw the estates of their fathers pass intact to their eldest brothers, the future presented the problem of finding socially acceptable careers. The choices might not yet have narrowed to the traditional handful—the army, the navy, the church, the bar—since in the seventeenth century none of these had quite become a profession in the modern sense. But in fact a landless young man who was neither scholarly, pious, nor martially minded was a prime candidate for a hazard of new fortunes by emigration.

Farther down the social scale, the yeoman might also try to enhance the value of his lands or the prospects of his children by taking fliers in New World ventures such as fishing and trading companies. If, in his emerging middle-class consciousness, America was not a haven for himself or his kin, he had no objection to investing his money there.

Fixed in the social mold below the landowning classes were the rural laborers, whose conditions became increasingly desperate as the era of the civil war wore on and were still a scandal as late as the nineteenth century. They lived in cottages not much different in quality, if one observer in the 1600s can be credited,

from the cabins of enslaved American blacks—"no other win-
dowes than to serve to let out the smoke, no other hangings,
than what the spider affords, no other bedsteads, or table-bords,
than the bare earth, no other bedding than plaine strawe, . . . no
other Couches, or Chaires, or stooles, or fourmes, or benches,
or Carpets, or Cushions, than what Nature hath wrought with
her owne hands, the groundwork being the earth, and the greene
grasse . . ." A farm worker received the equivalent of perhaps
fifty to seventy-five dollars a year in modern money, and lived
on a diet primarily of cheese, ale, and bread of a quality so poor
that it led one Londoner to remark: "What makes the peasant
grovel in his muck, humbling his crooked soul, but that he eats
bread just in colour like it?" His clothes were rags; he shivered
through a damp winter, worsened by a pinched supply of expensive firewood. (Not the least of America's attractions was expressed in 1629 by a settler who wrote from among its endless
forests: "All Europe is not able to afford to make so great Fires as
New-England.") From this existence, no improvement on the
condition of the urban poor, there was no exit for parents or
children, unless a youngster became apprenticed to a craftsman
and survived the risks of bad masters, floggings, and starvation
to rise to artisan's rank. Even then, his social status was likely to
improve little, for any attempt on his part or that of his wife to
dress or act like his or her betters might well be deemed, as one
writer expressed it in 1635, "pride and arrogance [which was to
be] most justly rewarded with shame, reproach, and scorn."

N ot that all of England groaned under oppression. There
were urban and country tradespeople, estate managers,
attorneys, shipowners, clerics, skilled butchers, brewers, gold-
beaters, sailmakers, and the like who were at ease in Zion, untouched by political combat and even willing to adjust their
religious practices to the prevailing winds. But it was also true
that for the large mass of English citizens of many classes, displaced or disaffected by civil brawls and economic upheavals,
there seemed little opportunity to hew out a more satisfactory
destiny. It was to such people as these that the promotional
literature of the colonies came as a revelation. They were the
ones whose eyes widened when they read in such pamphlets as *A
Plaine Path-way to Plantations* (1624) that every emigrant might
have a house "with one or two hundred acres of ground." They

stirred in the pews when ministers declaimed on the text wherein God spoke to Abram and said: "Get thee out of thy country, and from thy kindred, and from thy father's house, unto a land that I will shew thee." It was to them that John Smith spoke when, after a description of the marvelous sights of Virginia and his hair-rising adventures among its beasts and savages, he asked: "Who can desire more content, that hath small meanes, or but only his merit to advance his fortunes, then to tread, and plant that ground he hath purchased by the hazard of his life? . . . what to such a minde can bee more pleasant, then planting and building a foundation for his Posteritie, got from the rude earth, by Gods blessing and his owne industrie . . . ?" The boldness of Smith in referring to hazards of life and the need of industry was matched by other writers such as Captain Christopher Levett: "I will not tell you that you may smell the corne-fields before you see the Land; neither must men think that corne doth grow naturally (or on trees), nor will the Deare come when they are called, or stand still and look on a man till he shoot . . . nor the fish leap into a kettle. . . . But certainly there is fowle, Deare, and Fish enough for the taking, if men be diligente. . . ."

These writings were among the first notes of an American challenge to the restless and bold everywhere: come here, wrestle with the rich but forbidding land for your fortune, and what you win will be not only independence but new selves and new lives. Millions of migrants would answer the call in the centuries that followed the New World's first imprint upon the consciousness of the Old. The English who went out from the realm of James and Charles were not essentially different from the other "races" that followed.

Of the eighty thousand English (close to two percent of the population) who ventured out between 1620 and 1642 alone, not only to Virginia, New England, and Bermuda but to "Barbarie, India, Muscovie, and verie Calecute," it can be assumed that a goodly number endured the experience of some emigrants who arrived in London in need of board and lodging until their vessel sailed. They were taken in hand "by such men as we here call Spirits" and placed into boardinghouses, "where once being en-tred [they] are kept as Prisoners untill a Master fetches them off; and they lye at charges in these places a moneth or more before they are taken away." It is also safe to guess that under the very best of conditions, the stormy Atlantic passage in small, cranky, wet, foul, overcrowded sailing ships was terrifying. The supplies of hard bread and preserved meat that were carried aboard for use after the fresh provisions gave out (in a matter of days) usually became wet, moldy, and verminous. In their close quarters, the passengers quickly passed on plague, smallpox, and respiratory diseases to one another, while scurvy, arising from the lack of fresh vegetables, was another hazard. Sometimes, when a voyage was particularly prolonged by misfortune, discomfort escalated into nightmare. Not typical, perhaps, but always a possibility for an unlucky vessel, was the gruesome experience of the *Virginia Merchant*.

In 1649 the ship sailed for Virginia, with 350 passengers crowded into a hold designed for three hundred tons of cargo. It took twenty-three days to reach Teneriffe. From there the vessel labored to Bermuda. Even though some replenishment must then have been taken aboard, provisions were so low that when the ship was delayed further in a gale off the Carolinas, the travelers nearly starved. The "infinite number of rats that all the voyage had been our plague," one passenger wrote, "we now were glad to make our prey to feed on. . . ." A grown rat sold for sixteen shillings. At one point a "Royalist gentleman," Colonel Henry Norwood, was put on an island with several others to fend for himself. (Whether or not this was at his own request is not clear.) One of the women in the party died. The others were advised to save themselves by eating her, which they proceeded to do. This group reached the settlements on the York River only after twenty-two weeks of this horror.

In such premonitory agonies, then, the English families who were to become "old stock" Americans—First Families of Virginia, *Mayflower* Passengers, Builders of the Bay Colony— endured the transition between hemispheres. Once they arrived on American shores, their history tends to be absorbed into the traditional framework of institutional chronicles: the record of how communities, land-tenure systems, governments, churches, courts, and corporations were created, and of how diplomacy and war and internal migration expanded the boundaries of old settlements and inspired the creation of new ones. Yet there is another facet to the story. There is the matter of how the human material of colonies, the living souls who were "planted," chose their goals and dealt with the iron reality of

Printed by James Reeve

King Powhatan comands C. Smith to be slayne, his daughter Pokahontas beggs his life his thankfullnes and how he subiected 39 of their kings. reade the history.

This engraving of Captain John Smith's most famous close call appeared in his 1624 *Generall Historie of Virginia*. Trekking the wilderness in 1607, Smith was ambushed by Indians and taken to King Powhatan, chief of a thirty-two-tribe confederacy. According to the stalwart author's account, he was condemned to death but saved at the last minute when Powhatan's daughter, Pocahontas, threw herself between him and his executioners. *(Rare Book Room, New York Public Library).*

their new surroundings. These first English comers were not living Anglo-Saxon ancestral portraits but restless, frightened, angry, hopeful people, trailing sundry pasts behind them. The amalgam of new-settlement society was different for the different colonies, but a few serve particularly well as paradigms for later modes of migration.

Though it did not remain one, pioneer Virginia began as a company venture. Its initial settlers were brought out by a corporation as employees of different ranks, much as Irish and Chinese labor gangs would be imported to lay rails across the Great West in the 1860s. It was several years before Virginia's promoters sounded the call for stable, family-sized groups to take up private lands and plant farms in the wilderness.

Plymouth Colony, where the "Pilgrims" landed in 1620, and Massachusetts Bay, founded in 1629, represented a different design. The leaders of both colonies were bound cohesively by shared religious sentiments. They emigrated in groups, with two purposes in mind. One was the well-advertised motive (historically speaking) of creating an atmosphere free from official harassment in matters of worship. But they were likewise eager to build a stable economic base under their communities. In the case of the Puritan gentry who established Massachusetts, they could have remained in England as investors, reaping the profits of farms and fisheries whose harvests were gleaned by the sweat and perils of others. Instead, they chose to move to the hazardous New World themselves. Both Pilgrims and Puritans were forerunners of other groups that in later centuries set out from Europe, bought virgin land in wholesale tracts, planned towns, dealt out tasks and properties to members, and set their roots in fresh soil as corporate bodies (until, almost invariably, the frontier's attraction for rampant individualism broke them up). The script is a frequently repeated one of like-minded souls, huddled together for mutual security in new surroundings.

Pennsylvania and Georgia, founded respectively in 1681 and 1732, were of mixed parentage. Both were intended to return revenue, and from the start both offered opportunities for individual planters to purchase land and settle down to propertied futures, just as earlier arrivals had been doing in the New World for decades. But both these colonies were also at least partly Utopian. They were founded by strong men of philanthropic bent, who hoped that the good impulses in the human breast might prevail over the evil, especially in an experimental set-ting. William Penn and James Oglethorpe shared a dream that in a new world untainted by the clotted injustices of the past, a better life could be built by fallible mortals. The human mate-rial available to both men sometimes failed them, but their vision of America as the place where the human spirit could be refined to a new purity endured as a basic theme in the continu-ing story of migration to America. Whether the transplanting process was company-induced, part of a voluntary group plan, nursed by philanthropy, or simply inspired by individual ambi-tion, it rested on a kind of optimism about human prospects. Perhaps without such optimism the process would have been unendurable.

The first Virginians were living witnesses of what commercial ambition could project in the way of fantasy, given only scanty evidence to work with. The London Company, authorized to plant a colony anywhere between the 34th and 41st parallels North Latitude, had no clear idea what the land might produce. Its directors instructed the founding expedition, which left Eng-land in December of 1606, to establish a colony, look for a possible passage to the "South Sea," and explore the mineral resources of the area—which would include a search for gold. Yet the hope of turning Virginia into a gold-producing commu-nity or one that manufactured luxury goods of any kind was wildly unjustified. The initial phase of colonization was a brutal struggle for mere survival. The English "immigrants" who landed at Jamestown found themselves unprepared to survive a wilderness winter. Their inadequate supplies of food ran out, and the "bloudie Fluxe" and other diseases began to kill off the 104 men who remained after Captain Christopher Newport sailed back to England for fresh provisions, settlers, and tools. In the very midst of a land that offered, George Percy recalled, "a fruitful soile" and a great store of wild fruits and game, the adventurers who were not destroyed by disease endured famine. Their food was "but a small Can of Barlie sod in water, to five men a day, our drinke cold water taken out of the River, which was at a floud verie salt, at a low tide full of slime and filth. . . ." For five months they suffered this "miserable distresse," the liv-ing trying to shut their ears to "the pitifull murmurings and out-cries of our sick men without reliefe," several of whom died each night. ("In the morning, their bodies trailed out of their Cabines like Dogges to be buried.") Not until the Indians brought "Bread, Corne, Fish and Flesh in great plentie" was a reprieve for the group assured.

The London promoters, still hopeful, sent out German and Polish experts in the manufacture of glass, pitch, tar, and soap with the second "supply" of men and goods to Virginia. But in the face of the evidence, able observers on both sides of the Atlantic were beginning to realize that successful "plantations" required a different order of priorities. In Virginia itself, the controversial Captain John Smith, who was on the governing council from the beginning and was in charge of the new colony from September 1608 to September 1609, had decided that the horrors of the first year were not entirely due to God's dispensation but to bad management and laziness. "Most of our chiefest men," he reported in a hastily written pamphlet printed in England in 1608, were "either sicke or discontented, the rest being in such dispaire, as they would rather starve and rot with idleness, then be perswaded to do any thing for their owne reliefe without constraint. . . ."

Captain Smith was not reluctant to apply constraint. He put men to work planting and gathering for the common store, and kept them at work by the threat of imprisonment, whipping, and even hanging—a policy followed by subsequent governors for several years. He achieved these reforms in intervals between exploring expeditions, combats with the Indians, and a great deal of enthusiastic note-taking on the wonders of Virginia. Historians are still stung to debate by Smith. His own accounts of his colorful life include episodes that have the flavor of Baron Munchausen: captivity by the Turks when he was a soldier of fortune in Europe; an escape assisted by a lady—one of many—smitten with his charms; single combat with three Turkish champions, whose heads he cut off one after another; a journey into Russia, where he was reduced on occasion to beggary; and, of course, the famous tale of capture and condemnation by Powhatan, and rescue by Pocahontas. He may have been an inveterate liar, though the evidence is by no means clearly against him. What is certain is that his energy and drive in the early days of the Jamestown undertaking put indispensable backbone into the others present, even those who hated him. His zest for the virgin land, his absolute fearlessness in the face of its challenges, his dedication, from 1608 (when he was only twenty-eight years old) until his death in 1631, to "Virginia" and "New England," and finally his strong sense that life was spacious and inviting on the outer limits of civilization—all qualify him as a candidate for that select company of truly Americanized Europeans of the colonial era.

If Smith and his successors sensed that what Virginia needed was a more prosaic and workmanlike kind of migrant—a digger and builder, and not a simple fortune seeker—the company officials in London were beginning to react in somewhat the same way. The groups that were sent out in 1608 and 1609, the latter a contingent of settlers six hundred strong, included in their baggage many more items of hardware (andirons, tongs, spits, nails, bolts, hinges, latches, scales, and pots), supplies of such basic tools as augers, shears, knives, hatchets, hammers, and chisels, enough dried fruits and vegetables, cheeses, fish, meat, and flour to last out the first year, and seeds for the planting of cabbages, turnips, lettuce, onions, carrots, and the like against future needs. (There is no actual record of what the 1609 supply included, but inventories of later cargoes suggest the pattern.)

Still, it was touch and go whether the colony would survive. When Sir Thomas Gates, the new acting governor, arrived in May 1610, only some sixty settlers were left, and Jamestown was in ruins. The palisades of the fort were down, the gates sagged on the hinges, empty cabins ("whose owners, untimely death had taken newly from them," Gates wrote) had been dismantled for fuel, and the Indians were "as fast killing without as the famine and pestilence within." The town was abandoned in June, but a rescue mission arrived and coaxed the enterprise back to life. Four years later a solid economic foundation was laid when the first crop of tobacco was shipped back to the mother country. From then on, a shift in the quality, or more precisely in the aims, of the incoming migrants was discernible. For a long time, those already on hand continued to complain of the poor quality of the new arrivals, thus sounding another note that would be struck again and again throughout the history of immigration to America. While one settler wrote to London denouncing his superiors for sending "lascivious sonnes, masters of bad servants and wives of ill husbands," Sir Thomas Dale wistfully asserted that "this country" would be the equal of any in Europe "if it be inhabited with good people." Changes in policy were then in the offing that would attract those defined by Dale as "good people"—family heads, landowners, and skilled workers.

In 1614, Dale, by then governor, initiated a program of land-grant incentives amounting to perhaps three acres per person. Thereafter it became more and more common to offer the bait of cheap land to would-be settlers. About 1617, the company began to encourage groups of "adventurers" to band together in associations and migrate en masse. These "hundreds" (although that was not always the number involved) were expected to outfit themselves, and to include among their numbers not only tenants to work the land but also a minister, a physician, servants, and governing officials. They would be given much larger homesteads—as many as fifty acres for each member of the party—and the right to govern their estates, provided they made no ordinances repugnant to English law or the parent company's regulations. The offer of fifty acres for each immigrant landed, a gift known as a "headright," was later made to individual family heads, ship captains, and even single men who would get themselves across the ocean, a condition sometimes met only by signing a contract of indenture to work as someone's servant for a term of years, in exchange for passage money. It was an arduous route to landownership—but one open only in the colonies, not in England itself.

In effect, the Londoners were subcontracting the task of recruiting Englishmen to go to Virginia. They themselves continued to solicit municipalities for orphans, imprisoned debtors, and other social failures at home to make up the passenger lists of Virginia-bound ships. But they were moving toward a new system, wherein the colonizers would not be employees but citizens. Symbolic was a shipment of one hundred "young and uncorrupt maids to make wives to the inhabitants and by that means to make the men more settled and less moveable." What was emerging was not merely a plantation but a society. Many years later, emigration agencies that sent entire shiploads of workers and their families to the shores of the United States would be accused of dumping "hordes" of newcomers into the national community. Yet the practice had ancient and honorable American beginnings.

By 1624, when the London Company failed and the crown authorities took over the direct administration of Virginia, some five thousand white residents were there. Almost all had arrived during the preceding five years. There is no way of knowing how many had endured hunger, pestilence, and Indian attack as part of their personal experience of transplantation. Yet together they had created a community and written the first chapter in the record of the making of Americans.

The story of the small group known as the Pilgrims has been told so often, so inaccurately, and so sententiously that it seems impossible to endow it with a spark of novelty. Though it is not often considered typical of the immigration process, the leaders of the venture were Englishmen whose discontents at home led them along a rocky road of dislocation and severance from known patterns to the ultimate haven in a new land.

They were not huddled masses yearning to breathe free. Their story began in the little town of Scrooby, where William Brewster was postmaster at the beginning of the seventeenth century. It was not a lowly office. Brewster was charged with accommodating and expediting travelers on government business as they picked their horse-drawn way along the main route to and from London. The safe conveyance of official dispatches was his responsibility, and to its exercise he brought an unfinished Cambridge education and experience as an aide to Sir William Davison, one of Queen Elizabeth's secretaries of state. Politically speaking, Brewster was a loyal subject. In religious terms, however, he was a rebel in the eyes of English officialdom. Like his close associate, Pastor John Robinson, and a number of other Scrooby folk, Brewster was a Separatist. The Separatists went further than the Puritans; whereas Puritanism hoped to save the Anglican Church from corruption and heresy by the zeal of reform from within, Separatism advocated that its followers leave the Church of England entirely and form self-governing congregations of "saints," owing allegiance to no bishop, archbishop, or any ecclesiastical official. To the English who regarded church and state as inseparably joined props of the social order, such views were untenable. In repeated efforts to impose conformity, the law officers kept a close watch on the houses of the Scrooby Separatist congregation and even imprisoned a number of them. Such persecution drove many Separatists to flight, though it might mean the abandoning of homes and occupations.

This nineteenth-century painting by William
Halsall shows the *Mayflower*, covered with spray
ice, at anchor in Plymouth Harbor, while a
small boatload of Pilgrims heads for shore.
The ship remained anchored there for several
months, providing shelter for many Pilgrims
while their houses were being built. *(Pilgrim
Society, Plymouth)*

One memorable flight occurred in 1608, according to the recollections of William Bradford, who lived to become a governor of Plymouth Colony and to record his experiences in *Of Plimmoth Plantation*. Bradford and a number of his coreligionists fled to the Netherlands, at that time a model of tolerance to religious refugees (just as nineteenth-century England was to offer sanctuary to political fugitives from all over the world). They settled first in Amsterdam and then in Leyden, where they practiced such homely trades as brewing, baking, and brickmaking, followed the leadership of community pillars like Brewster and Bradford, and for more than a decade enjoyed "much sweete and delightful societie and spiritual comforte together in the wayes of God."

But even in the Promised Land there were the surrounding Canaanites. The Leyden Separatists appreciated the hospitality of their Dutch hosts, but life was hard for *émigrés* and strangers; moreover, the younger people were falling, as Bradford noted, "into extravagante and dangerous courses, getting the raines off their neks. . . ." The elders of the congregation regarded the extravagant courses as essentially Netherlandish. What they were facing, without quite realizing it, was the possibility of assimilation into their new milieu, and, like many small and zealous religious communities in the later United States—the Amish, for example—they resisted it. The course of resistance, for them, lay in further flight. After due and solemn deliberation, they made arrangements to move in a body to Virginia. The Separatist community consisted at this point of the original Scrooby migrants plus others who had joined them in the Netherlands. Not all the faithful, however, proved willing and able to undertake the risks of the journey or life in the wilderness, so that by the time of the departure for America less than fifty of them actually took ship.

In the textbooks, religious liberty looms as the only consideration in the minds of the Pilgrim leaders as the year 1620 approached. In fact, they were occupied with more mundane considerations. Not only was it necessary to secure permission from the Virginia Company and its various offshoots to establish a settlement in "Virginia," but it was likewise imperative that they accumulate a stake to get themselves settled and devise some form of activity that would render their colony self-supporting. The problem was one that racked thousands of later migrants. The Pilgrims' solution was to rely on fishing as "the cheife, if not the only means to doe us good," and to raise funds by a method that was a compromise with an unholy world.

They made an agreement with a company, numbering some seventy partners, in England. Shares were sold to some merchant-investors who would never leave England. Some of the Pilgrims themselves were able to buy shares. And finally, as plans for departure matured, a number of people were added to the passenger manifest who were neither shareholders nor veterans of life in Leyden, but who were simply going out to increase the labor supply of the prospective settlement. Thus the initial company of settlers contained a smaller number of "saints" from Leyden than of "strangers," many of them willing communicants of Anglicanism, who were seeking in the New World "not spiritual salvation but economic opportunity," according to one historian of the voyage. There was some sharp bargaining between the religious leaders and their business-minded sponsors over how much time the migrants might spend in working for the company and how much on their own account, and on how the joint property of all the shareholders—those who stayed and those who went—should be divided at the end of the contract period of seven years. But in the end it was all settled, and the gist of the agreement was that the Pilgrims plunged themselves into debt for seven years in order to win title to their New World estates, just as individual indentured servants in other colonies sometimes labored seven years for a master to pay off a passage and earn a "headright." (The *Mayflower* carried some of them, too.) Or, as the Pilgrims themselves might have pointed out, just as Jacob served Laban seven years in order to win Rachel.

With such details settled, the group left England in August on two ships—the *Mayflower*, of 180 tons burden, and the sixty-ton *Speedwell*. The *Speedwell* was so leaky and unseaworthy that the expedition was forced to return to port and abandon the vessel. One hundred and one passengers then crowded aboard the *Mayflower*, along with a crew of about fifty, and set out September 16, 1620, on their historic voyage. It was probably a better one, on the whole, than many later immigrants were to have. It took sixty-six days, during which the Pilgrims undoubtedly grew tired of constant wetness, unchanged clothing that must have reeked after the first fortnight, and a monotonous diet of bread, salt, beef, and beer. But the ship was clean, and only three or four crew members and one passenger died of illness, which was remarkable for the time. A boy, Oceanus Hopkins, was born at sea, and another, Peregrine White, on shipboard just before the landing in present-day Massachusetts. The saints and strangers had their quarrels, and the Pilgrims were especially disturbed by the profanity of one member of the crew. When he died suddenly of disease, they regarded it as "ye just hand of God upon him."

The details of the first landing on Cape Cod and the later disembarkation on the site of present-day Plymouth make up the prelude to a story much like that of the agony of Jamestown. During the relatively mild first winter, the men worked doggedly, putting up cabins of squared and sawed timber, storing food, and planting their few cannon. Weakened by their exertions and by an unbalanced diet, they fell prey to scurvy and typhus, and endured a ghastly period in their huts, during which the sick died off while the well performed the "homly and necessarie offices" they required. In March of 1621 an Indian came into camp, saying, "Welcome, Englishmen," a phrase he had learned from seasonal fishermen in Maine. Regaled with ship's biscuit, cheese, butter, wild duck, and brandy—and given a knife, bracelet, and ring—he departed to take the greetings of the Pilgrims to the Wampanoags. Subsequently the chieftain, Massasoit, appeared and made the acquaintance of the new settlers, who ultimately were taught the techniques of survival in New England.

By 1628 the colony was laid out on the slope of a hill along which two broad intersecting streets ran past houses, gardens, and stockades. It was patterned after an English village, predominantly lower-class (or at least lower middle-class) in flavor, with few formally educated men, ordained ministers, or evidences of schooling (though Brewster left a library of four hundred volumes at his death, and Bradford eighty). Yet they governed themselves more or less successfully. They were neither the saints they believed themselves to be nor figures in a pageant, but real people who had bootstrapped themselves into self-sufficiency in a wild new environment. They were the basic stuff out of which centuries of migration would be made.

Most of the leaders of the Puritan migrants to the Boston area in 1629 and later were wealthier and better educated than the Pilgrims, but the problems and processes there and in the other early colonies were similar. By the time the benevolent founders of Pennsylvania and Georgia undertook their plantings, the English migration was being mingled with other strains.

III

'This New Man'

Penn's Treaty with the Indians was painted by the Quaker Edward Hicks in the early 1800s. Penn's treaties stipulated fair payment for land and protection of Indian rights. *(Abby Aldrich Rockefeller Folk Art Collection, Williamsburg, Virginia)*

In 1782 a former soldier of France, lately a resident of Orange County, New York, published a book that he modestly entitled *Letters from an American Farmer*. In it he posed and answered a question that was of particular import during the transition from colonialism to nationhood in America:

> What then is the American, this new man? He is either an European, or the descendant of an European, hence that strange mixture of blood, which you will find in no other country. I could point out to you a family whose grandfather was an Englishman, whose wife was Dutch, whose son married a French woman, and whose present four sons have now four wives of different nations. . . . Here individuals of all nations are melted into a new race of men, whose labours and posterity will one day cause great changes in the world. . . . The American ought therefore to love this country much better than that wherein either he or his forefathers were born. Here the rewards of his industry follow with equal steps the progress of his labour. . . . The American is a new man, who acts upon new principles; he must therefore entertain new ideas, and form new opinions.

Thus did Michel-Guillaume Jean de Crèvecoeur, who had first come to North America to fight under Montcalm, lay his finger on the fundamental significance of the American experience. A new nation was emerging, without historic boundaries, ancient traditions, or a single, binding folk culture. The American future, like the westward-stretching continent itself, was an uncharted terrain of innumerable hazards and limitless possibilities. The American past was a patchwork quilt, made up of the customs, habits, taboos, visions, and memories of men and women drawn from a variety of national stocks. Most of them had been in the new land for less than three generations, scarcely time enough for new behavior patterns to sink roots below the level of conscious choice. Somehow, England's plantations had become colonies, settlements had become communities, companies of pilgrims and adventurers had become participants in a society. Thanks to a steady westward flow of transatlantic migration, that society was, as Crèvecoeur perceived, neither English nor European. "American" would do as a term for it, but the word was as yet not precise and definitive; rather it was suggestive and elastic, a white space on the map of mankind marked "Unexplored."

The tendency of classroom-taught history has long been to deal with immigration as a force in American life mainly after 1850. It will therefore come as a surprise to many to learn that perhaps a third of all colonial Americans in 1760 either were born abroad or had foreign-born parents. Accurate records were not kept, but the total colonial population in 1760 was about 1,600,000—a fourfold increase from 1713, when the Treaty of Utrecht opened a long period of peace. In that nearly fifty-year span, hundreds of thousands of Germans and Ulster Scots (Protestants of Scottish descent, from the northern counties of Ireland) came over. Of the estimated 200,000 blacks brought to American shores in the eighteenth century, perhaps half were landed during this period. (It is an unaccustomed twist of thought to consider a captive black, plantation-bound, an "immigrant." Yet in demographic terms such a treatment has its uses. For the settlement of "America" was a westward transatlantic shift of population groups in massive numbers, and of this movement a Fanti tribesman, groaning with seasickness in the foul hold of a slave ship, was a part as surely as any Puritan yeoman embarking with John Winthrop.)

Add to these numbers reasonable proportions of recent arrivals among the Huguenots, Acadians, Catholic Irish, Jews, Scots, Swedes, Hollanders, and other "foreigners" in Great Britain's North American mainland colonies on the eve of the Revolution, and it is a fair guess that at least half a million had made the ocean passage within the span of a lifetime.

This surge of newcomers had been a critical element in the great transformation of the provinces. The open sea lanes from Europe and Africa, as well as the open frontier, had effectively reshaped worship, deference, speech, the getting and spending of wealth, and the taking of ease. The political and juridical structure of the colonies remained essentially English, but the society was cosmopolitan.

An immigrant of 1760 debarked in a land where the early days of simple struggle for survival, the agonies of Jamestown and Plymouth, were only memories. Now he found cities, newspapers, courts, schools, legislatures, churches, roads, postal services, bookshops, finely furnished houses. Some of them were built and maintained by his countrymen, and his own presence continued to remold institutions. The thrust of German or Ulster Scot migration into western Pennsylvania transformed the life of that colony in ways that could not have been envisioned by William Penn. The impact of slavery on the economy of the South was measureless. In the compact, yeasty colonial cities, a handful of Scottish, Jewish, or French families with important mercantile connections could radically affect the distribution of social and political patronage. (Boston in 1740 had only 16,000 inhabitants, Charleston 6,800, Philadelphia 13,000, and New York 11,000.)

The motives, the drives, the particular distresses, and the "contributions" of each immigrant group are part of a kaleidoscopic pattern. But when the threads are unraveled, some gleam fresh and in distinct colors. The Germans—and in particular the Germans of Pennsylvania, where they constituted about a third of the populace in 1766—were the most conspicuous non-Britannic element in the colonies. Their mixture of piety and efficiency, mystic yearning and worldly realism, in matters of farming and business formed one important theme of future Americanism. The Ulster Scots brought to the back country, where they flocked, a toughness and Calvinistic communitarianism bred of their own troubled past. Both qualities stamped the future of a major American church—the Presbyterian—and the many colleges that it nurtured. Many colonial Jews and Huguenots were a commercial force in the port towns. Like the printers, ironmasters, and papermakers of German origin, they helped to diversify the colonies' soil-based economy. And as for the forced immigrants, the slaves, by 1760 they were already the bedrock of the Southern economy. To consider the story of all these groups is to feel the texture of American life as it took shape before political revolution confirmed the economic and cultural separation from Europe.

For America's Germans, the counterpart of the *Mayflower* was a roomy and seaworthy vessel of the West Indian service named the *Concord,* which dropped anchor in Philadelphia harbor on October 6, 1683. The families aboard were not the first Germans in the English colonies. Among individual settlers of Germanic origin who had appeared on the scene earlier, Jacob Leisler was already one of the wealthiest citizens of New York in 1684, with an estate of fifteen thousand guilders acquired by trade with the

Indians. In 1689 he would become involved in a revolt against royal authority in the province, and on a cold, wet May day in 1691 he would be hanged on a spot where Pearl and Centre Streets now meet in downtown Manhattan. But the *Concord*'s passengers were part of a group migration—the vanguard of armies of German, or *Deutsch,* newcomers, whose name would be corrupted by American tongues to "Dutch." Their John Smith, their Winthrop, their Bradford, was Francis Daniel Pastorius.

Their voyage probably had its origin in 1677, when William Penn traveled to Germany to make converts to Quakerism. He found a sympathetic audience among many German Pietists— believers like himself in a religion of inward vision, brotherly harmony, and worship undefiled by churchly ritual, pomp, and office. In 1681 Charles II of England gave Penn a province in America in lieu of sixteen thousand pounds owed to Penn's late father. Hoping to put his ideas into practice there, Penn published *Some Account of the Province of Pennsilvania* in the same year. The book was almost immediately translated for German readers, some of whom then formed a company to buy Pennsylvania land, and among those who heard their appeals for support was Pastorius.

A thiry-year-old graduate in law and theology from Altdorf University who had also studied at Strasbourg, Basel, and Jena, Pastorius could have applied his gifts to the pursuit of a comfortable career at home. But the prospective emigrants' descriptions of the idealized Pennsylvania-to-be, he later wrote, "begat a desire in my soul to continue in their society and with them to lead a quiet, godly, and honest life in a howling wilderness." Soon he himself was playing a leading role in recruiting German colonists for the Frankfurt-based company, and in the spring of 1683 he took ship for Pennsylvania to make advance arrangements. On shipboard he had a symbolic immigrant experience in meeting a Welsh physician, Thomas Lloyd, late of Jesus College, Oxford. Pastorius then knew no English and Lloyd no German, but the two American-bound scholars conversed amiably, in the tossing cabin, in Latin!

Penn's agents had sold the Frankfurt adventurers about forty-three thousand acres, and the newly landed settlers took part of the purchase in a tract about six miles north of Philadelphia. On it they began to build a city to be known as Germantown. It was the first American showcase for German orderliness, diligence, common sense about cash, and beehive closeness.

For thousands of Germans, careful attention to the sharp responsibilities of this world mingled with a mystical concern over the proper way to prepare for the next. German religious communities, harassed by authority in the homeland, migrated wholesale to await the Second Coming in the liberal air of Pennsylvania, where, Gottlieb Mittelberger reported, "not only is everyone allowed to believe what he wishes; he is also at liberty to express these beliefs publicly and freely." There were the Mennonites, whose founder, Menno Simons, taught them that true Christians shunned participation in government, refused to lift up their hands to slay others in war, dressed in a style that rejected worldly vanities, and swore no oaths. A colony of Swiss Mennonites settled near Lancaster in 1710. (The Amish folk of Pennsylvania are ultraconservative schismatic Mennonites.) There were the Dunkards, members of a sect of baptizers by total immersion, founded in Westphalia in 1708. Some time after their arrival at Germantown in 1719, the secession of some members led to the foundation of the Cloister of Ephrata, whereupon robes, tonsures, and liturgical rites appeared in the hospitable wilderness. Near Goshenhoppen, now Bally, were clusters of Schwenkfelders, originally a group of true believers from Silesia. Shortly before 1740, a colony of Moravians, or United Brethren, settled on a tract on the Lehigh River, purchased for them by their leader, Count Nikolaus Ludwig von Zinzendorf. There they built a community like that which they had formed on the count's estate at Herrnhut, in Saxony. To it he gave the Scriptural name of Bethlehem, and administered it through officials with the apostolic titles of elder, overseer, monitor, and, simply, teacher. Zinzendorf optimistically sent Moravian missionaries into the western wilderness as far as present-day Ohio, where they earnestly attempted with German polysyllables to bring God's word to their red-skinned neighbors.

The more firmly established German churches had representation in Pennsylvania, too. By 1733, Lutheran congregations in Philadelphia and elsewhere were requesting European-educated pastors. The German Reformed Church, essentially Lutheran, counted forty-six congregations in America in 1751. The German churches filled the settlements with their own jangle of religious argument (some of it printed on German presses) and also with the new sound of Baroque and classical music. Bach and Haydn came to America in the tongues and hands of German choristers and organists; Haydn's *The Creation* and *The Seasons,* for example, had American premieres in Bethlehem. And the religiosity and superstition of some uneducated Germans were reflected in the folk art that even today imprints its bright colors and intricate designs on rugs, furniture, pottery, wagons, barns, and farmhouses in the hilly countryside of "Dutch" Pennsylvania.

German colonists were sometimes brought over in groups by royal officials eager to add them to the always inadequate supply of labor. In 1710, for example, Governor Robert Hunter of New York recruited some three thousand "Palatines" (from the region known as the Rhenish Palatinate) whom he intended to settle in the Mohawk and Hudson valleys to produce naval stores—tar, pitch, rosin, and turpentine—for the Royal Navy. Their saga was painful. Nearly fifteen percent of them died of fever they contracted in the convoy that brought them across. Then they quarreled with Robert Livingston, on whose vast estates they had been settled. The issues were high rents and delays in permitting the eventual outright purchase of farms in the Schoharie Valley, which the Germans had been promised. Some of them, indignant and courageous, struck out for western New York on their own. In March 1713, one settler, John Conrad Weiser, chronicled, "did . . . the people (tho' treated by the Governor as Pharaoh treated the Israelites) proceed on their journey, and by God's assistance travel'd in a fortnight with sledges thro' the snow—which there covered the ground above three foot deep—cold and hunger . . . [to] the promised land of Schoharie." That particular Promised Land was plagued with frequent and fiery visits from the children of Canaan, the Indians, but the migrants endured it all. Promoters brought German and German-Swiss groups to still other colonies—to Germanna, Virginia, to New Bern, North Carolina, and to Purysburg, South Carolina, where they were variously supposed to smelt iron, weave cloth, produce silk, and cultivate vineyards.

Thousands of Germans continued to cross the Atlantic on an individual basis. Some paid their own passage, but others became part of a brutal flesh traffic in "redemptioners." Redemptioners were immigrants who had no money for passage or

The Pennsylvania Dutch brought with them the whimsical style of art displayed on the lid of this eighteenth-century box. These German immigrants fought to preserve their language and culture from outside influences. *(Museum of New Mexico Collections)*

subsistence. When they reached America, the ship's captain "sold" them as servants for a term of years to whatever buyers would pay the accumulated cost—according to the captain's reckoning! Unlike some immigrants who signed contracts of indenture while still in Europe or England, where they had some bargaining power with recruiting agents, the redemptioners, prisoners aboard ship until they were redeemed, were at the mercy of the captain. And the ship, by the end of the crossing, was apt to be a chamber of horrors.

The reason lay in the greed of shipowners who packed their passengers into the hold like herring—four to six hundred to a small vessel. What ensued was bitterly described by Gottlieb Mittelberger, one of that forgotten breed of immigrants who came, found the milk and honey lacking, and returned. Most of the passengers had exhausted their own provisions and pocket money in the long, exasperating, delay-filled journey down the Rhine to Holland and across to England, where they boarded their ships. They had no alternative to being jammed into dark, dank holds in bunks two feet by six feet; no effective means to protest against putrescent meat disguised by heavy salting, "fresh" water thick with filth, biscuits full of spiders' nests and worms.

With murder in his heart, Mittelberger, a schoolmaster and organist, held prayer meetings on deck when weather allowed, baptized five children, and commended to God's mercy the souls of those who died and were thrown over the side. At journey's end the redemptioners—starving, sick, exhausted—were in no position to resist any terms offered by the colonists who "liberated" them and carried them off as farmhands, domestics, and apprentices, with children and parents often going to different masters in permanent separation.

Yet the survivors—and every immigrant was, in a sense, a survivor of exile—persevered and endured. By the outbreak of the Revolution, it was estimated that there were as many as 225,000 "inhabitants of German blood" in the colonies. They had been in the new land, in substantial numbers, for more than a century by that time—longer than the majority of Poles, Italians, or Russian Jews and all their descendants were in the United States of the 1960s. And they had left a solid impress. Dr. Benjamin Rush—patriot, pioneer in psychiatry, exponent of equal education for women, and combative publicist, among other things—wrote, in 1789, a description of Pennsylvania's German inhabitants. He praised their well-built homes, their tight fences, their thoroughly cleared acres, and their well-tended gardens, noting that Pennsylvania was "indebted to the Germans for the principal part of her knowledge in horticulture." He admired their deep and solid farm wagons, under whose white tops the German farmers loaded the bushels of wheat and barrels of flour that they brought to market in such quantities as to make Pennsylvania the national breadbasket in the late eighteenth century.

They were at ease in Zion, belonging to the land. Many of their number would go on to distinguished careers as assimilated Americans. But it should be noted also that some of them added color to the national life by remaining entrenched behind traditional walls, too. They planted and pruned by conjunctions of the stars and phases of the moon, sought water with divining rods, and were not above begging talismans and incantations from witchlike crones to make the pumpkins fatter or the cows' udders fuller. In schools and churches they often clung to the mother tongue—successful, adjusted, and yet still solidly German.

The Scotch-Irish, to give them one of their names, were immigrants of a somewhat different breed. Even in the Old World they were borderers—fighting families sent out to hold a frontier against enemy aliens. About the time when the Jamestown settlers were starving and shivering with malaria, Scottish migrants were being settled on another "plantation," in Ulster, for the purpose of civilizing or at least containing the Irish, who even then were a thorn in the flesh of England for reasons described by Francis Bacon in 1601: "barbarous laws, customs . . . habits of apparel, their poets or heralds that enchant them in savage manners, and sundry other dregs of barbarism and rebellion." Sir Arthur Chichester, Lord Deputy of Ireland, had a method for dealing with the poetry-drunk rebels. Certain of their lords had lately risen in resistance to England. They were defeated, and their estates, largely in the northern counties collectively known as Ulster, were forfeited to the crown. Chichester decided that the settling of "colonies of civil people of England and Scotland" on these lands would plant the seeds of Protestantism and fidelity to London in the tough Irish soil.

So it was done, and by 1641 approximately 120,000 Britons had been "planted" in Ulster. The great majority of the settlers were Scots, not Englishmen, and were variously called Ulster Scots, Ulstermen, Scotch- (or Scots-) Irish, and sometimes (especially in emigration records and to the confusion of history) simply "Irish." They were not all "civil people" as Chichester had planned, either, which was possibly just as well in an undeveloped land with few roads and less law, as a contemporary saying had it. It was noted that many "from debt, or breaking and fleeing from justice, or seeking shelter, came hither, hoping to be without fear of man's justice," and that "iniquity abounded."

But the righteous had their supporting forces. As a historian of the Ulster settlement noted, the wicked might haste across the Irish Sea, but "God followed them when they fled from Him." Their righteous neighbors needed a certain measure of contentiousness themselves in order not to perish. God's pursuing agents were Scottish Presbyterian preachers, armored in a Calvinism that was stern even by seventeenth-century standards. More than a religion, Calvinism was a buckler against the world's snares. Holding man to rigid moral accountability before an angry God who had predestined him to damnation or salvation, it celebrated accumulation and diligence, and thundered against vanity and the flesh.

The Ulster Scots took their Presbyterianism with them, and therefore tended to live in closely knit communities, led in the paths of duty by their ministers. They wrestled hard with Satan, losing spectacularly when they fell and agonizing more loudly when they repented than Christians of milder temperament were accustomed to witness. They were a tough breed, as hard on themselves as on their enemies, and they had need to be sinewy, for enemies encompassed them. From Cromwell's era through the Glorious Revolution, Ireland was constantly a battleground of Protestants and Catholics. The Ulstermen won bloody victories at Enniskillen and Londonderry over forces loyal to the Catholic James II—and also planted the seeds of hatred between the "green" and "orange" Irish that still bears bitter fruit.

Then, at the moment of Protestant victory, the English government turned against the Ulstermen, who had begun to establish themselves as successful farmers, dairymen, sheep raisers, and weavers. English landowners and merchants secured the passage of laws forbidding the importation into England of Irish beef, meal, grain, wool, linen, woven goods, and many other manufactured items. The ports of Ireland were excluded from any sort of participation in the profitable colonial trade. Prices fell drastically in Ulster, and landlords attempted to make up the loss by raising rents. A calculated policy of keeping imperial profits exclusively in the hands of English merchants tightened the screws of adversity on the Scotch-Irish, and as depression fell like a rain of iron on the land, they began to swarm to America.

Sometimes whole congregations followed their preachers to the docks, after being inspired by sermons that promised goodly land to Abraham and his seed. The movement was heaviest between 1717 and 1785, with occasional peaks in years of bad harvests and consequent famines. Around 1750 it was estimated that nearly 12,000 Ulster Scots were reaching just Pennsylvania each year. For 1771–73 the total lay somewhere between 25,000 and 30,000, not including a heavy inflow from Scotland proper. Dr. Samuel Johnson and James Boswell, touring Scotland at that time, observed a rural dance in which the couples one by one joined a whirling circle, symbolizing "how emigration catches, till all are set afloat." Those who joined the overseas movement were, as the traveler Arthur Young saw it, probably the boldest and hardiest of their tribe—and also "probably the most mischievous." As it happened, they turned out to be superbly suited for the task that fell to them, that of subduing the colonial frontier.

Some went to New England, where a religious atmosphere congenial to their own might have seemed to guarantee a welcome. But the Lord's anointed had already filled up the greenest valleys there, and the Scotch-Irish were driven to the mountainous terrain of western Massachusetts, New Hampshire, and the future Vermont and Maine. (In New Hampshire they left a mark in the town of Londonderry, which produced six governors of the state, nine members of Congress, and five justices of the state supreme court.) But to the southward the younger colonies of Pennsylvania and the Carolinas begged for settlers, and the Scotch-Irish flowed into the so-called Great Valley, running from northeast to southwest, which forms a trough in the Appalachians and from which rise the rivers that flow down to the sea in Pennsylvania, Maryland, Virginia, and the Carolinas.

Rachel Levy, a descendant of well-to-do German-born Jews from New York, married Isaac
Seixas, of another great Jewish clan, and the
union produced the first American-born rabbi,
Gershom Mendes Seixas. Seeking the religious
freedom and economic opportunity that New
York and Philadelphia offered, the first European Jews in America still confronted discrimination but succeeded as individuals and as a
community. *(Frick Art Reference Library)*

They were not always scrupulous about land titles. James Logan, secretary of Pennsylvania Province—that is, agent for the proprietors, the Penn family—complained in 1730 of their "audacious and disorderly manner" in squatting on choice tracts such as the fifteen-thousand-acre Conestoga Manor, reserved by the Penns for themselves. Spokesmen for the Scotch-Irish, Logan wrote, replied that it "was against the laws of God and nature, that so much land should be idle while so many Christians wanted it to labor on and to raise their bread." Making a virtue of necessity, Logan wrote to his employers that it might be a good idea to populate the Indian-threatened frontier with the sons of those who had fought so gallantly in Ireland. Meanwhile, the Carolinas offered tracts for the taking, not yet pounced on by large companies or by favored friends of the governors or other speculators. Consequently, many Ulstermen moved on from Pennsylvania in long Biblical caravans—horses, hogs, oxen, kine, wives, children, and menservants and maidservants trudging ever further into the wilderness. In 1764 Salisbury, North Carolina, alone witnessed the passage of a thousand wagons, bound away for the mountains.

Once more the Ulster Scots were strangers in a hard environment, and they developed enduring protective ways. It was the Scotch-Irish who became the prototype frontier people. The men dressed in buckskins, moccasins, and caps of untreated animal pelts, rifles or muskets in hand, girdled about with belts into which were thrust powder horns, axes, and knives. The barefoot womenfolk in short linsey-woolsey gowns and petticoats grew prematurely leathery with work and suffering. Fighting hard, scrabbling for a living without respite, they moved through the forests like human scythes. Some did not move but became isolated in mountainous pockets, where they more or less gave up the struggle to get ahead and became the ancestors of the hill folk who would be discovered by ballad collectors and urban humorists in later generations. But most struggled to achieve something better than a "hog and hominy" existence for themselves and their children, and some succeeded. At least there was always respite from the grimness of life in the hunt, and in militia muster days, court days, election days, and other occasions for drinking, boxing, wrestling, and matching horses and men in races.

Ultimately the Scotch-Irish of the frontier fell into violent quarrels with the settlers in the older, coastal regions of the colonies—over the lack of protection against Indians, the sad state of back-country roads and bridges, and the tendency to underrepresent frontier counties in the colonial and later in the state legislatures. A tradition of polemical political discourse, laced with Scriptural zeal and rigidity, was maintained by a distinguished corps of descendants of the original Scotch-Irish settlers, among them men like Andrew Jackson, John C. Calhoun, James K. Polk, and countless others. By Revolutionary times, the Scotch-Irish were an inseparable part of the social fabric. Twice transplanted in a century and a half after 1600, they had found a home, a mission, and a style in America.

For the Western world's perennial strangers, the Jews, eighteenth-century America offered both a haven and a challenge. In Europe, the devastating pressure of restriction compacted the mass of Israel into self-sustaining ghetto communities. In the English colonies, however—particularly in liberal Pennsylvania and Rhode Island—Jewish cohesiveness and dedication to tradition had to stand the test of voluntary action. The use of adversity was not available to religious leadership; Jews could more or less blend into the larger social pattern, with some reservations, taking with them as much of their heritage, of their identity's core, as they thought to be consistent with success in the "outside" world. This is still the basic ground for understanding American Jewry. In the 1700s, as individual Jews in America began to taste the subtle mixtures of emancipation and traditionalism, assimilation and separation, they changed the quality of their lives and that of their Christian neighbors as well.

"Back in the old country," as the historian Jacob R. Marcus has observed, "the pious Jew, whatever his occupation, studied rabbinic literature, . . . prayed for the Messiah, and exulted in the martyrs who had died for the glorification of the Ineffable Name. Here, in colonial towns, in the dark forest, on the high seas, the man who had to flee from pirates, face the Indians, and dare the hazards of frontier life was surely not the same man who rocked back and forth, intoning the Talmud, in a German or Polish ghetto academy." He was not, indeed. Moreover, the "colonial town" to which he brought wine, furs, or cloth—and in which he built himself a synagogue—was not quite the same town.

The first group of Jews to land on North American soil consisted of twenty-three who were set down in New Amsterdam in 1654. An unconfirmed and possibly romantic legend says that they came on a French privateer, which had liberated them from a Spanish vessel that had in turn taken them from another ship. One thing is certain: they came from what had been a successful Jewish colony in Pernambuco (now Recife), a Brazilian city taken by the Dutch in 1630. The liberality of the Dutch had made their cities, both in Europe and in their colonies, havens for religious refugees of all kinds, including English Separatists (like the Pilgrims), French Huguenots, and Hispanic Jews. The latter were descendants of a once flourishing Iberian community of scholars, professional men, and traders. Persecution by the Spanish Inquisition, which was established in 1478, had forced Spain's Jews to become either Christians or Marranos—converts who secretly continued whatever Jewish practices they could—or to flee. Many of the exiles had established themselves as brokers, bankers, and shippers, in parts of South America and the West Indies that were not under Spanish control.

Pernambuco's Jews were from this background. The recapture of the city by the Portuguese in 1654 was a catastrophe for them. They dispersed, many bound for the homes of friends and relatives in French and English Caribbean colonies, where restriction was relatively light, and some to other Dutch outposts, including New Amsterdam.

Governor Peter Stuyvesant was no model of toleration. Under pressure from the Dutch West India Company, he allowed "these people" the right to "travel and trade to and in New Netherland and live and remain there, provided the poor among them shall . . . be supported by their own nation." Stuyvesant was determined to withstand the pressure of the Jews, who were anything but backward in measuring the extent of Dutch liberty. In 1655 he refused to permit Salvador Dandrada, Jacob Cohen, and several other Jews to trade at Fort Orange and along the Delaware River on identical terms with Gentile merchants. Next he refused Dandrada's application for the right to purchase a home in the city. But New Amsterdam's Jewish community had friends in old Amsterdam, and orders arrived the next year command-ing Stuyvesant to allow the Jews to trade and buy real estate (but not to open retail shops, become craftsmen, or hold public worship). Next, Asher Levy and Jacob Barsimson claimed and won the right to serve in the local militia, instead of paying a tax in lieu of enlistment as they had been compelled to do. Finally, they got full rights of citizenship, though Stuyvesant argued that "Giving them liberty, we cannot refuse the Lutherans and Papists."

The Dutch went, the English came, and the Jewish community grew. Most were Sephardim—Jews of Iberian origin—and a few were Ashkenazic, or German Jews. (The great subsequent Ashkenazic migration from Russia, Poland, and the Balkans was centuries in the future.) One by one, individual families began the process of succeeding in America. Success had a different meaning for each individual who experienced the process, but the case of Abraham de Lucena is illustrative if not typical. He imported Madeira wine and exported grain to Europe, bacon to Jamaica, and flour to Canada. He married one of his daughters to a man named Mordecai Gomez, a member of a New York Jewish mercantile clan with strategically placed representatives in Old World and West Indian trading and banking centers. It was a common thing among eighteenth-century mercantile families to create relationships in Amsterdam, London, Hamburg, or Lisbon, either by dispatching a son or nephew abroad or by strategic marriage.

Outside New York, Jews also won places for themselves as individuals and in groups. The keen interest of New England's Puritan founders and their descendants in the Old Testament was a source of closeness between some Yankee preachers and their Israelite neighbors. A famous friendship of the colonial period sprouted between the Reverend Ezra Stiles of Newport, Rhode Island, and Rabbi Haim Isaac Carigal, of the Jewish congregation in that city. They were drawn into contact by Stiles's interest in Hebrew and rabbinic lore, and corresponded throughout the rabbi's lifetime in Hebrew, Spanish, and English. Stiles eventually became president of Yale College, and once remarked to some students who objected to studying the Hebrew psalms that they "would be the first we should hear sung in heaven, and that he would be ashamed that any one of his pupils should be entirely ignorant of that holy language."

In a curious way, the Huguenots of colonial America were

somewhat like the Jews. They formed a small group with what contemporary sociology would call high status, income, and skill levels, and social cohesiveness. They were French Protestants, the majority of whom were expelled from France in 1685, when King Louis XIV revoked the Edict of Nantes, under which toleration had been granted to them a century before. Within two years of that date, 150 Huguenot families had come to Massachusetts, and there were other settlements in Rhode Island and Maine. Many of the refugees had been workers in silk and glass, silver and gold, wood and leather, and other fine crafts. The capital accumulated among Huguenot families enabled some to go into trade, and they made their deepest impress in the cities of Boston, New York, Philadelphia, and Charleston, where their family links to the trading ports of the Atlantic community (like those of the Jews) were invaluable. The honor role of Huguenot names is long and not always recognizable, because their assimilation was so complete that it often involved transformation of old family titles into something American. Apollos De Rivoire is hard to recognize as the father of Paul Revere, and the Bowdoins of Maine and Massachusetts are descendants of a Pierre Baudouin. John Greenleaf Whittier got his middle name from a Huguenot mother whose original family title was Feuillevert. The Faneuils of Boston, the Bayards and De Lanceys of New York, the Dupres and Ravenels and Legarés of Charleston and other South Carolina cities, attest how firmly the Huguenots became, in a short time, part of the colonial aristocracy of talent and property. If their impact on customs and religion was light, their weight in the economy was palpable—and a further evidence of growing colonial cosmopolitanism.

In a sense, one of the most fateful waves of immigration began in August of 1619, when, as John Rolfe recalled, a Dutch "man-of-Warre" landed at Jamestown bringing, presumably for sale, "twenty Negars." It was the start of a trade that went on for another 189 years (until 1808) with the law's sanction, and then, furtively, for fifty-two more, as naval patrols pursued "blackbirding" vessels, which sometimes escaped to land their forbidden cargoes in Chesapeake Bay or Gulf inlets. It is estimated that in the three hundred and fifty years from the sixteenth to the mid-nineteenth century, some fifteen to twenty million Africans crossed the Atlantic against their will.

Not all of them went to the United States. They also flowed to the West Indies and Latin America, mingling with Indian and Spaniard to form entire new population types. Their labor raised the great staple commodities—sugar, cocoa, coffee, cotton, tobacco, rice, and indigo—on which Western Europe prospered. In their millions, they exercised a tremendous transformative influence on North and South America alike. In the United States, from the start, their presence affected life in profound and intricate fashions. The exodus from Africa, in chains, was a haunted migration, whose ghosts have not yet been laid to rest.

To begin the story of immigration from Africa it is necessary to cut through thickets of mythology, grown in the soil of racial stereotypes. In Europe the causes that drove people to America were depression, war, and religious persecution arising out of the creation of modern states. In Africa, the decline of sub-Saharan federated empires set the stage. Some people will find it hard to believe that when Europe was in its "Dark Ages," around A.D. 900, a Central African empire of Ghana, known only to the Arab World, was at its height. In 1067 Al Bakri, a scholar living in Moorish Spain, wrote a description of the empire based on the records of traders and the tales of adventurers who for centuries had crossed the Sahara in search of Ghana's gold and salt. The rulers of the empire, wrote Al Bakri, could put "two hundred thousand warriors in the field, more than forty thousand of them being armed with bow and arrow." The major city of Aoudaghast was full of "fine houses and solid buildings," and when royalty gave an audience to the public, it was held in a pavilion crowded with pages holding gold-mounted swords, horses draped in cloth of gold, and princes "splendidly clad and with gold plaited into their hair."

By the middle of the thirteenth century, Ghana was superseded by Mali, whose leaders had long been converts to Islam. In 1324 Mali's greatest king, Mansa Kankan Musa, made the pilgrimage to Mecca. According to Al-Umari, a contemporary writer, he left on his journey with five hundred slaves, each carrying a staff of gold weighing six pounds, and with eighty to one hundred camel loads of gold, each weighing about three hundred pounds. Mansa Musa administered great cities—Timbuktu, Djenné, Walata—the "Milans and Nurembergs of the medieval Sudan," according to the historian Basil Davidson, into which caravans came "in stumbling thirst out of the north-

This 1819 illustration first appeared in a Pennsylvania-German tract, the *Neue Reading Kalendar,* devoted exclusively to excoriating the slave trade. The wide variety of German pious sects that gravitated to Pennsylvania were welcomed by the Quakers, who shared their strong religious and moral opposition to slavery. *(Rare Book Room, New York Public Library)*

ern desert with loads of copper and salt, Venetian beads, the sword blades of Europe and Damascus." But it was not until 1339, two years after Mansa Musa's death, that Mali first appeared on a map in Europe. Domestic and foreign wars and the greed of its rulers led to Mali's decline by the beginning of the fifteenth century. It was soon displaced in importance by the Songhai Empire, which had not reached its greatest heights when the Portuguese came to Africa late in the fifteenth century.

But the Songhai state was the last of a disappearing pattern. Raids by Moors from the north and by tribesmen from the African south were breaking up the old centralized empires. Meanwhile tiny West African "kingdoms" were emerging— Dahomey, Kongo, Benin—with whose princelings the Europeans dealt for ivory, pepper, gold, and slaves. And the "civilized" men who came in great ships from the north not only gave tools and other "trade goods" to the Africans but also firearms for them to use against one another. The various peoples of the West African coast—Mandingos, Fulani, Krumen, Ashanti, Fanti, Yoruba, Ibo—already separated by language and customs, did not unite against the invading slavers but remained isolated and vulnerable. "It was easy for slavers to set one group against another," a historian of the trade has written. "It was as though an invading force had arrived in Europe during the Dark Ages and had exploited the continent by pitting each feudal lord against his neighbors."

The European discovery of West Africa came just when the opening of the New World was creating a voracious demand for labor in mine and plantation. It did not have to be black labor necessarily. But Indians and white convicts, also available for forced work, proved difficult to manage for several reasons. The blacks native to the region extending from Senegal to Gabon suited the colonizers' needs far better—not because they were particularly docile or servile, but because they adapted easily to an agricultural way of life. They were themselves mostly farmers, not food gatherers or hunters, and they were acclimatized to hot latitudes. And they were already available as slaves.

Those who as early as 1540 were brought by the tens of thousands to Mexico, the West Indies, and other parts of Latin America were prisoners even in Africa. The Ewes, Yorubas, and other tribesmen who dwelt in the primary American slave-producing area along the Ivory and Gold Coasts were first made captives and then sold by other black men. Actually, slavery in an African kingdom might mean something different than it did on a Carolina rice plantation. Often it involved no change of home, tribe, or even status—merely the ownership by another of all the products of one's labor. Africans enslaved to other Africans were sometimes paying for crimes and sometimes taken in war. During hard times some actually sold themselves or their families into bondage to escape starvation. Some were kidnapped by slave catchers and traders; these predators usually were non-Europeans, for white men seldom ventured inland. Whatever the method of enslavement, the victims were a negotiable asset, sometimes sold by their own chiefs. It was a barbarous custom in European eyes but one that very conveniently excused the slave trade and that the Spanish, Dutch, and English readily turned to profit. It may be remembered that in Europe this was an era when jurisprudence still kept the rack and thumbscrew in its armamentarium, and exacted executions for petty crimes. Cruelty has no exclusive native land.

The lot of the African slave changed harshly once he was marked for sale to Europeans. Long coffles, sometimes made up of hundreds of slaves tied neck to neck by bark thongs, were marched down to such coastal ports as Popo, Lagos, Bonny, or Calabar, and collected in barracoons, or pens, to be bargained over. The collectors who served as middlemen between native slaveowners and slave-ship captains gathering a cargo were of varied backgrounds. Sometimes they were agents, or "factors," of great companies formed expressly for the trade, such as England's Royal African Company, founded in 1663 under the patronage of the Duke of York himself to furnish three thousand slaves annually to the colonies. Sometimes they were half-caste adventurers, free-lance agents of imperialism, trying to make their fortunes while struggling to preserve their own personalities against the rot of boredom, drunkenness, disease, insects, and the temptations of too easily available power and sex. It was with these men—the dregs of white society—whom the captain made arrangements to have his vessel "slaved."

Once the purchases were completed the horror began. Few slave ports had a wharfage, so ships stood offshore while huge canoes fought their way through the surf, laden with sixty to eighty terrified bound and branded Africans. The slaves were then packed into the holds as tightly as flesh could endure and more. Profit hunger inexorably dictated overcrowding; five and six hundred manacled blacks would be crammed into spaces as small for each as sixteen inches wide, two and a half feet high, and six feet long. Frequently they could neither sit upright nor even turn unless their neighbors turned too, spoon fashion.

In good weather they might be brought up on deck to stretch their legs twice a day and to be fed gruelly mixtures of yams, rice, corn meal, and manioc. But when storms arose, they were sealed below for weeks at a time in air so foul that crewmen fainted when opening the hatches. (Slave ships were distinguishable for miles by their stench.) In the darkness the miserable "passengers" had to wallow in pools of their own excrement, urine, vomit, and bloody mucus from ever-present dysentery. Disease might kill a quarter or more of a "cargo" in the six- or eight-week passage. Some conscientious captains, eager to preserve the merchandise, did attempt rudimentary sanitation measures, and it was remarked in defense of slave-trade skippers that they often took care of the blacks better than the masters of immigrant ships looked after their "free" passengers, from whom money had already been collected and whose fate was therefore a matter of indifference. Whether or not that was true, the miserable German or Irishman on the high seas had at least the consolation of thinking that in the long run he would be sweetening his lot in life. The terrified, uncomprehending African had no similar solace. Occasionally, in deep depression or stubborn resistance, slaves would throw themselves overboard if not watched carefully, or attempt suicide by refusing food. In the latter case they were flogged, or their lips were blistered with hot irons, or a cruel device called a speculum oris was hammered between their teeth to pry their mouths open, whereupon they were fed through funnels.

So, in dumb agony, the ancestors of almost all black Americans made the migration to America. The trade, at first only a trickle, swelled steadily under the twin stimuli of the Southern plantations' need for muscle and the enterprise of New England and middle-colony merchants who fitted out the slave ships. As many as a thousand blacks were imported into the Southern colonies each year at the beginning of the eighteenth century, and the total increased as new lands were opened to cultivation. In 1714 there were some 59,000 slaves in the North American colonies of Great Britain. Forty years later the number was 298,000. In 1790 the first United States census would count 697,681 slaves. Most of them were below the Mason-Dixon line, and in many areas of the South they far outnumbered the whites. A new social pattern had taken shape in less than a hundred years.

From the outset, the fate of the blacks was separate and inferior. No slave codes existed in the colonies early in the 1600s, and some historians have even speculated that when blacks first arrived, it was not taken for granted that they would all be slaves. In fact, some blacks were employed under ordinary contracts of indentured service. The English, however, knew from the start that the Spanish and Portuguese used blacks as slaves, and a work of 1623, published in London, explicitly referred to the "blacke people" whom the Spaniard carried "into the West Indies, to remaine as slaves, either in their Mines or in any other servile uses. . . ." Racial prejudice, ignorance, and fear, evidenced in a variety of ways, soon created the basis for a different, harsher treatment of black "servants" than of white. In Maryland, an act of 1639 spoke of the rights of "all Christian inhabitants (slaves excepted)"; nine years later, a ban was imposed on allowing "any Pagan" to carry guns. In a typical court case of 1640, three runaway servants were punished. Two had their terms of indenture extended by four years, but one, "being a Negro named John Punch," was to "serve his said master . . . for the time of his natural Life." Twelve years later another legal document recorded the sale of a black girl "with her Issue and produce . . . and their services forever." And in a historic departure from the practice in other slaveholding countries, Virginia in 1622 provided that the child of a slave mother and a white father should follow the status of the mother. In the future, there would be thousands of slaves to whom a mixture of "white blood" in their ancestry—superior though that blood was said to be—did not bring liberation or even any lightening of their burdens.

By 1700 the manacles had been fastened firmly on the African. And yet even at the beginning, somehow, the self-justifying myth that the "pagan" black could only grub and hoe under the lash was shredded by fact. The plantation was almost an isolated little society. Not only did it demand hands to prune and plant and dig; it also needed men to build and to repair the machinery of a primitive, self-contained economic enterprise. If the master had to make himself an amateur practitioner of law, medicine, and pedagogy, the slave likewise had to learn unaccustomed skills. As early as 1649 a description of the estate of a Captain Matthews of Virginia referred to his possession of "forty Negroe servants," whom he "brings . . . up to Trades in his house." Various documents listing deceased masters' assets showed that blacks in colonial Virginia and the Carolinas were coopers, carpenters, blacksmiths, and "mechanics"—a catchall name for artisans. Advertisements in eighteenth-century South Carolina newspapers showed black slaves practicing many trades—as shipwrights, cabinetmakers, wheelwrights, tanners, shoemakers, spinners, brickmakers, plasterers, painters, and glaziers, among others.

Artisanship was a pathway out of the most binding rigidities of slave control. A man with a manual talent could not be treated quite like livestock. Moreover, many plantation owners discovered that they could hire out their skilled slaves by the month or the year, much as one would rent tools to a neighbor. But "hiring out" involved, very often, permission for slaves to travel and to discharge tasks without supervision. In 1768 a Charleston man proudly offered to sell two or three black shoemakers who had "done all my business for nine years past." Another advertised the merits of a black man who "has been intrusted with the Care of a Shoemaker's Shop, without any Assistance from a White Man, for several years." Such facts, brought repeatedly to public attention, were poor props to the theory of the black's helpless dependence upon white leadership for his very survival. If further evidence of black potential was needed, it was to be found in the Northern colonies, where slaves were fewer in number but much more likely to be trusted with responsibilities as craftsmen's assistants and house servants than they were to be put to work in the fields. Some masters were even beginning to allow hired-out slaves to save their earnings and buy their freedom. Others were occasionally providing for the emancipation of slaves in their wills. The nucleus of a free black population was present and growing by Revolutionary times.

It was only a small beginning, however, and the trend of white attitudes was against any real upward steps for the African newcomers. Church people in the South occasionally made efforts to

"Christianize" the slaves, but it was difficult to achieve this without introducing them to concepts of spiritual equality and freedom, and possibly to literacy as well. That was dangerous; a Bible-reading black might be made restless by passages that related to such matters as the departure from Egypt. Training blacks in craftsmanship undoubtedly held the same perils. The black carpenter who learned enough arithmetic to measure his work was less likely to regard numbers as powerful and inaccessible white men's magic. It is hard to keep a little independence from expanding.

Law and custom among whites, especially in the South, militated against much work in educating the children of Africa; the feeling was summed up in a statement of Virginia's House of Burgesses in 1699, objecting to any massive efforts to convert the slaves as unprofitable because of the "Gros . . . Barbarity and rudeness of their Manners, the variety and Strangeness of their Language and the weakness and shallowness of their Minds." So ignorance was allowed to remain, and to become the excuse for further deprivation and continued ignorance. By 1776 a clergyman could say of the blacks of South Carolina that with few exceptions they "are to this day as great strangers to Christianity, and as much under the influence of Pagan darkness, idolatry and superstition, as they were at their first arrival from Africa."

It was probably a somewhat comforting rationalization for the continuance of slavery. But slave or free, the black presence in America was palpable. Each year, Southern whites became more deeply involved in the consequences of the slave trade. With each new black arrival or the birth of new black children, the habits, patterns, language, customs, fears, and unconscious beliefs of white Americans were being more surely molded by the biracial community's existence—even in terms of black subjugation.

The blacks, in short, had done what the voluntary migrants had done. They had become part of a new society. All of them—the peasants from the Rhineland, Sephardic Jews, Ulster Scots, Irish Catholics, and Huguenots—all these, like the powerless blacks, were being fused into a people. That was the development Crèvecoeur observed when he looked at "the American, this new man." It was a long-range development, on which the political revolution that began with the fighting at Lexington and Concord in the spring of 1775 merely superimposed a new form of government.

IV
A Question of Loyalties

Thomas Paine's pamphlet *Common Sense*, when it appeared in January 1776, helped crystallize many colonists' ideas about the possibility of total independence from Britain. And after the American Revolution Paine wrote *The Rights of Man*, which defended the French Revolution. *(Library of Congress)*

Among the immigrants who reached American shores in 1774 was a thirty-seven-year-old Englishman named Thomas Paine, a loner whose principal occupation in life seemed to be to fail at things. He was separated from his wife, he belonged to no church, and he had successively proved unable to earn a living as a sailor, grocer, tobacconist, corset-maker, and tax collector. His only assets on arrival were some letters of introduction from Benjamin Franklin, one of which he presented to Philadelphia's Dr. Benjamin Rush, a distinguished physician and political figure. Franklin had met Paine in London while the latter was attempting to persuade Parliament to im-prove the working conditions and salaries of his fellow excise-men. Franklin found Paine's political views, and the language in which he delivered them, unorthodox and interesting. So did Dr. Rush, particularly when the newcomer ardently pressed his conviction that the colonies should go beyond seeking better treatment from Britain and strike out without equivocation for total independence.

Dr. Rush had entertained similar notions himself, but he was not quite ready to risk "the popular odium" that conservative Philadelphia might heap upon the author of such a radical pro-posal. Paine, in contrast, had no roots in Penn's city and little to lose, so Dr. Rush encouraged him to write a pamphlet on the subject. When it appeared in January 1776, under the title *Common Sense,* a small-scale miracle ensued; as many as 120,000 copies were sold in three months, according to one estimate—a total far in excess of any reasonable expectation. It was as if Americans had been waiting for Paine's thudding sentences to jar them into confronting the implications of their own rebellion.

For page after page Paine hammered away at the sanctities of generations: monarchy, hereditary succession, loyalty to the mother country, government itself. As he warmed to his subject, his field of vision widened. All the world had a stake in the battles between redcoats and patriot militiamen. "'Tis not the affair of a City, a County, a Province, or a Kingdom; but of a Continent—of at least one eighth part of the habitable Globe. 'Tis not the concern of a day, a year, or an age; posterity are virtually involved in the contest, and will be more or less af-fected even to the end of time, by the proceedings now." Paine the wanderer, the defeated European, had grasped the continental and historical dimension of the American struggle, and flung it in the face of all humanity as a challenge:

> O! ye that love mankind! Ye that dare oppose not only the tyranny but the tyrant, stand forth! Every spot of the old world is overrun with oppression. Freedom hath been hunted round the Globe. Asia and Africa have long expelled her. Europe regards her like a stranger, and England hath given her warning to depart. O! receive the fugitive, and prepare in time an asylum for mankind.

An asylum for mankind! The phrase codified something already inherent in America, and made it a reason to fight; it far exceeded a demand for a voice in taxation or a fairer share in the profits of imperial trade. The United States came into being not merely as an emancipated colony but with certain commitments to that "candid world" which was to be addressed by the Declaration of Independence. In the eyes of at least some Americans in every later generation, their country would have a solemn obligation to serve as a model of what liberty could achieve in a commonwealth and also as a haven to those elsewhere to whom liberty was denied. Behind this faith was an awareness of how many men of "foreign" blood had helped to fuse provincial loyalties into American nationalism in the War for Independence.

The long crisis of empire that ended in revolt in 1775 was a time of special testing for those colonists not of English stock. In what ways would they respond to quarrels between London and provincial capitals over the "rights of Englishmen"? Would they remain aloof? Would they follow the tug of old-country loyalties and line up on one side or the other in solid phalanxes of Dutchmen for King George or Irish behind the Continental Congress? Or would they divide among themselves along lines of cleavage scored by geography, economic interests, local feuds, class ties, clan habits—just as other American crown subjects were doing?

In the blaze of gunfire it was this last pattern that leaped into clarity. Members of the immigrant groups split into opposed factions, and in so doing demonstrated—even when they took the Tory side—the overwhelming Americanizing effect of the environment. Had they stood in monolithic blocs, they would

86

have been loyal aliens, under whatever banner they chose. But when families, communities, and congregations of the foreign-born broke apart as "rebels" and "loyalists," they shared to the full the pain of national birth.

The Scotch-Irish, for example, followed their traditionally pugnacious leadership in divergent paths. In Pennsylvania, so many of them bore arms in the homegrown force known as the Pennsylvania Line that General "Light Horse Harry" Lee called it "the line of Ireland." Yet in Philadelphia in 1778, the command-ing general of the British occupation forces was able to raise a regiment made up almost exclusively of "Volunteers of Ireland"—men from all parts of the Emerald Isle, who had little in common but a desire to polish off Washington's half-starved army at nearby Valley Forge. What turned the Ulstermen toward British or American recruiting camps was often enough their reaction to the provincial leadership and their estimate of what would best overcome it. In Pennsylvania, those who fought on the side of independence hoped that collapsing royal authority would drag down with it the Quaker oligarchy whose pacifism and stinginess had left the frontier vulnerable to Indian raids.

In the Carolinas, however, the Scotch-Irish of the back coun-try nursed long-standing grudges against the tidewater planters, whom they saw as land-grabbing, power-hungry, haughty aris-tocrats, battening on God's poor. There, indeed, resentment ran so deep that when the planters chose the side of resistance, thou-sands of Scotch-Irishmen fought for the King, hoping that when the war ended His victorious Majesty would render justice by dividing the "rebel" landholdings among the faithful. Yet not quite all of the Carolina frontier's Scotch-Irish families took that road. In the district known as the Waxhaws, on the border be-tween North and South Carolina, a British officer reported the populace to be "universally Irish and universally disaffected." Among the disaffected was the son of a Carrickfergus farmer, who joined a militia company of dragoons in 1780 when he was thirteen years old, was captured by the redcoats the next year, and had his scalp laid open by a saber when he refused a British officer's peremptory demand to clean his boots. His sixteen-year-old brother died of smallpox contracted in British deten-tion, and his mother of typhus caught while nursing still other prisoners. His name was Andrew Jackson.

In New Hampshire, the outbreak of war stirred forty-six-year-old John Stark, whose father had come from Ulster in 1720, into instant action. A tight-lipped man of medium height, with strong features and keen eyes, he was a veteran of Rogers' Rangers, a hard-fighting frontier outfit of French and Indian War fame. Forsaking his farm, he rode to Cambridge, Massachusetts, and offered his services to the American army. For nearly two years he fought gallantly, but he *was* an Irishman, and no man to brook an insult, real or imagined. When Congress promoted several junior officers over his head, Stark resigned his commission in March 1777 and went home. But only four months later General John Burgoyne's army, slashing down from Canada toward Albany, raised the alarm in western New England. On July 18, New Hampshire commissioned Stark brigadier general and authorized him to raise a force and speed to the aid of Vermont. In twenty days he assembled more than fourteen hundred men, armed them, and hustled them through the mountains to Manchester, Vermont. A little more than a week later, he fell upon a British force at Bennington and devastated it, capturing nearly seven hundred men and killing their Hessian commander, Colonel Friedrich Baum. Stark made his way into the history books by allegedly crying out to his men: "There, my boys, are your enemies, the red-coats and tories; you must beat them or my wife sleeps a widow tonight."

The history books fail to add a significant minor note in the story. A year previously, at the Battle of Long Island, Stark's brother William had been killed in action at the head of a regiment—of loyalists.

Although the lessons of history are drawn from the behavior of aggregates, history itself is lived by individuals. The records of two German and two Huguenot families give human dimension to the story of how immigrants and their sons became participants in a war that would decide the fate of a continent. The names of these four illustrative and illustrious families are Mühlenberg (which soon jettisoned the umlaut), Herkimer, Laurens, and De Lancey.

The Muhlenbergs form what one author, Stephen Hess, has called an American political dynasty, whose achievement was to transport the colonial Germans—"speaking a different language, following different customs, suspicious of outsiders, prone to stand apart"—into full participation in national life via the avenue of politics. The patriarch was Heinrich (Henry) Melchior Mühlenberg, who arrived in Pennsylvania in 1742 to answer the cry of the colony's growing number of Lutherans for trained leadership. Mühlenberg was steeped in the profundities of classical theological disputation as taught at the universities of Göttingen and Halle. He was also a zealous organizer, and within six years of landing in Philadelphia had created the first Lutheran synod in America. Inside of ten years he had linked twenty congregations together at a price that included the wrenching of his own bones in endless, jouncing trips across the middle Atlantic and Southern colonies. In 1745 he united two branches of German immigration by marrying John Conrad Weiser's daughter. Weiser's family had come to New York's Schoharie Valley as part of the Palatinate settlement of the early part of the century. Weiser himself became spectacularly Americanized. He ran away from home, living with the Mohawks and learning their tongue (they bestowed on him the name of Tarachiawagon, "he who holds the heavens"). As a result he became a crack Indian trader, and an agent in dealing with the Indians.

Some of the wild Weiser strain passed to Heinrich Melchior's sons Peter and Frederick. Both followed their father's wish in becoming ministers (though Peter, the elder, did not complete the studies for which he was sent to Germany). But there obedience reached its high-water mark. Old Heinrich Melchior did not burn with revolutionary zeal. Instead he followed a German tradition in effect since the brutal Thirty Years' War, under which each prince set the religious style of his domain. Thus civil and religious authorities were partners. It was natural that the founding father of American Lutheranism saw George III as a sponsor of his efforts and shrank from challenges to royal authority. But Peter, off to take a Virginia pastorate in 1772 when he was twenty-six, drank of the intoxicating waters of protest. The German community he served elected him to the House of Burgesses, where he was influenced by the ideas of firebrands like Patrick Henry. Peter Muhlenberg became chairman of Dunmore County's pro-Revolutionary Committee of Public Safety in 1774. In January of 1776, if there is truth in a local legend, he ascended to the pulpit one Sunday, gazed firmly at his parishioners, and announced his text as Ecclesiastes 3:1: "For every thing there is a season, and a time to every purpose under heaven." He then went on to review the history of British oppression and build his argument. There had been a time to petition, and there was now a time to resist. There was a time to pray, and a time to fight. As the services ended, Pastor Muhlenberg impatiently ripped away at the ties of his gown, shrugged it back off his shoulders, and stood revealed in the uniform of colonel of the Continental Army. Simultaneously, the regimental recruiting sergeants, gathered by prearrangement outside the church door, launched into a clamorous, irresistible drum roll.

Transformed from pastor to warrior, Muhlenberg went on to carve out a distinguished combat record. He earned the nickname of "Devil Pete" in the course of several hard-fought engagements, and was in on the last act of the drama at Yorktown. On October 24, 1781, by now a brigadier general, Muhlenberg led an attack against one of two strong points anchoring the British lines. (At the head of his advance party was another immigrant, from the West Indies, named Alexander Hamilton.) At the end of the war, the former minister, now a hero to Pennsylvania's Germans second only to Washington, reaped his reward. He became a member of Pennsylvania's Supreme Executive Council, then its vice-president (under an early constitution), then a member of the First, Third, and Sixth Federal Congresses, and finally a Senator.

Frederick, the younger son, was of little more comfort to Heinrich Melchior. He had a congregation in New York, but he too immersed himself in radical politics—to such an extent that when the British occupied the city he was forced to flee to Philadelphia, where in 1779 he was elected to the Continental Congress. Less colorful than his brother Peter, he nonetheless was more influential politically than anyone in his family. After serving in the Pennsylvania convention that ratified the Constitution, he was elected to the First Congress—as was Peter—and was chosen first Speaker of the House of Representatives. He was then not quite thirty-nine, and his family had been in America for fewer than fifty years. The Congressmen who voted for him had, knowingly or not, made a powerful statement about the "asylum for mankind" that they were preparing to govern.

Heinrich Melchior Mühlenberg, who died in 1787, did not witness this particular family triumph, but he lived long enough to see his two older sons' rise in the "hurle burle" of politics, and possibly even to hope that the openness of American society would allow his many descendants distinguished careers. These

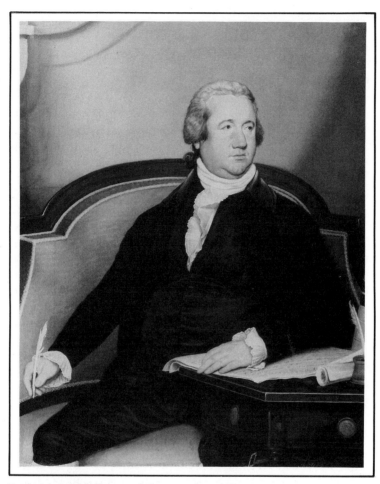

Frederick Muhlenberg, of the prominent German-American family that led the Lutheran community in Pennsylvania throughout the eighteenth and nineteenth centuries, was chosen the first Speaker of the House of Representatives in 1799. Fewer than fifty years before, his father, Heinrich Melchior, left his native Germany to establish the first Lutheran synod in America. *(National Portrait Gallery, Smithsonian Institution, Washington, D.C.)*

they did achieve, in law, medicine, science, religion, and education, providing a fresh level of meaning for the Revolution that the patriarch resisted and his heirs embraced.

Unlike Heinrich Mühlenberg, Nicholas Herkimer found the choice between resistance and rebellion neither painful nor unclear. New York's Mohawk Valley is a fruitful and gentle country of glacial soils pushed up into softly swelling ridges. In 1725, when John Herchheimer arrived in the valley, later known as Tryon County, it was thickly wooded and was controlled by the Iroquois. Patiently Herchheimer and his fellow Rhinelanders hacked away at the forest, planted flax, wheat, oats, corn, and rye in their seasons, built cabins and barns, and dreamed of a safe future for the children, such as young Nicholas Herchheimer, born in 1728. But by the time Nicholas had become a young man with the Anglicized name Herkimer, it was clear that security was still at least a generation away. Indian attacks periodically scorched the settlements. And there were other enemies, too, in the valley's great land-holding families, including those headed by Sir John Butler and Sir William Johnson. Their wealth, their control of trade with the Indians and with importers of European goods, their political connections, and their ability to hire and allocate the services of vitally needed artisans like millwrights and wheelwrights, all added up to something resembling feudal power. The German (as well as some of the Dutch, Irish, and Yankee) pioneers of Tryon County resented that resemblance. They turned to leaders of their own, like Herkimer, whose steady worldly efforts had enabled him to build a brick house—an impressive symbol on the relatively undeveloped frontier. They elected him a lieutenant of militia during the French and Indian War, then colonel, then chairman of the local Committee of Safety. In America, that could happen to the son of an untitled "Dutchman" easily—if he had the right qualities.

The Revolution tore the valley wide open. Many of the settlers believed that their best hope of safety lay in alliance with the powerful Tory families who had the crown's seeming protection. The Butlers and the Johnsons intended to convince everyone of the wholesomeness of that policy. They led raiding parties of white and Indian followers in savage strikes against nests of suspected revolutionaries. Herkimer had not hesitated for a moment to cast his lot with the enemies of royal rule. As a militia leader, he had his hands full defending settlements like German Flats and Stone Arabia against despoilment. Then, in the summer of 1776, he faced a new and more formidable enemy.

Late in July, a British colonel, Barry St. Leger, moved out from Oswego at the head of a force of five hundred British and Hessian troops, five hundred Tory rangers, and about a thousand Indians. His objective was to reach the Mohawk River and follow it down to Albany to join Burgoyne's main force there for the final thrust against the rebels. A week's march brought him to Fort Stanwix (renamed Fort Schuyler by the Americans) on the site of today's Rome, New York. There seven hundred and fifty colonials under two Dutch-descended officers, Marinus Willett and Peter Gansevoort, held him off. St. Leger threw siege lines around the earthen walls and log palisades of the fort, and Gansevoort and Willett sent messengers slipping stealthily out along forest trails for reinforcements.

Up from the southeast came the Tryon County militia, eight hundred strong, under the thickset, pipe-puffing Herkimer— "Old Honikol" to his troopers, who were also his neighbors. At Oriskany, eight miles from the fort, an ambush party was waiting for him. On August 6, they pounced from the woods in an explosion of hatred. It was Indian against Indian (St. Leger's Mohawks against some friendly Oneidas recruited by Herkimer), settler against settler, possibly even German against German. There were no flags and no trumpets—only the screams of dying men, many stabbed repeatedly after they fell and scalped while they were still conscious. Two hundred militiamen were killed and as many more wounded or captured. Herkimer's knee was smashed by a bullet, but, propped against a tree, he pulled his shattered troops together on high ground, where they held out against repeated assaults. Then rain fell, soaking gunpowder and men alike and halting combat. Later that day, the Tryon County militia retreated, carrying Old Honikol on a litter.

It was not complete defeat. While the fighting was at its height, Marinus Willett led a sortie into a British camp and destroyed or seized everything portable—including fifty brass kettles and a hundred blankets intended as gifts for the Indians— without losing a man. This discouraged the Indians mightily; they had little other motive but material gain for sacrificing braves in quarrels between the whites. Later, in the face of rumors that a huge American relief column was on the way, they abandoned St. Leger entirely, forcing him to retreat to Oswego. But Herkimer did not live to see this. Back at his brick house, a surgeon had crudely amputated his leg. Resultant complications proved too much for even his toughened constitution. He died ten days later, reputedly reading a Bible verse: "My wounds stink and are corrupt because of my foolishness." The settlers, who thought more kindly of his contribution than he, later named an upstate town and county in his honor.

Sometime after Louis XIV revoked the Edict of Nantes in 1685, two French Protestant gentlemen, probably unknown to each other, arrived in New York. They were Stephen De Lancey and André Laurens. What befell them and their grandsons superbly condenses two varieties of American experience. Stephen De Lancey remained in New York and married Anne Van Cortlandt, a daughter of a rich Dutch family. In 1703, their first son, James, was born. James went to neither France nor Holland, his parents' ancestral homes, for his education, but, as was proper for an aristocrat in the British colonies, was sent to Cambridge to acquire the accomplishments of an English gentleman, then to the Inner Temple to read law and to make friendships of future utility. Back in New York in 1725, he soon married Anne Heathcote, whose father was receiver-general of customs of North America. With this connection, James De Lancey was able to rise to the office of chief justice of the colony, where he earned the rather clouded distinction of presiding at the trial of the printer John Peter Zenger, a German immigrant, for seditious libel. In 1753 De Lancey became lieutenant governor, vigorously carried on feuds with such other great families as the Clintons and the Livingstons, in 1754 became a signer of the charter of King's College (later Columbia), and died in 1760.

His son, also named James, was sent to Eton and Cambridge, and entered the army on completing his studies. He took part in the French and Indian War, and indulged a country gentleman's passion for horse-flesh. Soon after his father died, Captain James imported the first English thoroughbreds ever brought to New York. He divided his time between caring for them, looking after real-estate investments on what is now New York's lower East Side, guiding the family's mercantile ventures, and managing the affairs of the "De Lancey interest," in effect a political party. From time to time he joined in objections to crown policies that adversely affected the family businesses. But essentially, James De Lancey had become an upper-class Englishman. When the fighting came, he sold out his stud and racing stable and moved with his family to England. The Revolutionary New York legislature, by acts of 1777 and 1779, confiscated all the De Lancey estates, ending the dynasty's participation in American economic life.

This seizure, of course, depended for its effectiveness on the triumph of the American cause, which two other De Lanceys were striving mightily to prevent. Captain James had a cousin, also named James—the son of Peter, old Stephen De Lancey's second son. This James, known as Colonel James, loved horseflesh not merely on the track but amid the thunder of the cannons and the heat of battle. After the British occupied New York in 1776, he organized a band of fifty mounted guerrillas who harassed the rebels in Westchester County. De Lancey's Horse was no plumed troop fighting a Walter Scott war. They plundered, they burned, and they specialized in raiding the herds of cattle that Westchester farmers had annually driven down to Manhattan markets. The patriots called them the Cowboys, a term that did not then have the meaning it was later to take on in the American West. De Lancey unrepentantly enjoyed such nicknames, and added his own to the string: "Colonel, Westchester Refugees," for one, and "The Outlaw of the Bronx" for another. But he had chosen the wrong side. At the end of the war he had to move to Nova Scotia, with many other Loyalists.

Both cousins had a dashing model in their Uncle Oliver, youngest of Stephen's sons, born in 1718 (only fourteen years older than Captain James, he was a good twenty-eight years senior to the Bronx Outlaw). Although a merchant like his brothers, Oliver was no model for the mercantile class; he was vigorous in contests and violent in language, a remorseless individualist who shocked two families by eloping with the wealthy Jewish heiress Phila Franks. He brawled his way through political service as an alderman, assemblyman, and member of the provincial Council, the legislative upper house. At the outbreak of the war, he raised a brigade of fifteen hundred Tories. As a brigadier general, De Lancey occupied the highest military position of any colonial loyalist in the British Army. (Patriots gave

On the issue of the term of citizenship required
in order to be eligible for election to the House
of Representatives, George Mason, one of the
framers of the Constitution, proposed a period
of at least seven years, four more than had
already been suggested. He was, he said, in
favor of "opening a wide door for emigrants;
but did not chuse to let foreigners and adventurers make laws for us & govern us." *(National
Portrait Gallery, Smithsonian Institution, Washington, D.C., S. Cooper Dawson, Jr.)*

his exalted status an ironic official recognition when they sacked his mansion at Bloomingdale in 1777.) The De Lancey battalions fought well but vainly. Oliver went into exile in the 1780s with his nephews and other kin.

André Laurens had spent an indefinite period of time in New York in the 1680s and possibly later, but had moved to Charleston shortly before 1715. The requirements of business life in America led his son Jean, a maker and supplier of saddles, to change his name to John. John's eldest son, Henry, born in 1724, was not sent to an English university, like the De Lancey youngsters, but he got the best education that tutors in South Carolina, hired by his prosperous father, could impart to him. He later went to London, to be sure, but only to make business contacts. In 1747, when John Laurens died, Henry returned to Charleston and soon entered an import-export partnership.

For some years Laurens shipped Carolina rice, indigo, and deer hides to ports in England, Holland, Portugal, Spain, and the West Indies, and in return received wine and slaves. As he prospered, he followed a Southern pattern of investing his profits in plantations, which brought a gentlemanly status that the countinghouse simply could not confer. Then the quarrel with England engaged him. Gouty, sensitive, and sarcastic, he made a tough and self-righteous adversary in a debate with British customs officials or with supporters of the governor in the provincial assembly, where he served almost uninterruptedly from 1757 to 1771. He then went to England for three years to supervise the education of his own sons, John and Henry. By then, whatever loyalty he had felt for English ways was cooling; outraged at what he thought was the corruption of the English ruling classes, he sent the boys away to school in Geneva and returned to Charleston.

In January of 1777 he was elected to the Continental Congress, and in November of the same year he was chosen president of that body, an office he held until December of 1778, when he was succeeded by John Jay, another Huguenot descendant. In August of 1780, Laurens set out from Philadelphia on the brigantine *Mercury* on a mission to Holland. His job was to interest practical Dutch bankers in advancing ten million dollars to the Americans and to negotiate a treaty of amity and commerce. Three weeks out of port, the *Mercury* was spotted and captured by a British warship. Laurens was taken to England. There he was treated as a state prisoner suspected of high treason. Louis XIV of France had expelled Laurens's grandfather as a disloyal subject who put faith above king. England's George III imprisoned Laurens as a renegade who put his home province above the throne. For fourteen months Laurens languished in the Tower of London, not seriously mistreated but in circumstances hardly healthful for a man of fifty-seven. Finally he was released in time to join the American peace commission in Paris, some months after his son John, who had returned home to join Washington's staff in 1777, was killed in action in one of the last skirmishes of the war in the Carolinas. In 1792, Laurens himself retired to one of his plantations, where he died after a long illness. (He had been elected to the Constitutional Convention but could not attend.)

The most surprising transformation from newcomer into patriot in the whole era, however, may have been that of Phillis Wheatley. In 1761, at about eight years of age, she was brought to Boston on a slave ship. A kindly merchant, John Wheatley, saw the little African girl standing terrified and nearly naked on the auction block, took a fancy to her, and brought her home to his wife. Taught to read, she developed into a poet whose work was primarily cast in neoclassic couplets, not quite adequately imitative of Alexander Pope's verses. Whatever their aesthetic deficiencies may have been, her verses found a publisher—a rather astonishing thing for any woman, white or black, at the time. Moreover, when Phillis, as ardent as any Boston follower of Sam Adams or John Hancock, sent a congratulatory poem to George Washington on his appointment as commander in chief, the Virginian wrote back: "Thank you most sincerely for your polite notice of me, in the elegant lines you enclosed . . . the style and manner exhibited a striking proof of your poetical talents. . . ."

Blacks participated in the Revolution in many ways, and this may have slightly sped emancipation in the North, though it is not easy to demonstrate the connection. There is a firmer possible link, however, between the role of the foreign-born on the ramparts and the pressures in the Constitutional Convention to allow immigrants quick access to equal political rights with native Americans. On the 8th, 9th, and 10th of August, 1787, and again on the 13th, the perspiring framers grappled with the question of the term of citizenship required for eligibility for election to the House or Senate.

George Mason of Virginia proposed a period of at least seven years for a Representative, arguing that he was for "opening a wide door for emigrants; but did not chuse to let foreigners and adventurers make laws for us & govern us." Three years (the original proposal on the floor), Mason held, was "not enough for ensuring that local knowledge which ought to be possessed by the Representatives." Yet when the question of the proper seasoning in Americanism for a Senator came up, Mason, though he argued for a fourteen-year requirement, confessed that he would ordinarily have contested for restricting the Senate to the native-born, "were it not that many not natives of this Country had acquired great merit during the revolution. . . ." It was a view that must have had some support in the group, though the only other delegate to be recorded explicitly on the subject was James Wilson of Pennsylvania, who noted that "almost all the General officers of the Pennsylvania line of the late army were foreigners. And no complaint had ever been made against their fidelity or merit." Wilson spoke with particular zeal. He himself was a Scottish immigrant, and it galled him to think that if "some gentlemen" had their way, he would be denied the right to hold an office under the Constitution which he "had shared in the trust of making." Moreover, his state, Pennsylvania, a colonial melting pot, had generously granted foreigners "all the rights whatsoever of citizens" after only two years' residence, and Wilson proudly pointed out that, possibly as a result of its encouragement of immigration, even though it was "perhaps the youngest settlement [except Georgia] on the Atlantic; yet it was at least among the foremost in population and prosperity."

The whole debate on the liberal proposals submitted by the Committee of Detail—three years' citizenship for a Representative, and four for a Senator—brought attitudes on immigrants and immigration into sharp focus. Charles Pinckney of South Carolina was fearful of permitting Senators, who had so much power in foreign affairs, to be drawn from non-native ranks. He reminded his classically learned colleagues of the Athenians' policy of making it death for any stranger "to intrude his voice into their Legislative proceedings." But James Madison, who yielded to none in his respect for ancient models, nevertheless denounced rules that would give "a tincture of illiberality" to the emerging national charter. "Great numbers of respectable Europeans," he remarked, "men who love liberty and wish to partake its blessings, will be ready to transfer their fortunes hither. All such would feel the mortification of being marked with suspicious incapacitations though they should not covet the public honors."

Pierce Butler responded with a defense of his South Carolina colleague's misgivings. Foreigners "without a long residence in the Country" (which the foreign-born Butler himself happened to enjoy) brought with them attachments to other countries, and "ideas of Government so distinct from ours that in every point of view they are dangerous." It was an idea picked up later on by Elbridge Gerry of Massachusetts, who was to make a long career out of distrust of Frenchmen, democrats, Southerners, the unpropertied, and strangers. Only the native-born, he declaimed, should serve in Congress, or else "persons having foreign attachments will be sent among us & insinuated into our councils, in order to be made instruments for their purposes." The "vast sums laid out in Europe for secret services," Gerry insisted, were a matter of common knowledge.

The aged Benjamin Franklin pleaded for the doctrine of asylum. He saw things from a cosmopolitan viewpoint; the people in Europe were friendly to the United States, and in the Revolution not only had many "strangers" (presumably men like Lafayette, Kosciusko, and von Steuben) served the rebel cause faithfully, but some had even taken part against their own countries: "When foreigners after looking about for some other Country in which they can obtain more happiness, give a preference to ours it is a proof of attachment which ought to excite our confidence and affection." He joined Madison in crying out against "illiberality."

That provoked a humorous speech from another Pennsylvania delegate. Tall, fleshy, and with a wooden leg, Gouverneur Morris was described by a colleague as one who "winds through all the mazes of rhetoric, and throws around him such a glare that he charms, captivates, and leads away the senses of all who hear him." His remarks, as recorded by Madison, began with a rebuttal to the charge of illiberality:

What is the language of Reason on this subject? That we should not be polite at the expence of prudence. There was a moderation in all things. It is said that some tribes of Indians carried their hospitality so far as to offer to strangers their wives and daughters. Was this a proper model for us? He would admit them to his house, he would invite them to his table, would provide for them comfortable lodgings; but would not carry the complaisance so far as, to bed them with his wife. He would let them worship at the same altar, but did not choose to make Priests of them. . . . He owned he did not wish to see any of them in our public Councils. He would not trust them. The men who can shake off their attachments to their own Country can never love any other. These attachments are the wholesome prejudices which uphold all Governments. Admit a Frenchman into your Senate, and he will study to increase the commerce of France; an Englishman, and he will feel an equal biass in favor of that of England.

In the end, the convention's decision was something of a retreat from the liberality of the first draft. No person could be a Representative who had not been seven years a citizen, and to become a Senator required nine. Yet the atmosphere created by the new state and national governments was, in the main, hospitable enough to continue to lure the disaffected of Europe, and it is estimated that 250,000 white aliens arrived in American ports between 1783 and 1815, most of them before the outbreak of the Napoleonic Wars. They came in search of the asylum that Thomas Paine had envisioned, and also, as always, in quest of less abstract advantages: work, cheap land, the chance to become shopowners, burghers, founders of thriving families.

They came largely from the same sources as the prewar migration. The Scotch-Irish and the Germans continued to furnish large numbers of indentured servants. (It was not until the early nineteenth century that the end came for that trade, which the British helped wipe out; they limited the number of passengers per ship—making it unprofitable for captains to pack the hold with nonpaying passengers who could be "sold" for their fare and costs on arrival in America—and restricted the emigration of skilled craftsmen, the kinds of servants most in demand. Moreover, the turmoil of war in Europe made recruitment of emigrants difficult and ocean transport risky. Finally, in 1819, the United States itself, by the Passenger Act, forbade the importation of indentured labor in order to remedy the abuses which made hell ships of the vessels carrying redemptioners.)

The German contingent also included several thousand Hessian prisoners, who remained in America instead of returning to the liege lords who had sold them like so many oxen. Besides these, some French, English, Scottish, and other settlers were enticed by agents of speculative companies that bought huge tracts of Western lands and desperately needed purchasers. One example was the Scioto Land Company, a syndicate with vast virgin acreages in Ohio. It employed Joel Barlow, a talented poet, ex-army chaplain, linguist, businessman, and radical pamphleteer, to enlist a company of Frenchmen who would bring Gallic civilization to the West. Barlow rounded up his culture bearers, who duly made their way to the banks of the Ohio River and founded Gallipolis in 1790. There they stayed until they found that their titles were defective and that their brave new world abounded in Indians, mosquitoes, malaria, violence, and ignorance, whereupon they abandoned the scene and their plans for producing wine, silk, and virtue in an undespoiled land.

As early as 1790, the first census takers enumerated a white population that modern scholars—using admittedly crude tests—estimate to be approximately 60 percent English, 9.5 percent Irish (both Ulster and southern), 8.6 percent German, 8.1 percent Scotch, 3.1 percent Dutch, 2.3 percent French, 0.7 percent Swedish, 0.8 percent Spanish, and 6.8 percent unclassified. The pattern was already so variously hued that Crèvecoeur could invoke "the American, this new man." And a German observer could describe America as housing a "promiscuous crowd of almost all nations in Europe." He predicted that such a mixture would "require a long fermentation before it will contain the spirit, the feelings, and the imprint of a united people." Yet the fermentation was already in process; French, Swedish, Welsh, Dutch, and German began to wane as languages used in church services and newspapers. De Witt Clinton, the mayor of New York, somewhat complacently but accurately reported in 1814 that "the triumph and adoption of the English language have been the principal means of melting us down." (It is intriguing to find the practical politician Clinton using that particular verb some ninety-five years before the playwright Israel Zangwill, an English Jew, used the phrase "the Melting-Pot" to describe the United States.

The new nation appeared to be embarked on a path of peaceful

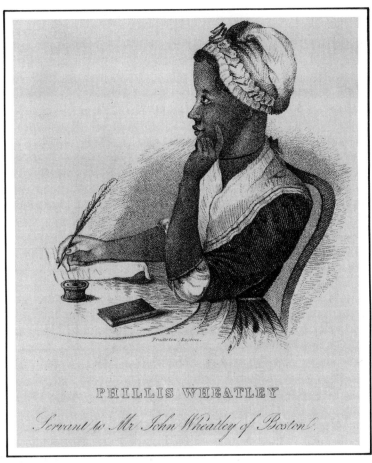

PHILLIS WHEATLEY

Servant to Mr John Wheatley of Boston.

Phillis Wheatley, "snatch'd from Afric's fancy'd happy seat" as a child, became a well-known poet whose work was published, a remarkable feat at the time for any woman. Being a slave in a land fighting for freedom did not, in her case, suppress the patriotism that welled up inside her and flowed out of her pen. In 1775 the devoted Wheatley sent a congratulatory poem to George Washington on his appointment as commander in chief. *(The New-York Historical Society)* assimilation of whatever fortune seekers and fugitives made their way into its extended arms. Yet from the start, as the remarks of men like Gerry at Philadelphia in 1787 portended, there was a dark underside to the welcome mat. KEEP OUT was written on it, in letters of pitch. In times of stress, there has always been a struggle to turn that side uppermost. The late 1790s were the first of such times. The question of immigration became entangled with European wars and revolutions, and with the development of the two-party system in American politics. An outburst of xenophobia splashed the closing years of the decade with hostility, which expressed itself in the passage of the Alien Acts—measures of firm rejection to all those who were in quest of Thomas Paine's asylum, or indeed thought in any way like Tom Paine on any subject.

When the First Congress enacted a "uniform Rule of Naturalization," as authorized in the Constitution, it provided that application for citizenship could be made after only two years of residence in the country. But almost immediately thereafter, events pushed the nation away from this generous policy. In 1792 the French Republic was established and war broke out in Europe—to continue, with only short intervals of peace, for twenty-three years. The policies of the Jacobin rulers of France drove thousands of their opponents into flight for their lives. Meanwhile, the monarchies of Europe trembled at the genuine threat that the virus of revolution might spread. In their attempts to effect quarantines, they vigorously harassed reformers of every kind. Political imprisonment and escape became increasingly visible features of public life. The Poles, the Irish, the Italians, all stirred restlessly under Russian, British, and Austrian masters. In Haiti and Santo Domingo the blacks rose against their plantation masters, killed (and were killed) by the thousands, and provoked a panicked dispersement of white settlers.

It was a time like the middle and later years of the twentieth century, an era of exile. And then, too, it affected immigration to America. As one historian, James Morton Smith, sums it up: "The neutral United States immediately became the haven of refugees. To its shores came discontented Englishmen, aristocratic Frenchmen, German Pietists fleeing forced military service, French planters escaping from West Indian uprisings led by

Toussaint L'Ouverture, and Irishmen in flight from British repression."

These castaways from the shipwreck of the old order arrived in the period when the United States was administered by the inherently conservative Federalists. Men like John Adams and Alexander Hamilton deplored democratic "excesses," especially in France. To exacerbate matters, the French, in their warfare with England, persistently seized or destroyed American ships trading with their enemy. The British did the same (thereby bringing about war finally in 1812), but in 1798 it was the French "spoliations" that were most abrasive. The infant United States Navy was actually in a state of undeclared war against France. Furthermore, three American envoys sent to Paris to seek a settlement had been treated with disdain, visited by three unofficial envoys (referred to in the publicly released account of the mission simply as X, Y, and Z), and told that they would have to bribe the French government with nearly a quarter of a million dollars before even hoping for satisfaction. The release of news of this "XYZ Affair" in April set off a wave of Francophobia in the United States. It was against this background that the Alien and Sedition Acts were passed.

The prelude was a stiffening of the naturalization law. It had already been modified once, in 1795, raising the residence requirement from two to five years. Now, three years later, the Federalist-dominated House Committee for the Protection of Commerce and the Defense of the Country brought in a measure for further amendment: this time to make the minimum residence before naturalization a full fourteen years, and to insist as well that five years elapse between a declaration of intention to be naturalized and the final award of citizenship. Some Federalists found the new proposal too mild, and hoped to exclude the foreign-born from voting and officeholding altogether. Among them was Harrison Gray Otis, a young Representative from Boston and the bright hope of Harvard's first post-Revolutionary graduating class. In 1797 Otis had declared: "I do not wish to invite hordes of wild Irishmen, nor the turbulent and disorderly of all parts of the world, to come here with a view to disturb our tranquility. . . ." He thus sounded a battle cry long to reverberate in Boston. (An Irish newspaper writer, taking up the challenge, metrically retorted with a threat that would actually be executed: "Young man, we would have you remember/

While we in this country can tarry,/The '*Wild Irish*' will choose a new member/And will ne'er vote again for *young Harry.*")

Otis did not prevail, any more than Republican opponents who could only succeed in making the bill nonretroactive, allowing aliens who had entered the United States before 1795 to apply for naturalization under the old law. But holding back for fourteen years a suspected future surge of naturalized voters was not enough to appease Federalist fears. President John Adams was informed that Frenchmen in Philadelphia were planning on May 9, 1798, to destroy the city by fire and massacre its inhabitants. A Federalist cleric, Jedidiah Morse, warned his congregation that the American "Jacobins"—that is to say, Jefferson's followers—were agents of a secret society called the Illuminati, which was dedicated to the destruction of all churches and governments.

To forestall such calamities, Congressional leaders drafted two bills. One, the Alien Enemies Act, providing for wartime restraint of noncitizens, was passed with little argument and formed the foundation of later American policy in this area. The other, the so-called Alien Friends Act, bore all the earmarks of a full-fledged witch hunt. As proposed by a Senate committee, it allowed the President to expel any foreigner on the mere suspicion of treasonable machinations. If the alien so deported returned and was detected, he could be imprisoned without trial at hard labor for life. Even those aliens not suspected and expelled could remain in the country only by securing a special Presidential permit, and would thereafter—even in peacetime—be subjected to surveillance. Moreover, any citizen who wished to "harbour, entertain or conceal any alien" had first to give written notice to a Federal court.

Jefferson warned that the measure was "worthy of the 8th or 9th century," and Madison commented that it was "a monster that must forever disgrace its parents." A letter writer to one newspaper wrote that he had seen, in a museum, an "American medal" inscribed with the motto "An asylum for the oppressed of all nations." "The gilding of this coin," he wrote, "is a little worn off and evidently shows base metal beneath." Another sardonically advised Irish refugees from British bayonets and nooses not to come to the United States, but to seek instead some country where "hatred to tryanny will not subject you to transportation without a trial by jury." The coast of Africa was suggested. Unlike Federalist Americans, it was implied, "the Hottentots are a hospitable people."

Before the President signed it on June 25, 1798, the bill was somewhat modified. The alien was given notice of a specific time within which he had to leave. If found in the United States after the deadline, he could stand trial, facing a maximum sentence of three years' imprisonment. During the grace period before his required departure, he could also present evidence in his favor, and might even receive a Presidential permit to remain in a specified place. If he was deported but returned and was found, he was entitled to a trial. If convicted, he could be jailed for as long as the President deemed necessary to the "public safety." While the amended act was an improvement on the draft, it was still a severely repressive measure, coupled in historical infamy with the almost simultaneous Sedition Act, which allowed for the jailing of those who in speech or writing brought the government "into contempt or disrepute." The best thing about the Alien Friends Act was that it was considered merely an emergency measure to be revoked after two years.

Happily, the actual enforcement of the act was haphazard. President Adams was loath to enforce it. He had long been a defender of the principle of asylum, and he was now compelled to eat his own words, explaining that while he believed in America as a refuge "for virtue in distress and for innocent industry, it behoves us to beware, that under this pretext it is not made a receptacle of malevolence and turbulence, for the outcasts of the universe." Some of the more conspicuous "agitators" who were the objects of Federalist suspicion solved the Presidential dilemma by leaving before proceedings were instituted against them—among them the historian Médéric Moreau de Saint-Méry, then a bookstore proprietor in Philadelphia, and Constantin Volney, a writer and former French National Assembly member. Both represented the colony of radical refugee intellectuals who were particularly irksome to certain patriotic Yankees. A blank warrant was issued for the arrest of the French economist Pierre Samuel Du Pont de Nemours, who was supposedly due to arrive in the country with a French delegation of visiting experts, but he delayed his landing until the act had expired. Otherwise, a distinguished industrial dynasty in America might have had a convict in its past.

The kind of fumbling application that unwittingly tempered the execution of the act is revealed in the story of the efforts to evict a French general, Victor Collot. Collot had been governor of the French island of Guadeloupe, which was captured by the British in 1794. Since Collot suspected that the Paris authorities might decide to punish him for his lack of revolutionary zeal, he asked his captors to allow him to go to the United States and remain there as a paroled prisoner of war, to which they agreed. While in America, Collot aroused American (and Spanish) anxieties by a long, leisurely trip along the Ohio and Mississippi Rivers, from Pittsburgh to New Orleans. It appeared to some that he was laying the groundwork for a possible French-organized "uprising" to seize Louisiana, then Spanish-owned. As a consequence, the American government had him kept under surveillance.

In October of 1798, Secretary of State Timothy Pickering, who was responsible for the execution of the Alien Friends Act, asked the President for blank warrants authorizing the arrest of Collot, Du Pont, and an associate of Collot's named Sweitzer. Then further deeds of heroism suggested themselves to him. He had heard from informants that another French general, Jean Serurier, was also in the United States, in disguise, and might attempt to contact Collot. So, in the fashion of police officials in a thousand melodramas, Pickering decided not to arrest Collot, hoping that he might lure additional game—Serurier—into his bag.

Affairs dragged on inconclusively until June of 1799, when it was reported that Collot was on the verge of leaving the country. Collot had in fact decided earlier that the new government in Paris would be in a forgiving mood, and had asked the British authorities for a passport to return to France. Pickering, then hoping to catch Serurier, had actually asked the British not to grant the request, and they had obliged him.

Now, however, Pickering was apparently ready to give up. Collot must be got rid of, Serurier or no Serurier. But he was reluctant to use the Alien Law, which he already considered a dead letter. President Adams, on the other hand, was eager to test it against the "pernicious and malicious intriguer." While they debated the issue, Collot moved to Newark, where he resided incognito. A Federalist judge, Elisha Boudinot, darkly reported to Pickering a series of "facts" and rumors of the kind that

108

have always delighted superpatriots. Collot subscribed to a violently Republican newspaper, the Philadelphia *Aurora*—and under an alias! He had an "intriguing spirit." He had criticized the government in conversation with a Frenchman named Boisobier, who had obligingly reported the fact to Boudinot. He had asked many questions about Frenchmen living in his neighborhood. And he had allegedly threatened that if war should break out between France and the United States, he would revenge himself on some of his local enemies.

Despite Boudinot's urgings, Adams and Pickering somehow failed to take action against Collot. The "intriguer"—if he was such—finally left under a British passport in August of 1800, and was allowed to come home by his government. An arbitrary law, tempered with doubt, inefficiency, and overreaching, had proved endurable for at least one alien.

The dawn of the nineteenth century brought a new administration to Washington, and the uncontested expiration of the Alien and Sedition Acts. The first fever of nativism had passed, and in the bustle of the Jeffersonian revolution, the issue was not raised again. The young republic entered a new era with a fresh set of attitudes toward the stranger at the gate.

V

Refugees, Rebels, and Romantics

The laying down of American's great railroad lines owes a greater debt to the muscle and sweat of thousands of Irish laborers than to machinery such as this steam shovel. *(American Geographical Society)*

On both sides of the Atlantic, the year 1815 marked a major turning point—perhaps the real beginning of the modern age. In Europe, the soldiers who had survived nearly twenty years of Napoleonic battles exchanged their swords for plowshares and beggars' cups, and a century of almost uninterrupted peace among the major powers began. Internal revolutions would work their effects on European life, but the destructive potential of international war would not be fully realized for another hundred years. In the United States, the momentum of the westward movement accelerated apace as the American people turned toward the immense, unprobed domain of forest, prairie, and mountain stretching to the Pacific, and began to settle it with a rush that carried them to California and Oregon within the span of a generation.

The pace of the era was set by the steam engine, an eighteenth-century creation that came into its own in the nineteenth. Powering paddle wheels and propellers, chuffing along tracks on land, it became the conqueror of oceans and of interior continental spaces. Before it, the forest melted and the mountains leveled, and the aboriginal life that hitherto had been hidden from modernity—of buffalo and Sioux, of zebra and Zulu—was doomed to subordination. Steam-operated machinery was the driving force behind a new world of goods—goods mass-produced with the prodigality of a god multiplying universes. And as all this new energy was released, all humanity stirred.

It was in such energized circumstances that an expanding global population began to move in mighty tides. Immigration to the United States is only part of the unfolding story of human development in our time. Between the census years 1820 and 1860, more than five million individuals came to American shores—a number greater than the nation's population in 1790. But other millions went to Australia, Latin America, Canada, and to European settlements in coastal North and South Africa. Still others severed their ancestral roots while remaining within Europe itself—the Irish going to England in search of jobs and the Germans seeking better lands in Russia, to take just two examples. On a shrinking earth that they did not yet think of as a crowded spaceship, people swarmed across the artificial lines drawn by political geographers.

European emigration to the United States grew each decade. In the 1820s there were 151,000 arrivals; 573,000 in the 1830s; 1,479,000 in the 1840s; and, in the last decade before the Civil War, when the country's total population passed the thirty-million mark, more than three million. Most of these immigrants—a point that would be labored at the end of the century but that attracted little notice before 1860—were from Northern and Western Europe. Some two million Irish took part in the 1815–60 migration, and a million and a half Germans, while around three quarters of a million came from England, Scotland, and Wales, along with smaller contingents from Switzerland, Scandinavia, and the Netherlands. During the same period there were also more than 112,000 known entrants from Canada and Newfoundland, many of whom undoubtedly were European-born. In addition, there was always a literally unchecked current of immigrants who went from Canada into the United States by walking across an unpatrolled border.

The forces that propelled dissatisfied Europeans toward Hamburg, Liverpool, Le Havre, and other popular embarkation points were many. Some were created by transient upheavals—political revolutions such as those in Poland, France, and Belgium in 1830, and in France, Germany, Italy, Austria, and Hungary in 1848. Each of them—and many abortive attempts to bring them off earlier—begot political exiles. Bad harvests and epidemics, religious schisms, and restrictive laws aimed at certain groups and classes impelled people to depart. The classic combination of many such factors was the Irish potato famines of the 1840s. The Irish already were politically helpless, punished in a variety of ways for their continued Catholicism, and desperately poor. Many who had not already fled their native soil were now chased out by starvation. But behind these crises were other, long-range developments.

One was a steady increase in the world's population, which aroused the gloomy apprehensions of the English economist Thomas R. Malthus. His *Essay on the Principle of Population,* published in 1798, attempted to prove that the populace would always outrun the food supply; thus war, famine, and plague were salutary checks. Besides furnishing somewhat specious arguments to a generation of economists who preached that wages had to remain at near-starvation levels, Malthusianism helped bring about a change of heart on the part of statesmen regarding emigration. Formerly, a nation's people were thought of as an economic resource to be husbanded, so that emigration, especially of skilled workers, was discouraged. But in the light of the population explosion, departing citizens were looked upon merely as fewer mouths to feed. Great Britain repealed most of its laws restricting exit by 1827; within twenty years Sweden, the Netherlands, and the German states had done likewise.

Ironically, an even greater impetus to migration came from industrialization, which helped to sustain the population increase. The same amount of labor could produce sustenance for far greater numbers of human beings in need of food, clothing, and shelter. But factory production and scientific agriculture were ruthless dislocators. Machines rendered hand skills obsolete, and suddenly weavers and shoemakers and metalsmiths, who once were proud guildsmen, found themselves displaced wanderers, trudging the world's roads in search of new work to do. Villages decayed as handicrafts that had once supported their menfolk were destroyed by factory competition. Improvements in the cultivation of the soil—new chemical fertilizers, selective breeding of herds, deep plowing, irrigation, and the like—made possible such miracles as the feeding of great multitudes by a relative handful of farmers, but they destroyed ancient security. Planned crop rotation, pest control, and the fencing that would maintain breeding conditions productive of the woolliest sheep, the meatiest steers, the most productive milk cows—all these innovations meant the end of common fields for grazing a whole town's livestock, of tiny plots laid out in patchwork patterns, of forests left standing to furnish firewood to all comers. And so the peasants who had eked existences from fragments of soil while following the customs of centuries were now driven to seek new lives wherever they could find them. Well-managed estates and eviction seemed to go hand in hand, and the more modern a country became, the greater were its swarms of likely emigrants.

Those who were ready to move were lured toward the United States by new enticements. Now the call came not only from promoters who walked the streets of German villages chinking money in their pockets but also from the "America letters" of men like Samuel Crabtree, who in 1818 averred in print that around Wheeling, Virginia, he saw "more peaches and apples rotting on the ground than would sink the British fleet," hogs without number, and an abundance of "tea, coffee, beef, fowls, pies, eggs, pickles, good bread" on the tables of the poorest families. Now the printed allurements of the broadsides struck off in seventeenth-century London or Amsterdam, replete with broken type and crude woodcuts of leaping Indians, were replaced by sophisticated handbooks citing land prices and travel routes. Some were issued by immigration bureaus, set up in the 1850s and afterward by population-hungry Midwestern states, and some by railways with land grants for new settlers. Michigan had an office for the promotion of immigration as early as 1848, and its first commissioner was instructed to spend half his time in New York and half in Stuttgart. Wisconsin, which created the post of Commissioner of Immigration in 1851, eventually found itself publishing pamphlets in seven languages and buying advertising space in such journals as the *Leipziger Allgemeine Zeitung* and the Tipperary *Free Press*.

Other, practical inducements beckoned toward America. Cheap passages were made possible by the booming trade in grain, cotton, and timber between Europe, Canada, and the United States. Passengers made up an attractive source of income for lightly laden westbound ships. The fare from Liverpool to New York dropped from twelve pounds to just over three between 1816 and 1846; that between Le Havre and New Orleans, from about 400 francs to as low as 120. Once one was in the Promised Land, reaching the interior was not expensive. To go from New York to Detroit in 1840, for example, by way of the Hudson River, the Erie Canal, and the Great Lakes, a traveler paid as little as eight dollars. An additional $6.50 got him as far as Chicago or Milwaukee. Rail transportation cost more but was still not prohibitive, although the accommodations for a two- or three-day trip on an "emigrant train" were apt to be Spartan—boxcars with benches but without any other amenities whatever, not even drinking water. Immigrants who ventured on the river steamers plying the Mississippi, Ohio, and Missouri rivers also paid little but endured overcrowding, sickness, and the chronic risk of fires and exploding boilers. Still, in the long run, for thousands of foreigners the promises were more potent than the risks.

Immigration became a wholesale shifting of peoples among nations pulled into ever-closer contact by transportation improvements. Inevitably, governments came to measure and control the flow by modernizing their pre-nineteenth-century statutes on the subject. The United States was no exception. The Federal government passed an act prescribing certain minimum standards for sea-borne passenger accommodations as early as 1819. Massachusetts (in a legal move later declared unconstitutional as an interference with Federal control of commerce) began collecting fees from immigrant passengers in the 1840s to pay the costs of administering a hospital for those who arrived ill. New York State required reports of immigrant arrivals, and in 1847 it set up a Board of Commissioners of Emigration to devise orderly procedures for receiving immigrants, registering them, assisting them where necessary, and protecting them from swarms of swindlers and pitchmen—representing boardinghouses, employers, and transportation companies—who previously had pounced upon them as they came down the gangplanks. In 1855 the board bought the building known as Castle Garden, at Manhattan Island's southern tip, and turned it into an immigrant reception station. It served that function until it was replaced by Ellis Island, under Federal jurisdiction, in 1892.

In the world-wide stream of migration, the supposedly "isolated" and "unsophisticated" United States stood with open doors. In 1860, states that led in recent immigrant populations were leaders in industrialization: New York and Pennsylvania, followed by Ohio, Illinois, Wisconsin, and Massachusetts. The states on the farthest frontier and the fifteen slave states attracted fewer newcomers from abroad. The South was particularly unattractive to them. Even for those who condoned slavery, the plantation system offered no industrial employment, while blacks preempted the chores often performed in the North by immigrant maids, cooks, teamsters, barbers, stevedores, janitors, and the like. Of the 4,138,697 foreign-born who lived in the United States in 1860, only some thirteen percent were found in the South—most of them concentrated in St. Louis, Baltimore, and New Orleans, where urbanization widened their opportunities.

The cities were a major lodestone for the new arrivals. Then as now, the streets were sensitive reflectors of social change. In 1860 an observer in the cities could see the homogeneous nature of

America's population being altered. St. Louis had a foreign-born contingent of sixty percent, and New York, Chicago, Cincinnati, Milwaukee, Detroit, and San Francisco were nearly half foreign-born. In New Orleans, Boston, and Baltimore, the proportion of immigrants was more than a third. The Irish and the Germans were particularly urbanized. There were exceptional groups, to be sure, such as the Norwegians, almost all of whom were cultivating prairie soil in Wisconsin, Minnesota, and Iowa. But the lure of the cities was evident.

The patterns of deployment were drawn by experience and the availability of jobs and land. The Scandinavians were attracted mainly to the prairies of the Midwest and to the North Central timberlands, which were much like the terrain they had known at home. Miners from Wales and Cornwall went to dig coal from the hills of Pennsylvania, or lead and iron from the earth of Wisconsin, Michigan, and Illinois. Germans farmed the Midwestern states—where bargains in already developed farmland were available as older American families pulled up stakes and moved farther west—or practiced such familiar skills as brewing in the cities. The Irish, however, rejected their peasant past and clung to the cities or fanned out along the lines formed by the canals and railroads then under construction, which offered work to unskilled hands.

Even before the fateful year of 1845, the lot of the rural Irish was squalor, with frustration for anyone who was ambitious. The genial qualities of the Irish are a tribute to good nature's triumph over bitter reality. Irish farmlands were fertile, but Irish eggs, butter, bacon, and flour were exported to pay rent to absentee landlords. The peasants relied for their own sustenance on what they could coax out of tiny plots that sometimes would have been barely adequate as urban back yards. Forty-five percent of all landholdings in Ireland in 1845 were less than five acres in extent, and more than ninety-three percent of all farms comprised fewer than thirty acres. Even these were subdivided as the population rose mysteriously—in a land largely without towns, industries, or medical care—to more than eight million in 1841, making Ireland the most densely populated country in Europe.

There was little that an Irish child could expect to attain beyond a tiny patch of sod. Catholics were forbidden to hold public office, purchase land, or attain rank in the army, the navy, or at the bar. There were no upper or middle classes into which talented youths could rise. Parents had to divide their poor lands among their sons or condemn them to starvation. It was only natural that thousands of youthful Irishmen should escape by emigration as fares were lowered and opportunities abroad beckoned. Even before 1845, an annual Irish movement to Canada and the United States was reaching occasional heights of 65,000 emigrants and rarely dipping below 30,000.

The great majority, however, stayed where they were, living lives that shaped the national character into patterns that would later remain largely the same in New World surroundings. Denied an open religious life that might change with the times, the Irish clung all the more stubbornly to the authority of their priests. Denied education, they grew more rooted in superstition. Outsiders so far as the law was concerned, they were often attracted to secret terrorist societies as the only means of dispensing popular justice against the informer, the exploitative landlord's agent, or the supplanter of an evicted tenant. Conspiracy was part of the very tissue of life; drinking, storytelling, and fighting were the alleviations of a frustrating existence. So despite all a vital spark was maintained, and its great supporter in the early decades of the nineteenth century was the potato, which could be cultivated with almost no skill or tools on the tiniest of plots. An acre and a half in potatoes could feed a family of five or six for a year. Any surplus could be converted to cash, which was then put by toward the purchase of a pig, and even perhaps a cow and some fowl. Peat was freely available to keep roaring fires going in windowless earthen cabins throughout the long cold and wet seasons. The housekeeping might be primitive, but the means of self-support were within reach of almost anyone.

It all rested, however, on the potato, which fed livestock and people alike. "What hope is there," an English official once cried, "for a nation that lives on potatoes!" None whatever if the crop was stricken, and in the autumn of 1845 that calamity fell upon Ireland. A blighting fungus, *Phytophthora infestans,* spreading rapidly, turned the leaves and roots of the plant black, pulpy, foul-smelling, and totally inedible. Not all the crop was affected at first, but in the winter of 1845–46, whatever had been harvested successfully was consumed or sold. The 1846 and 1847 crops failed completely, and those of 1848 and 1849 were but little better. Ordinarily during the growing cycle, Ireland lived on last year's harvest. Without that, Ireland starved.

The precise number of victims of starvation and epidemic disease is not known, but there certainly were hundreds of thousands and the total may have reached seven figures. Horrible scenes were enacted, like that described by a British ship captain who in 1846 saw thousands of persons writhing in the torments of diarrhea. In one hut he gazed at four adults and three children crouching, vacant-eyed and wordless around a fire, while a man and a woman lay dying in the next room. In cabin after cabin the living lay paralyzed, surrounded by their dead. Bodies were buried without coffins by exhausted relatives, only a few inches below the soil, soon to be unearthed by dogs and rats. Soup kitchens and public-works projects, relief ships, and donations of food (including large quantities from the United States) barely touched the edges of the misery.

The only hope offered was flight. Passage brokers who sent agents into the Irish countryside to sell space on chartered vessels found ready customers among those who could somehow scrape together the necessary pounds. "All with means are emigrating," noted one official; "only the utterly destitute are left behind and enfeebled labourers." The British government attempted to entice settlers to Canada with specially arranged low fares. The Irish, however, even in desperation, had doubts about going to a British colony—"a second edition of Ireland with more room." Thousands of them took advantage of the cheap rates for passage to the mouth of the St. Lawrence and free transportation upriver to Quebec, then set out to walk into the United States. It is estimated that the majority of the Irish who reached Canada made it only a way station.

The flood had begun. In New York, in the single eight-month period between May 5, 1847 (when the Commissioners of Emigration began to keep records), and the year's end, there were 52,946 Irish arrivals. The ailing were unloaded at Staten Island, where three hospitals and a workhouse for the destitute awaited them; the rest battled their way ashore through crowds of runners for boardinghouses (some of which were dens of thieves where the immigrant's little baggage and money were stolen from him and where he was fed and lodged in "a state of misery and wretchedness not to be borne or countenanced by any civilized community").

In a series of riots that took place during the
Great Famine, desperate Irish peasants looted
Galway's potato stores. Although other parts of
Europe suffered from the 1845 blight, hardest
hit was Ireland, whose economy depended too
heavily on the potato crop. The impact of the
Galway riots and other uprisings paled beside
the horrors and upheavals—the starvation,
death, and mass emigration—wrought by that
terrible famine. *(Radio Times Hulton Picture Library, BBC Publications)*

In Boston, during the same year of 1847, some 25,000 emigrants—three quarters of them Irish—arrived by sea and some 12,500 by land. But whereas New York was a city of more than 370,000, Boston's 1845 population had been only 114,366, which was increased virtually overnight by an impoverished, dependent third. Suddenly Boston was confronted by the problem of the slum, a full generation before it was to become a national issue. And because the problem was inseparably connected with the newly arrived Irish, a cruelly unfair association between degradation and Hibernian origins developed in the minds of some Americans. Confronted with alien poverty, they made the common error of blaming the victim for the disease.

It was inevitable that the Irish of Boston and New York should become the urban poor in short order. Penniless for the most part, they were unable to move westward and take up vacant farmland, even where the prices were rock-bottom—and even if they had not been thoroughly disillusioned with farming as a way of life. Single men could join work gangs bound for construction projects in the interior, but those who had families they chose not to abandon picked up the lowest kind of unskilled jobs: yard, street, and stable work for the men; and for the women, whose extra earnings were indispensable to survival, domestic service. Like other female migrants after them (black women coming to Northern cities from Mississippi farms in the twentieth century, for example), the mothers and homemakers of Ireland "went off," in the words of Oscar Handlin, "to serve at the table of strangers and bring home the bitter bread of banishment."

The scanty returns from such labor forced the Irish to live in places normally considered unfit for human habitation. Slumlords, the scavengers of every urban society, rapidly bought up cellars, stables, and sheds in alleys and yards, and rented them to the immigrants at gold-rush prices. A Boston Committee on Internal Health found that there were three-story houses into which as many as a hundred inhabitants were jammed; that a single room might house nine people; that thousands of Irish lived in cellars without windows or privies or a water supply— "in many cases huddled together like brutes, without regard to age or sex or sense of decency." In such an environment, it was noted, "intemperance and utter degradation reign supreme." So did cholera, which broke out in the city in 1849.

And so did the crime rate, which rose rapidly in the years immediately following 1843—particularly attempts to kill (up 1,700 percent), assaults on police officers (up 400 percent), and aggravated assaults with knives, dirks, pistols, slingshots, razors, pokers, hot irons, clubs, iron weights, flatirons, bricks, and stones (up 465 percent). Proper Bostonians reacted with predictable concern as to whether people who lived in such style could ever be redeemed for equal citizenship. Many of them nursed the idea that somehow the Irish freely chose their social position in the lower depths—a conception verbalized in the report of the New York Association for Improving the Condition of the Poor, which held that the Irish were "content to live together in filth and disorder with a bare sustenance, provided they can drink and smoke and gossip, and enjoy their balls and wakes and frolics without molestation."

German migration moved to a different rhythm from that of the hunger-harried Irish. The potato blight struck in the German states, too, but the growers were not completely dependent on the ravaged plant. Its impact, however, did jar a goodly number of farmers already hard pressed by bad harvests, taxes, falling prices, and disadvantageous changes in land-tenure systems. Thousands of them could be seen making their way to the emigration ports in the 1840s, in carts piled high with their belongings and pulled, according to a French journalist, by "starved, drooping beasts."

Emigrants such as these, patiently enduring salt fish, potatoes, and soup on the six- or eight-week trip from Hamburg and then fanning out into the interior, were much like their eighteenth-century forerunners who had Germanized Pennsylvania. The new century, however, saw a new kind of exile from the fatherland—the skilled craftsman seeking an American fortune (perhaps even with the idea of eventually returning home), and the member of the educated middle class who had been caught up in the new liberalism at home and had fallen afoul of the police and the courts, which were still on the side of absolutism. Not many of the German-born residents of America by 1860 were intellectuals, revolutionaries, businessmen, or bankers in either their former or their adopted land, but those who were gave a flavor to their communities and to American life as a whole that was not to be lost until the time of the First World

War. The essence of it was idealism, organization, love of culture, and a strong sense of communal solidarity. Its occasional austerities and rigors (especially felt by the children of German-American households) were softened somewhat by music and lager beer.

The romantic figure in the history of immigration is the lone pilgrim coming down the gangplank with his worldly goods on his back. From the time of the first colonial plantings, however, group settlements have been a persistent experience, and nineteenth-century Germans made their contributions to this tradition. Some of these communities collapsed under the divisive pressures of the competitive American environment. Others laid the foundations for prosperous townships.

In 1833, for example, a committee was formed in the university town of Giessen to plan an exodus to America. Its sponsors were children of the age of liberal nationalism. They included such men as Paul Follen and Friedrich Münch, alive with the faith that national consciousness bound people together in ethnic families, whose mutual trust and love would pave the way to universal kinship. It was an exciting idea, but the foundation for a united Germany could not be laid at a time when the great powers of Europe—especially Austria—preferred to see the German people divided among a cluster of small, relatively weak states. The Giessen planners hoped that in the interior reaches of America, far from the powerful Foreign Minister Prince Metternich's agents, they could create a community that would operate under American law but that would be "German from its foundations up" and a "model state for the whole commonwealth of man."

To this end, a shipload was gathered and dispatched to New Orleans in the spring of 1834. They were substantial citizens, able to finance their own passage and the cost of locating and purchasing a site. Soon after their arrival in Louisiana, reality began to erode the vision. There were quarrels over whether the settlement should be in Arkansas, Missouri, or Illinois. A decision was reached to go upriver to St. Louis, there to await a second shipload of migrants before choosing a final destination. But the steamer that was chartered proved incapable of the trip up the Mississippi's shallows and tricky channels. By the time two others were hired in its place, faith in the wisdom of the directors was waning fast among the settlers. Moreover, the milk and honey of the Promised Land was beginning to look most accessible to those who went it alone. One by one, families broke away to take up individual occupations and farms. A tiny remnant settled near St. Charles, Missouri, and some members of the second contingent from Germany joined them there. But most of the family heads in the new shipload also followed the example of the Israelites in the days of the judges: each did what was right in his own eyes.

During its nine years of independence, from 1836 to 1845, Texas attracted many German colonizers who were particularly fascinated with its low-priced land. The Texans were eager to populate their prairie stretches, and hard-working "Dutch" farmers promised just the kind of social and economic stability that a young "nation" seemed to need. In the early 1840s, settlements of Germans had been planted on the Colorado River by a nobleman from Holland, Felipe Enrique Neri, Baron de Bastrop, and near San Antonio by a French entrepreneur, Henri Castro. In 1842 a group of Hessian noblemen who called themselves the Mainzer Adelsverein contracted to buy a large tract on the San Saba. Prince Carl of Solms-Braunfels was involved in this undertaking, and in May 1844 he headed for the American Southwest to arrange things for an expected ten thousand colonists who would follow. In March 1845, after selecting and buying a new site, he founded the town of New Braunfels. Shortly, however, it was discovered that feudal honor was not impeccable. The prince had embezzled funds in his trust, and was removed. His successor, Ottfried Hans, Baron von Meusebach, signed a treaty with the Comanches, bought an additional tract on the Pedernales River, and carried the work forward.

By 1857 the Germans in Texas numbered thirty-five thousand. A local commentator believed that the colonies at Bastrop, Castroville, New Braunfels, and elsewhere would "remain German, with all their good points and all their bad ones, with all their wiseheads and their dunces, their fanatics and their philistines— they will remain German until, well, they are Americanized. History knows nothing of fusion, it witnesses only victory and defeat." But the landscape architect Frederick Law Olmsted, reporting in *A Journey Through Texas* (1857), found a pattern that suggested a blending of frontier and homeland: "You are welcomed by a figure in blue flannel shirt and pendant beard, quoting Tacitus, having in one hand a long pipe, in the other a butcher's knife; Madonnas upon log-walls; coffee in tin cups upon Dresden saucers; barrels for seats, to hear a Beethoven's symphony on the grand piano; . . . a book case half filled with classics, half with sweet potatoes."

Far to the north of Texas, another German model town rose at New Ulm, Minnesota, in the 1850s. It too derived its special character from the fact that in a time when Western development was largely in the hands of free-swinging promoters, land sharks, squatters, would-be magnates in rails, lumber, transportation and milling, and other wholly individualistic operators, it grew by plan. New Ulm was the product of German settlers who were already in the New World but who were looking for fresh opportunities—the German Land Association of Chicago and the Turner Society of Cincinnati. (Turner societies were the Anglicized version of the *Turnvereine*, associations of Germans ostensibly dedicated to the promotion of physical culture but really concerned with social and political planning.) New Ulm was situated on a six-thousand-acre site, and around the town itself 494 neat little four-acre plots were laid out for vegetable gardens. (Francis Pastorius had supervised the same kind of harmonious design for Germantown in the 1680s.) Parties of settlers arrived on the *Frank Steele,* a Cincinnati-built steamer plying the Minnesota River, and took up their assigned acreages. It was a far cry from Daniel Boone's day, but fully as significant in its power to implant civilization in the interior of North America.

A long with regularity, the German spirit was noted for pedagogy (and pedantry), diligence, and national pride. Many of the upper-class migrants of the 1820–50 era filled the bill as "model Germans." Often they were scholars who could have enjoyed careers in the expanding bureaucracy of the slowly modernizing German states, especially Prussia. But they had chosen to identify themselves with the drive for elected assemblies, written constitutions, national unification, the glorification of folk culture, and other goals of liberalism. Inevitably, frustration and failure turned them into refugees. Germany was without a major revolution until 1848. Then there was a rising in many of the constituent states, the summoning of an all-German parliament, and a roseate dawn of hope for a free, united, and progressive Germany. But the potential leader of the movement, the

King of Prussia, lost his nerve. Before 1848 was over, reaction set in. Newspapers and magazines were suppressed, liberals jailed, the German National Assembly at Frankfurt fell apart, and those who chose resistance were dealt with by the bayonet. A final wave of refugees—"Forty-Eighters"—joined those who had gone into exile before the dramatic year. Many of them chose America.

The early arrivals from this group included editors, scholars, and professionals. Somewhat like the German refugees of the 1930s, they found their educational attainments an actual burden in the hurly-burly of American life. Success and status in the New World seemed to go to men of action and to accumulators. Learning that could not be applied in the market place had little effect in advancing a man's fortunes. Some Germans (in both centuries) reacted to this discovery with contempt for American boorishness and refused to compromise with Yankee practicality. Others turned their hands to whatever they could and swam with the current, happily or otherwise. Not a few became successful and enthusiastic Americans.

Friedrich Münch, for example, one of the original members of the Giessen Society, tried agriculture in Missouri for a time. Americans had a name for this kind of *émigré* who trod furrows while ruminating upon metaphysical mysteries—"Latin farmers." Numbers of them were supplied to the frontier by the German colonization societies, both in Europe and in such American cities as Pittsburgh, Chicago, and Cincinnati, which bought land and sped the wanderers onward. Münch eventually graduated from the Latin-farmer ranks into journalism and literature. Fellow intellectuals likewise found themselves appropriate niches, if lucky.

Francis Lieber enjoyed a distinguished career in academic groves. Lieber was a firebrand when he came to the United States in 1827, having already fought in the Waterloo campaign (at the age of fifteen) and in the Greek War of Independence. He was the guiding spirit of the first *Encyclopaedia Americana* (1829–33), and from 1835 to 1856 he taught history and political economy at South Carolina College, now the University of South Carolina. When his liberal opinions finally proved too much for the conservative slaveholding establishment, he moved to New York and Columbia University, where he became a political theorist and teacher.

Whereas government in the abstract engaged the mental energies of Lieber, Gustav Philipp Koerner found the day-to-day life of bread-and-butter politics to his taste. Koerner, born in 1809 to a Frankfurt am Main bookseller, matriculated at the University of Jena in 1828. He subsequently studied at Munich and Heidelberg, and at each place kept up his contacts with the vigorous student movement for German unification. Such a course leads to trouble as the sparks fly upward; inevitably, when there was a brief uprising against the government in Frankfurt in 1833, young Koerner was involved. When it failed, he went into exile. After a look at St. Louis, Koerner decided to try his luck elsewhere. He may have found the city on the Missouri all too Germanified for his taste, as he was an outspoken opponent of those who were trying to create islands of German separatism in America. He settled in Belleville, Illinois, and engaged in the practice of law—the great avenue to professional, social, and economic advancement in nineteenth-century America. Koerner soon drifted into politics and campaigned for the Democrats in 1840 and 1844. He was then made a justice of the Illinois Supreme Court. Finally, in 1852, he was elected lieutenant governor.

K oerner's career is a smaller-scale version of the life and times of the man who may be the quintessential German-American, Carl Schurz. Schurz has been described by one recent writer as "a man so laden with statesman-like virtues"—honesty, clarity, independence—"that it would be almost comforting to find a flaw or two in his character." He began his political life as an idealist swimming against the current in Germany, and he ended it as combatively as ever, denouncing his fellow Americans for their indecent imperialism in subjugating the Philippines. Skinny, bespectacled, bearded in later life, he looked more the schoolmaster than the man of action, but his record belied his image.

Schurz was a university student in Bonn when the revolution of 1848 broke out. He was an enraptured follower of Professor Gottfried Kinkel, poet and prophet of the New Germany; a nineteen-year-old spirit coiled to spring at a touch. The right moment came one day when he was bent over his desk working on a dramatic treatment of the life of Ulrich von Hutten, a noble Renaissance writer, scholar, and controversialist. A friend dashed in with the news that the French had just ousted King Louis Philippe. Schurz flung down his pen and rushed out to join in the rejoicings of his liberal brethren. "That was the end of *Ulrich von Hutten,*" he recalled later. "I never touched it again."

The following spring found Schurz in a situation calculated to take the romance out of revolution. With other troops of the temporary government set up by liberals in the Rhenish provinces, he was shut up under Prussian siege in the fortress of Rastatt. When the garrison commander decided to surrender, Schurz escaped through a sewer that led under the walls to the fields outside. After a near-drowning, near-starvation, and concealment in a farmer's loft with soldiers scarcely inches away, he crossed the border into France and eventually joined a large group of German refugees in Zurich. But he was not finished with the Prussians. Professor Kinkel was being held in the prison at Spandau, and Schurz rescued him in what appears to modern eyes to be a scenario for an adventure film.

Under an assumed name, Schurz traveled to Berlin. There, posing as a doctor, he made contacts that finally put him in touch with a bribable officer of the guard. On a November night in 1850, Schurz waited outside the prison while the professor came sliding down a rope that had been smuggled into his cell. Then he and Schurz hustled into a waiting getaway carriage. If the American environment was one that yielded its gifts most freely to the man who could improvise courageously, Schurz passed his citizenship test that night.

He did not go to the United States directly. First there were a few months of journalism in Paris. Then, following his expulsion from France in the spring of 1851 by the police of President Louis Napoleon, he lived in England for more than a year, meeting many other liberal exiles but finding the country unchangeably foreign. Despairing of liberalism on the Continent in the foreseeable future, Schurz set his course for America and landed in New York in September 1852. Moving to Philadelphia with his bride, he set about learning English by diligently reading Thackeray, Shakespeare, Macaulay, and the Philadelphia *Ledger* —never skipping a paragraph, and never failing to consult the dictionary when a word was doubtful. In 1856 he moved on to Watertown, Wisconsin, and plunged into the study of Blackstone (the starting point of a nineteenth-century legal education)—and into the management of an insurance company, the nurture of the weekly newspaper *Deutsche Volks-Zeitung*, service as an alderman and Commissioner of Public Improvements in Watertown, partnership in a Milwaukee law firm, and campaigning for the newly founded Republican Party. By 1860 he was to the German Republicans of Wisconsin what Joseph was to Potiphar: whatsoever was done in that house, he was the doer of it. Abraham Lincoln's reward for Schurz's efforts in securing the Wisconsin vote for him was to appoint Schurz Minister to Spain.

Schurz's subsequent career defies summary. Eager to be part of the crusade against slavery, in 1862 he resigned from his post in Madrid and was commissioned a brigadier general of volunteers. He served diligently and bravely, though not always successfully. After the war he returned to journalism and eventually moved to Missouri, whose legislature elected him to the United States Senate in 1869. Schurz became increasingly disenchanted with what he thought of as boodling and vengefulness in the Republican Party during Reconstruction. In 1872 he was one of the leaders of a Liberal Republican insurrection that attempted to deny renomination to President Grant. It failed to make a dent in the victorious totals of the hero of Appomattox, but when Rutherford B. Hayes became President in 1877, he appointed Schurz his Secretary of the Interior.

From this vantage point Schurz conducted a vigorous war on the patronage system of filling government jobs. Though his enemies denounced him as a sinister foreigner, trying to substitute Prussian bureaucracy for the time-hallowed spoils system, he saw his principles triumph in the creation of the Civil Service Commission in 1883. In 1884 he abandoned the regulars again to support Grover Cleveland, as a protest against the Republicans' nomination of James G. Blaine, about whom clung the aroma of too many favors done for railroads and other corporations. In 1896 Schurz was a Republican once more, defending the "sound dollar" against the crusade of William Jennings Bryan for unlimited coinage of silver. And in 1900 he was denouncing William McKinley's conversion of Americans into empire builders. During and between these various campaigns he had done duty as an editor of the New York *Evening Post* and *Harper's Weekly*.

Schurz had the incorruptibility and the pugnacious honesty of an Adams. The stereotype of the German in our century is that of a man whose tongue may speak of liberty while his soul is

Robert Owen, a British saddler's son who made
a fortune in textile manufacturing and wrote
numerous expositions of his principles of educational philanthropy, himself received a formal
education only until he was nine years old. In
1825 the Utopian Socialist started a planned
colony, New Harmony, "an enlightened social
system which shall gradually unite all interests
into one, and remove all causes for contests
between individuals." *(Bettmann Archives)*

always ready to click heels to authority. But Schurz wrote from Spain during his diplomatic service there: "I cannot endure people who abase themselves as they do here; and I am embarrassed when all manner of honors and reverences are hurled at my head. Nowhere can I feel right save in a country where the people stand erect in their boots." In his fifty-four American years, Schurz neither bent a knee nor allowed his heels to emit the ghost of a click.

By mid-century it was already a commonplace of American life that Cincinnati, St. Louis, and Milwaukee were heavily Teutonized. In 1840 the Germans of Cincinnati owned five thousand houses and cast a third of the city's votes. In the following decade, the German language was given parity with English in the local schools. Milwaukee was often called the German Athens. Forty thousand Germans contributed to the rise of Wisconsin's population from 3,600 in 1830 to 300,000 in 1850, and many settled in the lakeside city, where they brought German newspapers, choral groups, *Turnvereine,* coleslaw, and pumpernickel, and introduced the names Schlitz, Pabst, Blatz, and Miller to the American scene. St. Louis's German population made the city an island of free-soil sentiment in a slaveholding state. In other cities, too, the German influence was abundantly evident. It is not surprising to learn that New York had 100,000 Germans in 1860, supporting not only a congeries of beer gardens but also twenty churches, fifty German-language schools, ten bookstores, five printing establishments, and a theater; nor that the Germans of Philadelphia were sufficiently strong in voice and number to hold a choral festival, or *Sängerfest,* as early as 1846. Two years later, in New York, the Germania Orchestra, a pioneer American symphony organization, was launched. And it may be somewhat disconcerting to those who believe that the pre-1860 South was a homogeneous land of English-descended "natives" to find that Germans flourished there. In Richmond as early as 1840, the local German population held a festival in honor of Gutenberg. Seventeen years later, the unveiling of a bust of Baron von Steuben was attended by a German rifle company, a German singing group, a Schiller Society, a *Turnverein,* and a German dramatic club. In 1860 more than one of every six people in the future capital of the Confederacy was of German origin. Louisville had three German newspapers in the 1850s. Nashville, Mobile, and Natchez all had German social clubs and professional men. Charleston, deeply marked as it was by the culture of planters who followed eighteenth-century French and English Caribbean models, nevertheless counted 1,200 Germans in 1842. New Orleans had many German inhabitants, and, as we have seen, Texas had several colonies of Germans even before it became a state.

Wherever the Germans were able to take hold on something like their own terms, their impact was palpable. It was something that could be measured in dollars when German skills raised and operated breweries, glass factories, binderies, packing plants, sawmills, and machine shops in the valleys of the Ohio, the Mississippi, the Missouri, and their tributaries—those streams that not long before had flowed through wildernesses. It was something that left names on the land and pictures in the mind, too.

Thus the Germans of the nineteenth-century migration and the people-hungry American economy and society met and altered each other. And as with the Germans, so with the Swiss, the Dutch, the Scandinavians, and the other new arrivals. Each group found ways of interweaving its characteristic styles with the needs of a young country. Each group tended to respond to some mood of the American moment, and help it to expression in reality—whether it was the quest for a perfect society, or westward expansion, or the liberation of technology to create a triumphant capitalist order. There were always foreign faces in whatever caravans moved, physically or intellectually or through politics or investment, toward new horizons.

Among the most colorful of the European promotions of the young century were the vest-pocket Utopias that were conceived in the Old World to be realized (or, more often than not, unrealized) in the New. Native Americans themselves were fertile in devising models of the good society. It was natural. America had no past to speak of to enchain its nobler aspirations, but it had an almost empty continent as a stage on which to act out dramas of social invention. Revivalism fed the fires of millennial hope. Scarcely a county lacked its evangels of an American Zion. But it was not only religious frenzy that begot perfectionist fantasies. The lingering spirit of the French Revolution led some rationalist dreamers to meditate the creation of the perfect state, deep in the wilderness, minus priests and kings—the shrine of reason, unprofaned by bayonets. George Rapp and Robert Owen are two faces on opposite sides of the coin of Utopianism. One was deeply and mystically religious, the other totally opposed to any vision not supported by rationally considered pragmatic evidence. Yet each essayed an American projection of his dream of the good society, and by coincidence their creations occupied the same piece of ground.

"Father" Rapp was born Johann Georg Rapp in 1757 in Württemberg and grew to be one of those solid Pietists whose records checker German religious history. Somehow, engaged in farming and in raising a son and a daughter, he acquired the dangerous habit of reading and deeply pondering on philosophy and theology. Soon he began to feel that the forms of church worship interfered with the true communication between believers and the Holy Spirit. The preaching of that doctrine got his followers jailed and earned him the opposition of the state church. So, like English Puritans a century and a half before him, he became a Separatist (after his fashion), and then, thanks to his patriarchal qualities, a Separatist with a following of about 830 persons. In 1803 he journeyed to America to seek a suitable haven, and most of his flock joined him there the next year.

Pooling their resources, the Rappites bought five thousand acres of wild land some twenty-five miles north of Pittsburgh, on which they established the Harmony Society. Its principles were plain: wants to be supplied from a common store, dress to be simple, social distinctions to fade in the interest of common purpose. In two years of hard work they built more than fifty houses, a church, schoolhouse, sawmill, gristmill, and tannery, barns, workshops, and a distillery that produced excellent whisky. In 1807 a portentous new revelation came to Rapp: celibacy was the true and sanctioned path for the faithful. Those who could not accept this tenet quietly withdrew from the community. Those who could but were already married remained together and practiced restraint. Those still chaste went on as before—or so, at least, they claimed. Asked many years later if there were safeguards built against temptation, an elder replied: "None at all. It would be of no use. If you have to watch people, you had better give them up." A subsequent ordinance enjoined the sacrifice of tobacco, too—and a somewhat jocose commentator later remarked that this was "a deprivation which these

Germans must have felt almost as severely as the abandonment of conjugal joys."

In 1814, a series of agricultural setbacks convinced Father Rapp that the Pennsylvania locality was less than ideal. The Rappites then sold the original site for $100,000 and bought thirty thousand acres on the Wabash River in Indiana. There they built the town of Harmony and once more went through the process of raising homes, shops, and buildings, and bringing smiling prosperity to the rude creek bottoms. Success followed virtue nicely. They even recruited new members and rose to a strength of something between seven and eight hundred community members. Unfortunately, however, the swamp mosquito was no respecter of faith. Agues and fevers beset the community. Moreover, Father Rapp had a practical eye for such worldly factors as the slow development of southern Indiana, which kept the settlement inconveniently far from good markets. The neighbors were unfriendly and showed little prospect of becoming sources of future profit. And last, the Harmonists themselves grew restless; a move would reassert their unity. For all these reasons, Rapp put Harmony on the market in 1824, and a buyer was almost immediately found in a Briton, Robert Owen, who paid $150,000 for the land, buildings, and all other assets. The Rappites, it should be recorded, moved out to build Economy, near Pittsburgh, which flourished for years. Visitors found the paterfamilias Rapp holding court in a fine brick house, bands serenading crowds in the orderly streets on Sundays and summer evenings, and factories distinguished by the presence of vases of flowers on each worker's machine. The tempter finally entered into Eden in 1831, in the form of a newcomer who styled himself Count Maxmilian de Leon and who eventually led a secession that ruined the old colony.

Back at the renamed New Harmony, Robert Owen was undertaking some remarkable alterations in the world. He was himself an inordinately successful self-made textile manufacturer, whose model Scottish factory town of New Lanark was the wonder of social reformers in that era of industrial cruelty. He had deliberately created a planned and paternalistic laboring community because of a profound belief in environmentalism— or what would one day be called behaviorism. It was Owen's credo, as explained in numerous pamphlets and speeches, that the infant responded totally to his nurture. Owen would tell fascinated audiences of middle-class English and Americans that if they had been brought up at the foot of the Rocky Mountains by Indians, they would be redskins to the core, or, if exposed from infancy to the culture of China, they would be mandarins and coolies in all but pigmentation. This apparently rigid doctrine led in the direction of great expectations. The evil that men did came from wrong or outmoded ideas and from irrational religion. Replace an environment of error with one of truth, and man would leap into his natural state of virtue. Owen hoped to try nothing less at New Harmony. "I am come to this country," he announced in April 1825, "to introduce an entire new system of society; to change it from an ignorant, selfish system to an enlightened social system which shall gradually unite all interests into one, and remove all causes for contests between individuals." Then he returned to Great Britain, leaving affairs in the hands of deputies, among whom were his sons.

Theoretically, New Harmony was to rework the old Rappist surroundings to conform to various ideas of Owen's. There were to be four main buildings arranged around a central square. Kitchens, laundries, and refectories were to be communal. Schoolrooms, laboratories, concert halls, and ballrooms would be placed with geometric precision at corners and in the centers of the buildings. Rooms for married couples would occupy the lower floors; the upper would be reserved for single persons and for children—who, at the age of two, were to be removed from the confusing influences of their parents and educated by the community. Education, in the first American coeducational system, would include music, history, drawing, astronomy, geography, botany, and agriculture. The community as a whole would hold property in common, recognize the equal rights of all, and devote its nonworking hours to moral lectures, dancing, singing, and military drill. (How the last would be reconciled with perfect equality seems not to have been specified.) Owen, like most perfectionists, was suspicious of individualism; one of his cherished ideas was that all the communitarians should wear uniforms—pantaloons and collarless jackets for the men; pantalets tied at the ankles with short slips over them for the women.

The history of New Harmony need not be spelled out in detail. A gathering of intellectuals made its collective way down the Ohio and up the Wabash to partake of the feast of reform. It included a distinguished geologist, a chemist, an artist, assorted European pedagogues, the zoologist and entomologist Thomas Say, who had been curator of the American Philosophical Society, and others whose conjoined abilities led someone to dub the keelboat that brought them on a January day in 1826 "a boatload of knowledge." They worked under an elegantly drawn-up constitution, called the Community of Equality, that divided productive labor into neat categories (agriculture, manufactures and mechanics, science and education, literature, domestic economy, general economy, and commerce) and contained a kind of declaration of community objectives calling for cooperation, sincerity, kindness, courtesy, order, health, and learning. These high objectives notwithstanding, Owen's Utopians were all so hopelessly impractical that the original community fragmented and then failed in a very short time.

Many equivalents of Harmony and New Harmony were founded by visitors and settlers from Europe. In their quest for the impossible the European projectors of ideal communities were demonstrating once more the deep connections between American and European experience in the modern age. It was an age of men set on edge by the possibilities of their ever more powerful technology. Especially in a new land, nothing seemed impossible to the god-men who made, and still believed they controlled, the machine.

VI

Entering the Partnership

This gathering of Norwegian Lutherans was photographed outside a church in Blue Mounds, Wisconsin, about 1875. At first, immigrant churches consisted of single nationalities. *(State Historical Society of Wisconsin)*

When the Israelites found their way into the Promised Land, their program for dealing with the local inhabitants was simple and approved by God. They slew the natives or drove them from the choicest spots. The European settlers in America applied something of the same human-relations technique to the "inferior" Indians, but when they dealt with white predecessors they did not consider that they had such an option—at least, not often. In general, native American and newcomer had to adjust to each other somehow, and that process of mutual adaptation was one of the great shaping forces of life in America.

Historical tradition sketches the process as a one-way street: the immigrant was "Americanized" as a result of his contacts with "old stock" Americans, of different blood from his. Reality supplies a more labyrinthine map of interplay. New immigrant arrivals mingled with a "native" population that also included their own countrymen who had arrived earlier and those countrymen's offspring, who had grown up sharing two cultures. Successful sons of Irish Catholic settlers looked warily on post-famine shanty dwellers fresh from the old sod. "German Latin" farmers and "Forty-Eighters"—freethinking and worldly—found themselves sharing community institutions with Germans who had migrated for religious reasons and were still bound to the pieties of their past. Frenchmen whose forebears had helped to settle Louisiana met with refugees from revolutionary upheavals in the French West Indies, and found that they had little except language in common, and less than language with Frenchmen from Canada.

Moreover, the different immigrant groups seeking styles of their own while conforming to American life were actually re-defining the term "American" by their participation. The process was fluid and continuous, and left indelible marks on the national character.

In the so-called immigrant churches, for example, an interesting drama was played out. The first act saw planted in the wilderness a largely ethnic church—one whose members were drawn heavily from a single nationality. The second act revealed a relaxation of doctrine and practice, as a new generation grew up in an American setting. In the third, fresh arrivals from the same immigrant stock burst on the stage, outraged at the old church's falling away from orthodoxy, and often brought on a turbulent scene of heresy charges and secession. The prototypal script was written in the churches of New England—planted by Puritan "saints," then broadened to accommodate the less zealous children of the founders (who were not as sure of their salvation), then scourged by revivalists.

German Lutheranism is another model case. Not all German settlers worshiped in the Lutheran fellowship, but those who did, especially in the eighteenth century, clung zealously to Old World formulas, rituals of faith, and even language. "Since it has pleased Thee," said a liturgical statement of the German churches in Pennsylvania in 1786, addressing the Almighty, "by means of the Germans, to transform this state into a blooming garden, . . . help us not to deny our nation, but to endeavor that our youth may be so educated that German schools and churches may not only be sustained but may attain a still more flourishing condition." Yet God had other designs. Following the pattern set by "Americanizers" like the Muhlenbergs, German Lutheran pastors in the United States drifted away from a concentration on doctrine into the currents of good works. They joined in associations to promote worthwhile causes, exchanged pulpits now and again with non-Lutheran shepherds, took sides on political questions, and seemed unmoved while English steadily displaced German as the language of worship. In the 1840s, a voice was raised in prophetlike anger to chastise them. It belonged to C.F.W. Walther, sometimes known as the "Lutheran Pope of the West." Himself a relatively new arrival, Walther scorned both the secularism of the German intellectuals who had become prosperous in the new country and the apostasy of German churchmen who allowed themselves and their congregations to become involved in such crusades as abolitionism. What had such things to do with "the ancient true Church of Christ on earth"? From a base in St. Louis, Walther harried the liberals and eventually organized the conservative Missouri Synod. This schism was not the only one to rend the Lutherans; ultimately they split into Northern and Southern branches, just as did the Presbyterians, Baptists, and Methodists.

In effect, American freedom and space and social conflicts had imposed themselves on Lutheranism and broken it along certain lines that were not so much religious as political and cultural.

The subdivision would probably not have taken place without continued immigration and the stresses it created. At the same time, the existence of more than one kind of Lutheran "denomination" among which German-Americans (and non-Germans, too) could choose served to strengthen the American religious pattern of variety and diversity.

Patriarchs of immigrant churches flourished in American soil in the 1800s. T. N. Hasselquist, a farmer's son in his native Sweden, was trained as a pastor, crossed the sea, and began a ministry in 1852 among scattered Scandinavian farmers in Illinois. Often he held services in such makeshift surroundings as barns. But adversity stimulated him. Soon he had established the *Hemlandet* newspaper, a society of Swedish Lutheran missionaries, a seminary, a printing press. He sought out parishioners with the zeal of a born fisher of men who knew his America. The Illinois Central Railroad wanted purchasers for lands granted to it by the national government. Hasselquist promoted himself to the railroad as an agent, wrote tirelessly to friends, ministers, and editors in the Northeast and in Sweden, and sent emissaries as far as Quebec and Montreal, where they met Scandinavian newcomers and told honeyed tales of rich acres and Lutheran neighbors awaiting them in Illinois. Hasselquist's Scandinavian Evangelical Lutheran Augustana Synod waxed prosperous on such efforts, and, except for the departure of a number of dissident Norwegians in 1870, remained untroubled by secessions.

The process by which religious traditions were given new shapes in the multinational American setting also touched the ancient faith of the Jews. Reform Judaism came to the United States as an import from Germany. Its Moses was Isaac Mayer Wise, born in Bohemia in 1819, educated in a rabbinical school and at the Universities of Vienna and Prague. Wise grew up in heady times for Jews in German-speaking countries. During intermittent periods of liberalism, they were allowed, if they chose, to emerge from the ghettos, attend public schools, and participate in professional and political life more freely than ever before. Yet it was difficult for them to reconcile this liberation with the rituals by which the Orthodox Jew testified to his chosenness—the distinctive dress, diet, holidays, prohibitions, and prayers that every waking moment demanded. Thousands of German Jews found an answer in a new idea, namely that the ethical and historical content of their religion could be separated from such trappings as beards and side curls, forbidden Sabbath fires, prohibited pork, and the swaying, incomprehensible, rapid-fire Hebrew chanting of liturgical poetry. They made this belief the foundation of a new kind of religious life, which enabled them to move less distinctively and thus more comfortably among their non-Jewish brethren, and to build temples where such novelties as organs, choirs, and preaching in German were permitted.

Those Jews of the new persuasion who migrated to America from German states naturally brought their views with them. Isaac Mayer Wise did more. He joined his Germanic Reform Judaism to American religious liberalism, in a kind of second assimilation of a faith already assimilated. He became a devoted reader of the works of Unitarian and Transcendentalist thinkers such as New England's William Ellery Channing and Theodore Parker. Channing and Parker believed that God was a God of reason, and that mankind was essentially virtuous but was sometimes betrayed into error by compounds of ignorance and superstition. The university-trained Wise agreed; he privately lamented "the disappearance of Judaism in . . . Polish-cabalistical rabbinism and supernaturalism," and raged that "poor Hebrew reading and indecorum were as necessary an accompaniment of Jewish orthodoxy as was dog Latin of Catholic orthodoxy, and the poorest imaginable translation of the Psalms of Scotch Presbyterianism."

From a post as the rabbi of Congregation B'nai Jeshurun in Cincinnati, Wise directed the campaign for an American Judaism worthy of the best that nineteenth-century idealism had to offer. He led in creating a rabbinical training school (Hebrew Union College), an organization of rabbis (the Central Conference of American Rabbis), and a congregational association (the Union of American Hebrew Congregations) that would work together to perpetuate Reform Judaism when its German-speaking founders had passed from the scene. Yet by the time this work was completed, in the 1880s, a new wave of European Jews was washing over American cities. They were from the *shtetls*—the tiny villages of Russian Poland and western Russia; they had been restricted to that region and to the most humble occupations by the edict of the Czar. They were lower-class, uneducated in anything non-Jewish, mystical, superstitious, suspicious of the entire Gentile world, crabbily argumentative—in short, the reverse of everything that Wise, the apostle of reason and the enemy of parochialism, stood for. Yet by sheer numbers they made American Reform Jews a minority elite—one more example of mass migration's power to disrupt well-established patterns in the nation's life.

The most fascinating story of the relationship between American immigration and American religious life, however, is unfolded in the records of the Catholic Church. Its founding fathers in the thirteen colonies were Englishmen; Frenchmen and Germans, in their turn, became its most visible supporters. Finally the Irish arrived, and they came to conquer. Though they were followed in the parishes by Italians, Poles, and Latin Americans, for a long time the ethnic flavor of the Church of Rome in the United States was that of corned beef and cabbage. By the end of the nineteenth century, the Irish had created the situation in which St. Patrick's day was in part a Catholic, in part an Irish, and in part an American holiday.

The political and spiritual center of the church that the Irish found in the 1840s was Maryland, where the Calverts had placed it two centuries earlier. The first American archbishop, John Carroll, was a distant cousin of the Charles Carroll who signed the Declaration of Independence. The then Father Carroll was chosen Prefect-Apostolic in America in 1784, and he built an organization sturdy enough to withstand and absorb heavy inflows of newcomers in succeeding decades. Frenchmen swarmed into the fold, thanks to the Louisiana Purchase of 1803 and to slave uprisings in the West Indies that drove large numbers of refugees into American havens. Early German migrations included numbers of Catholics, and by the 1820s the infiltration of still other nationalities had confronted the church fathers with an unprecedented situation. One historian has noted that "an Irish Lutheran, a German Episcopalian, a French Metho dist, a Swiss Baptist, and an English Mennonite might then have been thought something of an oddity, but no one thought it strange to see men of all five nationalities occupying neighboring pews in a Catholic church of New York, Philadelphia, or Baltimore. Willy-nilly, the American Church had become catholic in the broadest sense. . . ."

Although they admired its universality, the first Irish on the scene lost no time in asserting their desire to see the church pay attention to particular national prejudices in assigning clergymen. In 1803 a group petitioned Carroll to replace their German priest, Father Helbron, who did not "know how to utter himself in the English tongue," with someone who could understand "the Irish language." If none should prove available, the supplicants added, they would as soon "depend on providence a little longer than get a German priest."

French priests were not considered a notable improvement. The Irish-born Bishop of Charleston, South Carolina, John England, spoke for the majority of his countrymen when he declared in 1835:

> The Irish are largely amalgamated with the Americans. Their principles, their dispositions, their politics, their notions of government, their language and their appearance become American very quickly, and they praise and prefer America to their oppressors at home. The French never can become American. Their language, manners, love of *la belle France,* their dress, air, carriage, notions, and mode of speaking of their religion, all, all are foreign. . . . The French clergy are generally good men and love Religion, but they make the Catholic Religion thus appear as exotic, and cannot understand why it should be made to appear assimilated to American principles.

The bishop himself was one reason for Irish success in church leadership. He was the firebrand offspring of a Cork tobacconist and had supped on hostility to the British from his childhood. After studying for the priesthood, he was assigned as a chaplain to prisoners awaiting transportation to exile in Australia. Immediately he became a vigorous spokesman for better treatment of these prisoners. In the Cork *Mercantile Chronicle,* he damned the British in ways that made church officials, wincing, set him down as one who "lacks sacerdotal meekness, and prudence." There was a place for hotheaded young clergymen: in 1820, he was ordered to Charleston, in the wilds of America. He plunged into the currents of Americanization without a backward look. He applied for citizenship almost before he had recovered his land legs, and was soon off to Washington to meet and admire such American worthies as President James Monroe and Secretary of State John Quincy Adams. In 1826 he was well enough

142

known in the capital to be invited to address the House of Representatives—the first priest so honored.

It was Bishop England's belief, in 1831, that before half a century had elapsed, Catholicism would "extensively flourish" in the "land of steady habits." And it did, thanks to the dedication of thousands of Irish settlers. They streamed into America faster than the church could train pastors or build tabernacles for them, and so, like others before them, they held services conducted by laymen (a "dry Mass," they called it) or by missionary priests in whatever place might be available—basements, stables, haylofts, billiard parlors, firehouses, storage rooms, and even saloons, with the bar hidden by blankets. As fast as pennies could be collected, houses of worship rose. "Hundreds of churches have been erected in a few years," wrote one priest in 1850, "and the country studded from Maine to Key West and from N. York to Minnesota with convents, hospitals, schools and colleges, erected mainly in the cities, by Catholic servant girls living at six dollars a month, and in the country by Catholic laborers working on the railroads and canals, at a dollar or a dollar and a quarter a day." The supposedly shiftless Irish contributed their savings and their sons alike to the faith. In Brooklyn in 1826, there was a small Irish community; the men, mostly navy-yard workers, organized themselves into the Erin Fraternal Association. One of them, Patrick McCloskey, was the father of a boy, John, who became the first American cardinal. George McCloskey, a milkman, had two sons who also entered the church; one was made the Bishop of Kentucky, and the other the first head of the American College in Rome.

It was no wonder that the Irish came somehow to identify opportunity, the church, and the United States as elements in a kind of social trinity. "In Ireland," said one pastor, "a father often wept to think that his children would grow up, and never be able to rise above the conditions in which they were born—Here there is no honor, no station, no eminence they may not aspire to." Hence, a faithful Irish Catholic immigrant would no more think of avoiding naturalization than of skipping Mass. Girls were advised by the priests to look for piety, sobriety, and citizenship in their suitors.

The Americanization of the Irish church, or the conversion of Catholicism in America to something Irish—it is difficult to say which description is more accurate—went on at a rapid pace.

The most notable leaders in the American hierarchy in the latter part of the century were authentic sons of St. Patrick. New York's Archbishop John Joseph Hughes was from County Tyrone. The first American cardinal, as noted, was John Mc-Closkey; the second, James Gibbons, was born to Irish parents in Baltimore. Archbishop John Ireland, of St. Paul, Minnesota, had a singularly appropriate name and was Kilkenny-born.

Archbishop Ireland sounded a proud boast at the Third Plenary Council of the American church in 1884:

> There is no conflict between the Catholic Church and America. I could not utter one syllable that would belie, however remotely, either the Church or the Republic, and when I assert, as I now solemnly do, that the principles of the Church are in thorough harmony with the interests of the Republic, I know in the depths of my soul that I speak the truth.

Archbishop Ireland's faith in America was so complete that he was known to utter views that bordered on the heretical. "An honest ballot," he once said, "and social decorum will do more for God's glory and the salvation of souls than midnight flagellations or Compestellan pilgrimages." So zealous was he in quest of assimilation that he was among those indirectly rebuked in a letter issued by Pope Leo XIII in 1899, *Testem benevolentiae,* wherein so-called "Americanizers" were warned that too much adaptation of doctrine to local and modern conditions led to falsehood and error.

With the Irish in the ascendancy, the 1890s found many German Catholics in the United States beseeching the church for priests who spoke their own language, just as the Irish themselves had once done. It was even suggested by a German Catholic layman, Peter Cahensly, secretary of the Archangel Raphael Society, that the church would grow faster in America if parishes, schools, and bishops were clearly separated and assigned by nationality.

Rome never accepted this idea. "Cahenslyism" was antithetical to the unity of the believers in the true faith. But this kind of controversy contributed to ethnic discord in the United States. When two suffragan bishops were appointed for the heavily German Catholic church in Minnesota in 1889 and both proved to be Irishmen, Archbishop Ireland exulted: "Thank God, we've dished the Dutch!" The Vatican, of course, would not have seen the matter in that light, and Ireland himself was not so much anti-German as he was intensely committed to the idea expressed by a New York priest in 1851: "Is it not clear and evident that the children of Ireland coming hither in such numbers are the great element of Catholicity in this country?" There could be no doubt that Irish immigration had profoundly affected the course of Catholic history in the United States, and accordingly the destinies of a major segment of the people called Americans.

To a church, pride of nationality was a two-edged sword. It could hold congregations tightly together, and it could also turn away potential converts of other tongues and customs. But the political organizer usually had no such dilemma to face: the party was roomy enough for everyone, and a vote for the right ticket in any language was welcome. The road to advancement for thousands of immigrants lay through the precinct clubhouse, where their accents were a positive advantage. Prior to the Civil War, it was the Germans and the Irish who profited most by the nation's discovery of the ethnic vote. In the major cities entire blocks and election districts were composed of families who spoke in a brogue or in gutturals. Here, clan loyalties could create compact followings for leaders who stood out, and such "armies" of friends were the negotiable currency of politics in the age of universal suffrage.

The major impact of the Germans was on the state and national elections in Illinois, Wisconsin, and Missouri, as shown by careers such as those of Schurz and Koerner. In St. Louis and Cincinnati, among other cities, they also cast a long shadow over local government. Yet the Germans do not furnish the perfect illustration of ethnic politics at work on the street corners. Their clannishness was not usually intensified by the enmity of their neighbors. And when they lined up to vote in phalanx it was apt to be temporarily and over a specific issue: in resistance to temperance laws that would deny them Sunday pleasures in the beer gardens, for example. Or if, in some rural areas, they voted against land speculators and mortgage holders along with their Scandinavian or Scottish or Canadian friends, the binding force was their interest as farmers rather than as foreigners.

With the Irish it was different. Their political machines were sometimes built in advance of the issues that put them in mo-

This photograph of Carl Ferdinand Wilhelm
Walther, the Lutheran clergyman from Saxony,
was taken in 1885, two years before his death.
Referred to at times as the "Lutheran Pope of
the West," Walther exhorted pastors to uphold
the traditional doctrines of Old World
Lutheranism in the face of a rising tide of
secularism and liberalism. *(Missouri Historical
Society)*

146

tion, and displayed a cunning architecture that rose out of the very nature of the Irish urban experience. For one thing, the hostility of the old-stock Protestant community caused the Irish to cling together. The neighborhood was their world; the leader who was faithful to friends and family, generous with help to the unfortunate, and much in evidence at neighborly functions like wakes was a man to be admired, trusted, and followed. The judgment of outsiders on him was unimportant. If he was in politics, what he said did not matter; he earned votes simply by what he was.

For the opportunistic young Irishman, politics, in one writer's words, "like baseball, prizefighting, and the Church, was a career open to talents. . . . Like every other profession, it was expected to reward its practitioners with money, prestige and, if possible, security." This point of view did not automatically predispose Irish politicians to dishonesty, but it clashed ringingly with the "genteel" conception that government should be high-minded, disinterested, and inexpensive, in order to spare the taxpayers from too many exactions on their working capital. The "proper" Americans who became political reformers thought that expertise and a willingness to leave economic problems to solve themselves were the twin hallmarks of the worthiest candidate in an election, and they were willing to scuttle party loyalties to vote for a man who had those virtues. To a good practical politician, be he Irish or any other kind of nationality, such blackhearted ingratitude appeared far more scandalous than spoilsmanship. The exiles from Erin did not invent a political style tailored to man's unconquerable self-interest, but they were at home with it. New York's ward-heeling George Washington Plunkitt was a good example; he told a reporter around 1905, "There's only one way to hold a district; you must study human nature and act accordin'."

New York City became a cultural and political mecca for the Irish—as it would be for many other immigrant groups—early in its modern history. The Irish on the scene around 1800 drifted naturally into an alliance with Jefferson's followers. Republicans, being supporters of France, were foes of Great Britain—a sure guarantee of popularity with wearers of the green. One prop of the Jeffersonian organization in New York was the Society of St. Tammany, founded by old-stock Americans in 1789 for fraternal purposes. By 1817 it was a potent political club, already known after its meeting place, Tammany Hall. In that year, one of its gatherings to nominate a candidate for a Congressional seat was broken up by a group of Irishmen who demanded the honor for someone from their ranks. The effort was unavailing; even two years later the society was noted for a streak of antiforeign feeling. But in 1821 a new New York State constitution removed the requirement that voters be property holders. That was, perhaps, the beginning of Irish power. Its emergence coincided with the political revolution that brought Andrew Jackson to the fore as the symbol of the common man's yearnings. The Irish were natural Jacksonians. The Whig Party, which opposed Jackson's Democrats, was itself broadly based, but its backbone was composed of the successful: manufacturers, land speculators, bankers, transportation-company owners; it had strong appeal for clergymen, teachers, doctors, and other professionals. These were the people whose kitchens the Irish swept and whose horses they drove, and the opportunity to equalize things a bit at the polls was irresistible. In a local election in 1827, it was alleged, two hundred Irishmen under the protection of a pistol-packing party leader deposited three ballots apiece for a candidate favorable to Old Hickory. In 1834, Irish toughs in the Sixth Ward (known as "the bloody ould Sixth") battled Whig legions in the streets fronting both parties' headquarters for three days. It took the arrival of militia with bayoneted muskets to cool things down. A Whig paper commented sarcastically that voting was, after all, "an affair of Americans" and that "foreigners must needs work themselves into a fury, and attempt to settle the question by club law."

Nonetheless the New York Irish were on their way, and they were sped along the path of electoral influence by a Whig governor, William H. Seward, who raised an issue involving the perennially sensitive question of who should control and pay for the city's schools. In 1840, New York City's public-education bills were paid by a private organization, the Public School Society, run by benevolent upper-class citizens who collected money from both public and private sources for the purpose. They steadfastly refused to provide funds for any Catholic parochial schools. Seward was from upstate Auburn, and as solid a member of the white Protestant establishment as could be found, but he was appalled to learn that about half of New York City's

Catholic children were receiving no schooling at all. Firm in the nineteenth-century progressive belief that the classroom was a useful agency of social betterment, he proposed to the legislature that the Public School Society be ordered to finance the parochial schools on a pro rata basis. "I desire to see the children of Catholics educated as well as those of Protestants," he said, "not because I want them Catholics, but because I want them to become good citizens."

The legislature refused to act on his request, and the Public School Society and the city's Common Council both resisted the Irish demands, which Seward had inspired, for a share of the school fund. The issue was fought with the usual heat on both the Catholic and "secular" (i.e., Protestant) sides, and in the struggle the Irish organized with a new sense of purpose. In the autumn of 1841 a new legislature was to be chosen. Both the Whig and Democratic parties rebuffed the Irish vote, and named pro-School Society candidates in New York City. Thereupon the then Bishop Hughes summoned a mass meeting four days before the election and got a parochial-school slate nominated. It took enough Irishmen away from their Democratic allegiance to give the Whigs a thin edge, showing that the church could hurt the party in a contest of allegiances.

Although the new state legislature created a public school system, it expressly forbade making payments to schools teaching "sectarian doctrine." The church in New York then went to work laying the foundations of a privately supported network of schools, which in the long run served its purposes better. Another important result was that Tammany accepted the lesson that the Irishman's ballot could not be taken for granted. They began to pass out to their "Paddy" constituents what one writer nicely styles "a host of petty jobs, which it was their small ambition to hold: marshals, street inspectors, health wardens, lamplighters, firewardens, dock masters, weighers, clerks . . . each vested with that official authority, no matter how small . . . by virtue of which they were raised to the white-collar class." Nor was private employment neglected. "I know every big employer in the district," Plunkitt was to say in defense of his profession, "and in the whole city, for that matter, and they ain't in the habit of sayin' no to me when I ask them for a job."

As the Irish poured in they were naturalized and marshaled in Tammany ranks. Their enemies writhed; in his diary former

Mayor Philip Hone made the angry observation in 1843 that Bishop Hughes deserved "a cardinal's hat at least for what he has done in placing Irish Catholics upon the necks of native New Yorkers." In 1868 the New York *Tribune* sneeringly wrote: "It is rumored that Judge McCunn [who owed his election to Tammany] has issued an order naturalizing all the lower counties of Ireland, beginning at Tipperary and running down to Cork." The wave would not recede. Tammany leaders seized on the Irishman's natural gregariousness; they helped in the formation of glee clubs, baseball teams, benevolent societies, and militia units, and then reaped the harvest of loyalty.

By the end of the Civil War, Tammany had become for all intents and purposes totally Irish. At that time its boss was William Marcy Tweed, who sprang from Protestant Scottish, not Irish, roots but had grown up with Irish cronies. Tweed's ring having bilked the city of an estimated thirty million dollars in six years, he was finally unhorsed by newspaper exposures. He was convicted on 120 counts, ranging from grand larceny to conspiracy, and died in jail. Among the members of his ring were Peter Sweeny and "Slippery Dick" Connolly, Irish to the tips of their sticky fingers. The Tammany reins then passed to "Honest John" Kelly, a brother-in-law of Cardinal McCloskey. In 1886 the role of boss was bestowed on Richard Croker. Like Tweed, Croker came from Protestant stock, though at least he was Irish-born, and he joined and remained in the Catholic Church throughout his life. He discreetly betook himself out of the country after a series of threatening investigations, and he laid his bones in Irish earth in 1922, leaving five million dollars behind him. His successor as Tammany's top sachem was Charles Murphy, who carried into the modern era the Irish banner that flew over the Hall. By then there was truth in one writer's remark: "Ask an Irishman, and he will probably tell you that St. Tammany was a younger brother of St. Patrick who emigrated to America for the purpose of taking a city contract to drive all Republican reptiles out of New York."

Religion and politics, then, were two areas in which the catalytic mutual impact of "new" immigrants, "old" immigrants, and "natives" worked upon one another to create a particularly American style. It was inevitable that hostility should be a part of this formula. The United States was self-consciously the land of refuge for the homeless and tempest-tossed. But at every stage there were those crying aloud that the native-born in America constituted a family with unique hereditary gifts for self-government—and that to admit outsiders into the home as equals would dilute and corrupt those precious qualities. This belief was shared both by aristocratic old families, guarding their view of America like a precious jewel, and by violent men at the bottom of the social ladder who saw in every newcomer from abroad a competitor for jobs. The hostility was particularly strong in times of national stress.

So, just as xenophobia had surfaced when Federalism and Antifederalism were being codified in political parties, it emerged again in the 1830s, 1840s, and 1850s, when partisan passions were high and there were many anxieties about the course that the ship of state was sailing. The first shots in the nativist campaign were directed at Catholics in particular. This was not surprising; the Pope was a foreign prince, and in innumerable Puritan sermons, dating back to the beginnings of New England, he had been denounced as the Antichrist. Hatred of Rome was a tradition. In 1830, in New York, the Reverend George Bourne founded a newspaper, entitled *The Protestant*, to fight "Romish corruptions"; in the same city the Protestant Association was formed the following year; and in Boston, the Reverend Lyman Beecher used his middle-class pulpit to loose the fateful lightnings of his oratory against a suspected Catholic design to subvert America.

Angry words led to action, and action blazed—literally—in Boston, where Irish homes were occasionally set on fire under the goad of oratory like Beecher's. One climax came on the night of August 11, 1834. On a hill in rural Charlestown stood a convent of Ursuline nuns, who operated a school to which a number of wealthy Bostonians—most of them Unitarians—sent their daughters. This made it doubly provocative to mobs: it was run by Papists and utilized by the rich. Late in July a very upset young nun had left the convent. Then she returned. Rumors circulated to the effect that she had run away, had been forced to go back, and was even then a prisoner in a dungeon. Shortly a crowd gathered at night, roaring and gesticulating in the light of a pillar of fire created by igniting a pile of tar barrels in a nearby field. Then the rioters broke into the convent, drove out screaming pupils and white-faced nuns, set the building ablaze, and watched it burn to the ground.

A nother milestone in the march of bigotry came in 1836 with the publication of two books by Maria Monk: *Awful Disclosures of the Hôtel Dieu Nunnery of Montreal* and *Further Disclosures.* The prurient mind is especially grateful for sensations that come packaged as instruction, and the young Canadian woman's work was a rich diet for those who savored sex in print. She told of how she had become a nun, and learned that her duty was to "obey the priests in all things," including "criminal intercourse." The babies born as a result of such liaisons, she wrote, were immediately baptized, killed, and buried under the convent floor. Many tales of abduction, seduction, secret passages from priests' bedchambers to nuns' cells, and similar Gothic devices filled the books' pages. Though the author was probably demented, and the books were soon shown to be frauds, true believers in Papist perfidy were readily convinced.

In 1844, rioting scarred the streets of the City of Brotherly Love. Early in May, a Protestant society called a meeting in Kensington, an Irish working-class area, to protest a school-board ruling that permitted Catholic children to use their own Douay version of the Bible in school. As the upholders of the King James translation crowded into a meeting hall near an Irish volunteer fire company, shots rang out and at least one Protestant fell to the ground, mortally wounded. It was a signal for turmoil. Before dawn streaked the sky over Kensington's chimneys, the windows of many an Irish home had been shattered by rocks. That day and evening the crowd returned to the attack, this time firing private houses. Soon whole blocks in the Irish district were crackling and blazing; pitched street battles were fought amid choking clouds of smoke, while a nativist newspaper shrieked: "Another St. Bartholomew's Day is begun in the streets of Philadelphia. The bloody hand of the Pope has stretched itself forth to our destruction." A special police force was finally formed to restore order, but fresh fighting broke out early in July, escalating to a confrontation in front of the Church of St. Philip de Neri in which both the crowd and the defending militia had—and used—cannon; thirteen people died and fifty were wounded.

"WHAT ARE YOU LAUGHING AT? TO THE VICTOR BELONG THE SPOILS."

This 1871 cartoon by Thomas Nast helped bring about the downfall of "the Tweed Ring," led by Tammany Hall's Grand Sachem, William Marcy Tweed. This corrupt political machine took over New York in the mayoralty election of 1865 and created a kingdom of graft. It won the hearts and the votes of the local Irish by issuing tickets printed PLEASE NATURALIZE THE BEARER, to be presented by immigrants to Tammany judges. (Harper's Weekly)

In the 1850s anti-Catholic feelings blended with a general assault on foreigners. A tumultuous decade, it opened with the Southern states threatening secession and closed with the threat near validation. It witnessed bloodshed in Kansas and at Harpers Ferry, riots as fugitive slaves were captured in Northern towns and then rescued by abolitionists, the collapse of the Whig Party, the birth of the Republican organization, a boom in railroad and factory building, threats of war in Central America, the "opening" of Japan, even literary explosions—*The Scarlet Letter, Leaves of Grass, Moby Dick*. The times were fluid and fearful; much of the fear was focused on the more than three million immigrants who entered the gates.

The litany of charges was familiar. The aliens dwelt in slums, loved wickedness, drank to excess, sold their votes. "They bring the grog shops like the frogs of Egypt upon us." "America has become the sewer into which the pollutions of European jails are emptied." Elections had been turned "into an unmeaning mockery where the rights of native born citizens are voted away by those who blindly follow their mercenary and selfish leaders." What was novel in the 1850s was the emergence of influential national organizations to bind together those who scorned the aliens, and the launching from those platforms of a temporarily successful political movement.

The founding fathers of nativist clubs had imaginations that were richly romantic; Tom Sawyer was no more giddy with the incantatory power of ritual than the officers of the Order of the Star-Spangled Banner, founded in 1849. To enter its ranks a new member had, first, to swear that he was born of Protestants in the United States, was not married to a Catholic, and would support only native-born citizens for all offices of honor, trust, or profit. Then he had to remember secret passwords, mysterious grips, and strange devices for carrying on the great work. Meetings, for example, were announced by the clandestine distribution of heart-shaped pieces of paper to the members— white for routine occasions, red if danger threatened. There was a "cry of distress" to bring help from other members, much like the "Hey, Rube!" of the carnival. There were secret gestures like a baseball coach's signals; as an instance, if two people in the order were with strangers and one began to speak too freely, the other reminded him of security precautions by drawing the thumb and forefinger across the eyes. Since all of the initiates were supposed to disclaim any knowledge of the order's very existence, they soon acquired the name of Know-Nothings. Presumably this secrecy was to protect members from reprisals. But in the political climate of 1854, it was inevitable that the Know-Nothings should forsake their protective cover in order to enter candidates' names in elections.

The organization of the order, providing for local, state, and national councils, paralleled the committee structure of the parties; and the apparatus of newspapers and speakers that united partisans of the Whigs and the Democrats was not hard to duplicate in those simpler times. The Know-Nothings came out fighting, and astonished themselves and the country. Their candidates in 1854 won control of the governments of Massachusetts (where they swept every state office and nearly all the seats in the legislature) and Delaware. In Pennsylvania a coalition of Whigs and Know-Nothings won the election. The next year the Know-Nothings conducted successful campaigns in Rhode Island, New Hampshire, Connecticut, Maryland, and Kentucky; they came close to victory in Virginia, Alabama, Georgia, Mississippi, and Louisiana, and they ran well in New York and Pennsylvania. They were probably helped in 1855 by the growth of another nativist league, the Order of United Americans.

However, despite the nature and origins of the movement, the Know-Nothing victories did not signal a sudden, massive revulsion against immigration. Local issues had much to do with the election results. In the border states and in the South, many voters were eager to dodge the slavery question. They disliked abolitionists and slavocrats with equal intensity; the Know-Nothings had taken no national position on the question and provided a fine refuge for neutrals. The Democratic Party was splitting into Northern and Southern factions, and many Democrats sulked in Know-Nothing tents or used them as halfway houses on the road to turning Republican. Whigs found in Know-Nothingism a life raft as their party broke up and sank.

For all these reasons, therefore, the motley collection of politicians elected as Know-Nothings (under such party labels as Americans or Native Americans) never united on a program dear to anti-alien hearts. Some in the Congress of the United States submitted a bill requiring a twenty-one-year residence period prior to naturalization, but it died in that dungeon of much other legislation, the Judiciary Committee. The "Americans" could not even secure passage of legislation to forbid the admission of paupers, criminals, idiots, lunatics, and blind people to the country. In the states the record was little more impressive; even in Massachusetts, where the government was nearly all Know-Nothing for a year, the most they could achieve was a pair of laws confining officeholding to the native-born and voting to those who had resided in the land for twenty-one years and were naturalized. Both acts were repealed by succeeding legislatures. The Massachusetts Know-Nothings hastened their own extinction by creating a "Nunnery Committee" to investigate convents, schools, and seminaries, and to see if indeed they harbored helpless white slaves of the Vatican. The body of legislators chosen behaved so grossly and consumed such huge quantities of food and drink at public expense that the chairman was expelled from office. In Massachusetts, the nativist enterprise went down to the sound of laughter. And when the American Party ran the ex-Whig Millard Fillmore for the Presidency in 1856, he floundered to defeat, receiving only Maryland's electoral votes.

Nativism and its political offspring had transiently electrified groups of voters, but the American people seemed to agree with Abraham Lincoln, who in 1855 gave a classic reply to the question whether he was sympathetic to Know-Nothingism:

> How could I be? How can any one who abhors the oppression of negroes, be in favor of degrading classes of white people? Our progress in degeneracy appears to me to be pretty rapid. As a nation, we began by declaring that "*all men are created equal.*" We now practically read it, "all men are created equal, *except negroes.*" When the Know-Nothings get control, it will read, "all men are created equal, except negroes, *and foreigners and catholics.*" When it comes to this I should prefer emigrating to some country where they make no pretence of loving liberty—to Russia, for instance, where despotism can be taken pure, and without the base alloy of hypocrisy.

Then, in 1861, a new sound was heard in the land that aroused foreign-born and native population alike—the gunfire of civil war. The immigrants and their offspring reacted to the emergency with promptness and generosity—sometimes stimulated by the offer of bounties, certainly, but primarily in what was once more a proof of what had already been proved,

156

namely, that the majority of immigrants considered the United States to be genuinely their country, and its trials their trials. It has been estimated that the two most numerous groups of "foreigners," the Irish and the Germans, between them contributed at least 370,000 troops to the armies of the Union. Some of these warriors were integrated into ordinary army units, but others were grouped in special companies, regiments, and even larger formations. Early in the war it was a common practice to raise volunteer forces composed entirely of men from a particular locality or occupation or nationality. For their part, the Irish formed units bearing such names as the Irish Rifles and the Mulligan Regiment, and sometimes even marched into battle with a flag of green carried next to the national colors. There were ten regiments made up wholly of Germans in New York, six in Ohio, six in Missouri, five in Pennsylvania, four in Wisconsin, and three in Illinois. One German romantic hero of the war was Brigadier General Ludwig Blenker—sometime jeweler's apprentice, medical student, volunteer in the revolutionary armies in Germany, and now a merchant in America and a lover of good things. In his mess tent, champagne and beer flowed as if the Virginia wilderness were the Black Forest and were populated by Teutonic knights—an illusion strengthened by the ringing Germanic commands of the officers in his brigade. Compared to Blenker, political generals of German extraction like Carl Schurz or professionals of German descent like Godfrey Weitzel were prosaic.

Some military organizations, rather than being ethnically exclusive, were spectacularly mixed. While the 23rd Wisconsin could count companies of Swedes, Irish, and Germans, New York's Garibaldi Guards boasted a Hungarian colonel, an Italian lieutenant colonel, a German surgeon, and companies designated as "hussars" and "carabinieri." The Adjutant General's muster rolls unimaginatively listed this miniature Foreign Legion as the 39th New York, but on parade it carried with dash a set of regimental colors (the same as those in the Hungarian flag) presented by Garibaldi himself. A New York cavalry regiment was for a time commanded by a genuine Italian count, Luigi Palma de Cesnola (who later became director of the Metropolitan Museum of Art in New York), and another unit from New York, the Gardes Lafayettes, had French, German, Italian, and Spanish names on its roster.

The Confederacy had exotic soldiery, too, especially from Louisiana. Almost from the first days of New Orleans, the city had been an international port and a mingling ground for adventurers from Latin America, Europe, and the Mississippi Valley. The 1st Louisiana Regiment claimed to have representatives of thirty-seven nationalities in its ranks; a single company of the 10th Louisiana listed soldiers from Austria, Corsica, England, France, Germany, Greece, Ireland, Italy, Martinique, Portugal, Scotland, Sicily, Spain, and Switzerland. When the 13th Louisiana marched through New Orleans, the home of many of its volunteers, cries arose from the crowd: "Oh, Captain, for the love of God, let Patrick go home with me. I have a good dinner cooked for him. . . ." And "Mon Dieu, Lieutenant! let my lil' Garçon, Jules, go my 'ouse. His petite sis-ter seek." At the top levels of command, Jefferson Davis had five generals born in Ireland, including one, Patrick Cleburne, whose brother served in the Union Army.

There were, of course, foreigners who stayed home on both sides of the fighting lines—who profiteered and evaded taxes, sowed discontent among the troops, pretended that the whole conflict did not exist, or denounced the war. Less than two weeks after Irish troops had fought brilliantly at Gettysburg in July of 1863, thousands of Irishmen in New York City staged a draft riot that lasted for four destruction-filled days. They were outraged at a conscription act that allowed the rich to buy exemptions from army service but forced the poor—themselves—to fight a war for "niggers," who might some day claim a share of the unskilled jobs that were their sustenance.

Yet by and large the immigrant communities bore their share of the burden of the terrible war, which Lincoln, in the Second Inaugural Address, suggested might be God's punishment for the sin of two and a half centuries of black enslavement. Thus the newcomers participated in the nation's guilt and expiation. In 1858 Lincoln had noted that Fourth of July celebrations honored the brave grandfathers and great-grandfathers of his audience for establishing a nation that was prosperous and free. Then he added:

> We have besides these men—descended by blood from our ancestors—among us perhaps half our people who are not descendants at all of these men, they are men who have come from

Europe—German, Irish, French and Scandinavian—men that have come from Europe themselves, or whose ancestors have come hither and settled here, finding themselves our equals in all things. If they look back through this history to trace their connection with those days by blood, they find they have none, they cannot carry themselves back into that glorious epoch and make themselves feel that they are part of us, but when they look through that old Declaration of Independence they find that those old men say that "We hold these truths to be self-evident, that all men are created equal," and then they feel that that moral sentiment taught in that day evidences their relation to those men, that it is the father of all moral principle in them, and that they have a right to claim it as though they were blood of the blood, and flesh of the flesh of the men who wrote that Declaration [loud and long continued applause], and so they are. That is the electric cord in that Declaration that links the hearts of patriotic and liberty-loving men together, that will link those patriotic hearts as long as the love of freedom exists in the minds of men throughout the world. [Applause.]

The men of foreign birth and extraction who died on the nation's Civil War battlefields, to save or to break a Union their ancestors had not made, were in a sense validating Lincoln's faith that the Declaration of Independence had made all of them "native Americans."

VII
Run, Work, Beware

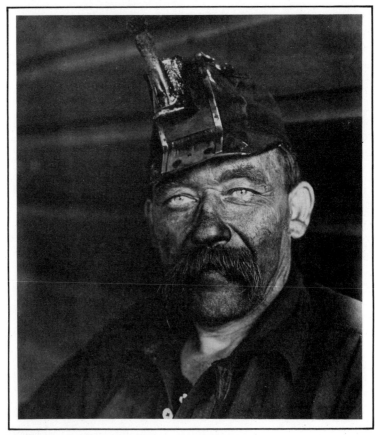

Rapidly expanding steel mills and coal mines offered large-scale employment to unskilled immigrants, like this Polish track layer who worked in the Pennsylvania coal fields. *(Lewis W. Hine, International Museum of Photography at George Eastman House)*

After the Civil War, a flood of immigration washed over the American land. The steam-power revolution continued to add its driving energy to the forces that propelled migrations. Railroads probed deeper into parts of Europe that were until then still locked in medieval patterns, and into areas of North America yet untouched by white civilization. The transatlantic passage shrank to less than two weeks, the train journey across America to about a week. The flow of migrants widened and deepened, and seemed on the verge of engulfing familiar American social landmarks.

The steady increase in the number of newcomers was both an effect and a cause of the explosive industrial growth of the United States. The immigrant ships brought manpower and consumers, critically needed to create and to buy the products of the rising factories. At the same time, each spurt in the nation's productivity created new jobs and new opportunities. The word went back from the "foreigners" who had spent a year or two in America that dollars were waiting to be earned. Along with letters describing the American scene went remittances and steamer tickets. Yesterday's immigrants quickly became the vigorous recruiters of tomorrow's.

The biggest annual migration before the Civil War was 427,833 in 1854. The total was not surpassed until 1873, when 459,803 entered the gates. In 1882 a new record of 788,992 was set. Then came a deluge. Seven times from 1883 through 1903 the yearly total passed half a million, and only twice in that time did it drop below a quarter of a million. The all-time high was reached in 1907—1,285,349 souls—and in the period 1905 through 1914 the million mark was exceeded six times. (Fiorello La Guardia, who would later be elected mayor of New York, worked as an interpreter at Ellis Island in 1907, and he remembered clearing an average of five thousand immigrants a day in some periods of heavy traffic.)

Between 1860 and 1900, more than thirteen and a half million immigrants arrived. Between 1900 and 1930, another eighteen million landed. In seventy years, the total of entering migrants was greater than that of the entire population of the United States at the time of Lincoln's first election. Such a massive absorption is more than an incident in history: it is, in the words of one scholar, "one of the great outstanding facts of our national life." The marks are still on the nation's economy and psyche. Moreover, the post-1880 immigration set off more far-reaching reverberations than any ingathering that had preceded it. The foreign-born, in 1910, made up nearly fifteen percent of the total American population, which was not a substantial increase over the more than thirteen percent of 1860. But the actual numbers were far greater, and the faces, the accents, and especially the economic roles of the aliens had changed markedly. As the forces of modernization rolled over Southern and Eastern Europe, they drove thousands of uprooted families before them to ports of embarkation. Not all of these exiles chose America as their new homeland, but those who did found, in overwhelming numbers, that their natural environment thenceforth would be the city and the factory. Economic necessity dictated that pattern: the jobs and opportunities were concentrated in cities. But as a result immigrants became tangled in disturbing complications in American life created by urbanism and industrial upheaval. And to make matters worse, some Americans blamed them for creating the problems in which they were snarled and pointed the finger of accusation at their strange nationalities, religions, or—a vague term—races.

Statistics encompass the facts, if not the emotions, of the big change. In 1870 total immigration to the United States was 387,203. About eighty-five percent of it—328,626 people— came from Europe, and more than ninety percent of *them* came from the British Isles, Scandinavia, Germany, Belgium, Switzerland, Holland, and France. Southern and Eastern Europe were hardly in the picture. The sprawling Austro-Hungarian Empire sent only 4,425 immigrants to the United States; Italy fewer than 3,000; Russia a mere 907; and those areas under Ottoman rule or suzerainty, including the present-day Bulgaria and Rumania, yielded all of six. Poland was divided among Russia, Austria-Hungary, and Prussia, but the immigration officials, attempting until 1899 to keep a separate count of incoming Poles, found only 223 of them in 1870. There were fewer than 1,400 arrivals from Greece, Spain, and Portugal together.

A young native American of 1870, therefore, stood an excellent chance of living out his life, even in a city, without ever meeting a foreigner other than someone German, Irish, or perhaps Swedish. His chances of encountering an Italian, a Pole, a Greek, or one of the Central European peoples with such exotic-sounding names as Magyars, Slavs, Croats, or Slovenes were remote. Nor would alien presences necessarily upset him. Both natives and foreign-born were widely dispersed over a still rural countryside. Nearly three quarters of the total population of some forty million lived in communities of fewer than 2,500 residents. With that much elbow room, differences between peoples were not so noticeable, not so irritating, as they would soon become.

Only thirty-seven years later the same American, in late middle age, would find a wholly different picture. In the peak year of 1907, approximately 1,200,000 Europeans passed through the various checkpoints maintained by immigration authorities (the majority being handled at Ellis Island, which was opened in 1892). But now nearly a million came from the domains of the Czar, the Sultan, and Emperor Franz Josef of Austria-Hungary, and from around the Mediterranean. More than 335,000 came from Central Europe—Bohemians, Serbs, Poles from Galicia, Slovaks, and many more ethnic varieties from a region that was itself an enormous mixing bowl of peoples. Nearly 260,000 came from Russia, a heavy proportion of them Jews. The Italians numbered some 285,000. Rumania, Bulgaria, and what remained of the Turkish Empire on European soil accounted for 36,510, but there were thousands more from the still Turkish Near East—Syrians, Greeks living on islands under Turkish rule, and Armenians fleeing from severe persecution. And then there were Portuguese, Hispanic-Americans, French-Canadians, and other familiar and unfamiliar faces in the procession, and almost all of these new arrivals remained in the increasingly crowded cities.

The balance had shifted at just about the end of the old century. The preponderant share of European immigration now came, and continued to come until 1924, from areas that had sent practically no one to the republic when it was young. The hypothetical American who lived out his adult years between, say, 1870 and 1910 was bewildered, to say the very least, by the sights and sounds and smells of urban neighborhoods full of Lithuanian Jews, Ukrainian Catholics, swarthy Italians, dark-eyed Greeks, heavy-featured Poles and Slovaks. He could not relate them to anything in his own past experience or to the American history that he had read in his schoolbooks. He fell naturally into the habit of calling these strangers "new" immigrants, and he wondered if they would ever really "become Americans"—if they had the toughness and commitment, the self-improving drives and the political savvy of the "old" immigrants, the Scandinavians and Germans and Irish, whose names were now familiar on tax rolls and on police forces, in legislatures, in advertisements for businesses they owned.

These anxieties, which persisted as the twentieth century unfolded and eventually led to a program of immigration restriction, arose from sources that ran deeper than racial antipathies. The sheer mass of the new immigration was unsettling. It was as if a family took on a cluster of new poor relations every month and had to review its budget and its living arrangements accordingly. Moreover, the period from 1890 to 1917 was one of angry national strife. Lockouts and strikes splattered the industrial scene with violence. Depression haunted the middle and lower classes. Reformers brooded about the vast power concentrated in railroad and industrial combines whose assets were counted in billions. Crusading journalists bared the ugly features of graft and corruption in boss-ridden city and state governments. Many Americans uneasily recalled Thomas Jefferson's gloomy observation that cities were to the body politic what sores were to the human physique. The "new" immigrants—crowded into slums and company towns, working at the lowest levels of skill and reward in the industrial order and carrying all the stigmata of poverty, from poor health to crime and alcoholism—seemed to embody the fulfillment of that warning.

But the concept of an old and a new immigration masked the fact that the newcomers from east and south were not fundamentally different from those who had come before them. Like all pilgrims, they included in their ranks the good and the bad, heroes and opportunists, born leaders and natural failures. Not only would they in time become Americans; they were already Americans when they took ship.

The process must have begun for thousands of Pasquales and Giuseppes with a realistic look at life in southern Italy. The march of progress faltered as it moved down toward the toe of the boot-shaped Italian Peninsula. In Calabria (the toe of the boot), Apulia (the heel), and the island of Sicily, rainfall was uneven: months of drought baked the soil, and the vegetation was as tough as the scrawny goats that tore at it for sustenance. Then came heavy rains, carrying away the earth in great slides— because most of the trees whose roots would have held in the life-giving water had long ago been cut down. Some rainfall remained in swamps, over which the anopheles mosquito whined in ominous triumph. The south Italian peasant fought a constant, losing battle against malaria and nature's whims.

Society gave him little help. By the time that national unity was achieved, in 1870, the Italian government had forced the breakup of great church-held estates in the south. But the land fell mainly into the hands of the well-to-do. These landlords rented their estates piecemeal to peasant farmers and abandoned to agents the day-to-day management of the land while they themselves courted the pleasures of Rome and other European cities. Two thirds of all landlords in Sicily in 1900 were absentees; in Calabria the figure was two fifths. The estate managers cheated and bled the tenants as dispassionately as leeches. Life was a daily struggle for a bit of bread soaked in oil and salt; government officials seemed to be merely successors to the conquerors who for many centuries had kept appearing on the scene to take the lion's share of the crop, sleep with the women, and hang the more rebellious men. Priests married the living, buried the dead, and promised heavenly consolations, but greater help than that was seldom available.

In sum, life was what it was in Ireland, for example—a continuing demonstration that half-starved tenants cultivating worn-out lands could not rise far above an animal existence. There was no escape except in the coffin or the emigrant vessel, and the more ambitious ones of course chose the latter route. Even before 1900, Italians—many from the north, too—had been migrating in large numbers to Latin America, North Africa, and the more industrially developed countries of Europe. After the turn of the century, stories began to spread that jobs were plentiful in the United States. Between 1900 and 1910, more than two million Italians chose to find out for themselves whether that was true.

Not all were poor. Not all were tenant farmers. Among these migrants, for one, was Constantine Panunzio, the offspring of an attorney, who came from Molfetta in Apulia. His father had an abiding faith in the power of the chastising rod to shape a child's life correctly. Young "Costantino" was beaten, tied to a bedpost, and kept on a bread-and-water diet when he seemed to deviate from the course—planned by his grandmother—that would lead him to become first a priest, than a teacher, and finally a statesman. But father and grandmother were fighting a losing battle. Costantino had unwittingly taken his first step on the road to America one day when he wandered down to Molfetta's harbor and saw ocean-going ships riding at anchor. Despite all their rust and scale, to him they looked like proud, venturous galleons. He yearned restlessly for the sea, and in the turbulence of his desire became a schoolboy delinquent: robbing vineyards, playing truant, shirking confession, rattling handfuls of hard candy off girls' windows, setting off firecrackers in public streets. His father used every trick in the jailer's catalogue, from thrashings to compulsory jobs—in a foundry, a soap factory, a blacksmith shop, an electrical-supply plant—hoping that a taste of manual labor would make his boy savor the comforting benefits of a priestly life. It was of no use. In 1897, when Panunzio was thirteen, the paterfamilias gave in to his young rebel and permitted him to join the crew of an Adriatic coasting schooner.

Five years later, Panunzio sailed into Boston on the brig *Francesco* and promptly jumped ship to escape a tyrannical captain. After five days of sleeping on benches, he was led by a French sailor, whom he met in a park, to Boston's North End Italian colony, where he was allowed to sleep, on credit, in a bed he shared with three men and many bugs. Promptly he found that an Italian beginning a career in the New World could only expect to find work with the "peek and shuvle"—which he said were his first two English words, as he spelled them. Within a few weeks the young firebrand was digging holes for a living. Eventually he would move on to become a logger, farm hand, college student, and social worker. He was one specimen of the "new" immigrant.

Another was Louis Adamic, of Blato, Carniola, in Austria (later part of Yugoslavia). The process began for him, too, when he was a boy. In the village wineshop he heard the returned *Amerikanci*—who wore black derbies, celluloid collars, and loud neckties—boast of their New World achievements. America was a "Golden Country—a sort of Paradise—the Land of Promise," huge beyond imagination, prodigal in surprises, and above all, able to furnish white bread and meat, even on weekdays, to peasants' children. But by the time Adamic was eleven, he had already heard another side of the story. A townsman, Peter Molek, returned from the mines of Pennsylvania with an asthmatic cough, a body twisted by rheumatism, and a warning that America was a jungle that swallowed people unless they were strong and wise enough to save their money and return home. Molek even showed him a book about immigrants just like himself and what befell some of them in the New World. It was by a man named Upton Sinclair, and was called, in fact, *The Jungle*.

Yet four years later Peter Molek's health was better, and he was ready to go back to the scramble of American life. Louis Adamic was anxious to go, too. He had spent three years at school in Laibach (later Ljubljana), and he had not lost the American fever. He had eagerly read such books as *Stric Tomova Koča (Uncle Tom's Cabin)* and *Zadnji Mohikanec (The Last of the Mohicans)*, and copies of a Slovenian-American newspaper, *Narodni Glas*, which he borrowed from a classmate, Yanko, who got them from a brother in America.

Yanko and Louis were members of a students' club where Slovenian nationalistic speeches foamed and intoxicated like beer. One afternoon they found themselves in the streets of Laibach as demonstrators for Slovene self-determination—singing, shouting slogans, pulling down German signs from above store windows, and preparing to crown the local statue of Franz Josef with a cuspidor. Suddenly a detachment of Austrian cavalry, with sabers drawn, appeared on the scene. Someone threw a rock; a command ripped out; then there was the heart-stopping rattle of shots. The students scattered pell-mell for the safety of doorways and alleys. But Yanko Radin would never reach sanctuary. He fell with a bullet through his head. Adamic, kneeling over his friend's body in a daze, was arrested. Now he was more than halfway to becoming an American.

He was released from jail after a few days, but he was expelled from the government-run school. The family tried to enter him in the Jesuit seminary in town, but the boy could not face ten years of confinement, prayer, somber clothes, and airless cells. "No more school for me," he decided: "I was going to America." His father was outraged, but his mother interceded. Late in 1913, Louis Adamic sailed for New York on the *Niagara*, out of Le Havre.

167

The Italian Panunzio and the Slovenian Adamic became Americans via the road of rebellion. For Mary Antin's father, of Polotzk, in the Russian section of Poland, the incitement to emigration was not so romantic. It was simply failure. But then, in a sense, life for a Jew under the Czar was something of a continual exercise in failure. What separated men from one another was the boldness with which they did something about it.

Sentimentality casts a fond aura today around the *shtetls*—the little villages from which the ancestors of millions of American Jews came less than three quarters of a century ago; but all the performances in the world of *Fiddler on the Roof* cannot disguise the fact that the *shtetls* were, in a sense, prison compounds. Russian Jews were required, in the 1890s, to live within the Pale of Settlement, a rigidly limited area. In periods of official liberalism, some exceptions were made for a small number of Jewish intellectuals, businessmen, and factory workers. But the privilege was often arbitrarily revoked; most of the time it could only be sustained by constant, humiliating petitions to an insulting bureaucracy, and also by plenty of bribe money. In the villages of the Pale, Jews confronted a barbed-wire snarl of high taxes and restrictions on landownership and the choice of professions. As a result, they were forced into competition with one another in the authorized lines of work. An oversupply of tailors, butchers, bakers, peddlers, grocers, barbers, tinsmiths, capmakers, tinkers, harness makers, carpenters, wagon drivers, and other petty tradesmen fought for pittances with a savagery Darwin would have recognized.

Russian Jews took what consolation they could in the intense practice of their religion. Cut off from contacts with a changing world, they became increasingly introspective, mystical, superstitious, and parochial in their faith. And there was little opportunity to break out, even where there was a will. The great world beyond the synagogue was closed—and threatening. From it came harsh decrees and the hard-fisted tax collector. From it came the dreaded conscription officials who would take Jewish young men away for military service that, prior to 1874, lasted twenty-five years. As soldiers they would be forced to abandon Jewish practices and thus became dead in the eyes of their own community. Far better, then, if one could not bribe the conscriptors, to use the brutal services of the "crippler," who would cut a

Mary Antin, a Russian-Jewish immigrant who came to the United States as a young girl, felt America's welcome profoundly and later wrote *The Promised Land* about her experiences in her new homeland. For her and other European Jews, America became a haven from squalid ghettos and a religious persecution so heinous that it routinely took the form of physical torture. *(Library of Congress)*

boy's heel tendon, slash an eyeball, or pierce an eardrum, inflicting hours of pain and terror in youth to spare a lifetime of horror and despair. The outside world, too, was the Gentile peasantry that lived inside as well as beyond the Pale—coarse, uneducated, bibulous men who every now and then, egged on by priests and officials, went on a rampage in the Jewish quarter—burning, beating, knifing, and raping. The pogrom was to Russian Jewry what the lynch mob was to Mississippi blacks: the ultimate threat, the always possible disaster.

Like all Jewish children in Polotzk, Mary Antin learned what helplessness was at an early age. When a tiny neighbor, the boy Vanka, threw mud at her, she ran to her mother and was told resignedly: "How can I help you, my poor child? Vanka is a Gentile. The Gentiles do as they like with us Jews." The second time it happened she did not run to her mother but took shelter, saying to herself, "Vanka is a Gentile." The third time, when he spat on her, she wiped her face and thought nothing at all. She even learned, when she saw Vanka coming while she was eating an apple, to hold out the core to him with a false smile that made her "feel black inside."

Her father, meanwhile, was practicing the same abasement as he bent and smiled while filling the palms of excise officers and policemen with bribes. He had been a scholarly boy, slated for a life of Talmudic meditation, in which effort he would have been supported by the contributions of less gifted mortals. But when he grew up he found that such piety was not to his taste. The great world called him—at least what little of it was open to a Jew—and so he forsook study and went out to make his living at a series of occupations. He succeeded at none. He got a permit to travel in Russia and was, for a time, assistant superintendent of a distillery. Then he inherited his father-in-law's dry-goods store in Polotz, and life went very well for a while. But a series of illnesses in the family wiped him out. Candlesticks, furniture, dresses, featherbeds were sold or pawned. There was a brief respite while he worked at another job, as superintendent of a gristmill; then desperation—in the midst of which came an offer from an emigrant-aid society: they would get Antin to America.

He went off penniless, leaving a family on the brink of starvation. He wife kept them from going over the edge by peddling; the children took odd jobs (Mary herself was unhappily and unsuccessfully apprenticed to a milliner); relatives gave their mites. The father continued his restless shifting from venture to venture in Boston, where he had landed, and with undaunted optimism borrowed enough money to send steamer tickets back to Polotzk. The family left town by train, with half the Jews of the village thronging around to cry farewell, to remind them of the perils of the sea, to shout messages for relatives in American towns near Boston such as "Baltimoreh," to wave colored handkerchiefs, and to assist in loading featherbeds and baskets of kosher food aboard. Weeks later, after many miles of rail and steamer travel, delousing, disinfecting, labeling, pigeonholing, and confinement in Hamburg and presumably in Boston too, they all stepped out into the New World.

P anunzio, Adamic, Antin—three names among millions but each illustrating a pattern of deracination. At first glance, most of the twentieth-century international migrants were an unpromising lot. Even the conscientious and helpful people from the various national immigrant-aid societies and from the settlement houses that sprang up in slum neighborhoods were now and then discouraged when they saw their charges come down the gangplanks. Most Eastern and Southern European immigrants were uneducated, poorly dressed, easy marks for disease, superstitious, unskilled—and terrified. The *looked* like the wretched refuse of Europe's teeming shore.

Yet they were far from beaten. Like the German redemptioners of the 1750s or the Irish of the 1840s or, for that matter, like the old American families who had yoked up oxen for every new frontier from the Connecticut Valley to Oregon, they may well have been unputdownables, survivors by instinct. A person who responds to failure by seeking out a new challenge in a strange environment is anything but defeated. Even those whose hopes in the New World never were fulfilled or who returned to the old country or became permanent dependents had at least had the courage to dice once with destiny.

The newcomers brought with them the fruits of a hard background. Life was a question of pushing and shoving to get one's share. Officials were enemies. Deceit and coercion were sometimes indispensable to keep a roof over the head, a loaf in the pantry. Some genteel Americans might have outgrown such directness, though their ancestors would not have been shocked— those who had gulled British customs collectors, swindled the

Indians out of the choicest lands, duped investors in unsound banks, and used every possible quasi-legal advantage to undermine business competitors. We read Henry Adams lamenting that he, the descendant of Puritans and Presidents, was less fit for modern American life than any "Jacob or Ysaac" from Cracow, who had a keener instinct, a more intense energy, and a freer hand for getting on in the world than he did. While this remark was made in distaste and fear, its import was that the immigrants were contributing a fresh vitality to the land. Henry's equally gloomy brother Brooks thought of the immigrants as the possible equivalent of the barbarians, who overthrew Rome and infused a decayed civilization with new blood—a left-handed compliment if there ever was one.

But the immigrants were not coming to pull down the monuments of American life; they were, in fact, to become deeply involved in building new ones. Whatever cultural and social assets and shortcomings the newcomer brought to the scene, he had an economic role to play. His labor power was vital, particularly in heavy industry.

So much attention has been focused on the immigrant urban laborer that there is danger of overlooking the "foreigner's" role in the final agricultural conquest of the Great Plains. Europeans played a crucial part in that process. Sometimes they came on their own, and sometimes they were recruited by state immigration bureaus or by railroads with land or services to sell. In 1874, for example, the management of the Santa Fe line heard of the imminent arrival of a group of hard-working Russian Mennonites. They were related to the German Mennonites who had come to Pennsylvania in the eighteenth century; but *their* ancestors had elected to go east instead of west, and had accepted generous grants of land from Catherine the Great, who had an interest in seeing southern Russia well populated. Originally, the Russian colony of Mennonites had been exempted from most taxes and all military service, but early in the 1870s Czar Alexander II stopped that. The Mennonites thereupon shopped about for a new place of refuge. By correspondence they learned that some of their American brethren had moved to a treeless but fertile Beulah Land named Kansas. On a September day a first contingent arrived in New York, to be met by agents of the railroad. If the Americans had any impulse to laugh at the Mennonites' styles in beards and clothing, they suppressed it by reminding themselves that the newcomers had brought gold drafts worth two million dollars with them. Eventually the Santa Fe sold the Russians about a hundred thousand acres of land, but only after sweetening the bargain with such services as chartering a steamer to bring belongings from Russia, hauling building material free for one year, liberally granting passes to Mennonite ministers, and using the corporation's considerable influence in Topeka to get state legislation exempting the Mennonites from any future militia-duty requirements. In return the Mennonites, year after year, sent carloads of good farm produce—primarily hard, red Turkey wheat—rolling to market.

A t the turn of the century another railroad mogul, the Great Northern's James J. Hill, also took a hand in the migratory process. A bearded, one-eyed prophet of Far Western development, Hill believed that the northern Great Plains, the Rockies, and the Pacific Northwest might be made to blossom with prosperity (in which his line could share) if it were settled and farmed with techniques suitable to a normally dry area. He sent agents to England, Scotland, Ireland, Wales, Finland, Denmark, Norway, Sweden, Germany, and Russia—agents bearing pictures and pamphlets in the native tongues—and invited all men of spirit to share the banquet of timber, grazing land, and soil that God had spread. By the thousands, Europeans jumped at the bait. Hill had no land to parcel out and sell, but the government was giving away farm land under the 1862 Homestead Act, and he could offer other inducements—fares as low as thiry-three dollars or less from Chicago to any point on the line, and special packages such as the low-price rental of a complete freight car, into which the westward-bound Swede or Bohemian was permitted to put all his household goods and farm machinery, fifty bushels of grain, up to twenty hogs and sheep, as many as ten head of horses, mules, and cattle, feed for the stock in transit, 2,500 feet of lumber, five hundred fence posts, a small portable house, and even trees and shrubbery. Such advantages made it reasonable to try one's luck.

Yet for every homesteader who possessed at least the initial skill and capital to begin a farm, there were dozens of immigrants who arrived with little more than the clothes they had on. Most of them were categorized by the authorities as "unskilled workers." For thousands of Polish, Italian, and Balkan peasants this was an inaccurate statement. They were, in fact, farmers without farms or prospects. Some managed—often with the help of charitable societies—to find their way to the land, either as separate owners or in agricultural colonies scattered from New England to California. And some, after long and grinding years of industrial labor, put aside enough to buy run-down farms in New England, New York, New Jersey, and Pennsylvania, and started to raise fruit, poultry, or vegetables.

The majority of those arriving after 1890, however, underwent a transition common throughout the modern world. They became part of an industrial urban lower class. Hard times, high taxes, poor soils, competition, droughts and floods and earthquakes, had all combined to make life oppressive on the old European farms. Those countries where industry was taking hold needed labor acutely, and the word went out that hands were wanted in mine, mill, loft, logging camp, packing plant, road-building crew and cannery, fishing fleet and freight yard. Two or three dollars, even for a twelve-hour day, sounded like a vast improvement on whatever life had to offer in Zyrardów or Catania. The immigrant went to where the pay dirt could be found. And for a nation such as the United States, in the midst of a long-term bloom, he was pay dirt himself.

The pattern of immigrant dispersion tells the story. The foreign-born were drawn into the magnetic field of the country's industrial heartland. As early as the 1890s Chicago, hog-butcher to the world, freight-handler, stacker of wheat, and maker of steel, had more Germans than any cities in Germany except Berlin and Hamburg, more Swedes than any place but Stockholm and Göteborg, more Norwegians than any town except Christiania and Bergen. Cleveland, where John D. Rockefeller and Marcus A. Hanna and others made their fortunes in oil and coal and iron and lake shipping and public transit, had 100,000 foreign-born; Detroit, a manufacturing town even before the advent of the automobile, had 80,000. New York, already a center of garment making and other light industries in 1900, numbered 1,260,914 foreign-born—almost a third of the city's total population; by 1910 the number had swelled to nearly two million—Russian Jews comprising the largest single group, followed by the Italians, the Germans, the Irish, and the "Austrians." Twenty years later, when the foreign-born in the nation as a whole totaled greater than fourteen million, fully half of that

174

Many young immigrants attended schools like
New York's West 52nd Street Industrial School,
here photographed by Jacob Riis. "The public
school," Mary Antin said, "has done its best for
us foreigners. . . . You should be glad to hear
of it, you born Americans, for it is the story of
the growth of your country; of the flocking of
your brothers and sisters from the far ends of
the earth to the flag you love." *The Jacob A. Riis
Collection, Museum of the City of New York)*

number were in the heavily urbanized Northeastern states; another fourth were in the North Central states, concentrated mostly in the industrial sections of Michigan, Ohio, Illinois, Indiana, and Wisconsin.

T he post-1900 arrivals naturally tended to cluster where able-bodied males were most in demand. They took up coarse grades of labor, while the earlier immigrants and the native-born workers climbed the occupational ladder. A 1900 tabulation of white male breadwinners showed that among those of German origins, about one in six worked as a nonfarm laborer, or in a mine, mill, or factory; among the Scots, about one in five; of the English and Welsh, approximately one in four; of the Irish, nearly one in three. But almost half the Italians and some sixty-three percent of the Hungarians fell into the category of laborers. Moreover, there were some spectacular concentrations by area. In Pennsylvania in 1900, nearly fifty-nine percent of the whites mining bituminous coal were foreign-born. In three anthracite-producing shafts in Lackawanna County, more than seventy-five percent of the employees were Slavs; not surprisingly, it was reported that "scores of collieries . . . cannot work when the Slavs observe a religious holiday."

The Italians seemed to find their way to the railroads and to urban construction projects as predominantly as the Slavs went to the mines. There was a natural tendency, once a nationality group had made inroads in a field, for fellow countrymen to gravitate to it. The Italians, too, were fed into the labor market in especially large numbers by the *padrone* system. The *padrone* was an Italian who arranged for passage, greeted new arrivals in their own tongue, got them settled, then sent them out in gangs to various jobs, collecting board money from the immigrants at one end and fees from the employer at the other. Once the *padroni* had established contacts in a particular industry, they tended to funnel their lucrative stream of greenhorns into it until saturation was reached.

"Where do you work-a John? On the Delaware Lackawan'" went the question and answer in a mocking popular song. "John"—or rather, Giovanni—worked on a host of railroads that needed muscle as the network reached its maximum expansion of some 254,000 miles in 1916. A Bureau of Labor study routinely noted that "one of the great lines of railroad reported an increase in its construction and track gangs of 41 percent in 1906 over 1905" and that "the men employed were all Italian immigrants." In the 1890s the Erie Canal was modernized. Back in the 1820s, when Clinton's Ditch was first being dug, the lowly Paddies grubbed and shoveled their way across New York State, and died of malaria in droves. Of 12,500 laborers engaged in the updating project seventy years later, 10,500 were Italian. The Italians built large sections of the subways of New York and the street railways, waterworks, and sewer systems of hundreds of cities that were coping with an explosive growth in the first two decades of the new century. They carried pipe, and they poured concrete in Baltimore, Bridgeport and Buffalo, Pittsburgh and Providence, Erie and Hoboken and Jersey City, Schenectady and Springfield and Syracuse—the smoky industrial towns where much of America's wealth was created but little of it was enjoyed. They were also quarrymen, cigar rollers, glassworkers, and employees in clothing factories—where, one Rochester, New York, manufacturer smugly noted, they were "as cheap as children and a little better." Some, like others before them, rose out of ditches and from benches to become foremen, contractors, and suppliers themselves. Some chose to work as waiters, barbers, and shoemakers or as grocers selling vegetables, olive oil, cheese, salami, zamponi, and pasta to other Italian Americans and to other Americans willing to educate their palates.

Those immigrants who were lucky and persevering could expect some reward for their efforts that offered at least a partial fulfillment of the expectations they brought to America. But the way was hard and steep. America's early industrial age was prodigal of resources, and tended to waste human beings as carelessly as it did forest land or pure water. Unskilled workers—and especially recent immigrants—were in a jungle, just as Peter Molek had said to Louis Adamic. They were the prey of the unscrupulous employment agents who collected their money and then loaded them on trains with fake "passes" to nonexistent destinations. They lived in ignorance of what few rights they had against the company-town landlords and storekeepers who bilked them. They were buried and drowned in mine disasters, burned in factory fires, crushed and maimed by unsafe machines in the care of negligent foremen, and they died painfully of lung diseases without the awareness that there might be legal and political avenues of redress. They were forced by the meagerness

their incomes to live in squalid urban tenements, or in mi-
rant labor camps like those characterized by one government
inspector as showing "an absolute disregard for comfort, health,
morality, and justice." The "new" immigrants learned that the
New World's prizes demanded enormous sacrifices and that there
was no guarantee of victory for themselves or their posterity,
even with unsparing exertion. If their own experience did not tell
them, they had only to look around them and see impoverished
Anglo-Saxon fifth- and sixth-generation Americans in the coal
towns, or in the South, or in pinched but proud rural New
England.

Yet there was a chance, provided one did not get discouraged
and give up the pursuit, and if one *did* give up certain other
things. A guidebook aimed primarily at Jewish immigrants
summed it up well. The author appeared to promise eventual
success, but with evident misgivings. He told his readers:

> Hold fast, this is most necessary in America. Forget your past,
> your customs, and your ideals. Select a goal and pursue it with all
> your might. No matter what happens to you, hold on. You will
> experience a bad time but sooner or later you will achieve your
> goal. If you are neglectful, beware for the wheel of fortune turns
> quickly. You will lose your grip and be lost. A bit of advice for
> you: Do not take a moment's rest. Run, do, work and keep your
> own good in mind.

Forget the past—forget customs and ideals—run, work, beware!
This was a new kind of counsel for immigrants. And it was
difficult advice to follow, for men of ordinary frailty. Even the
enthusiasts whose faith in America was not shaken by sweatshop
labor and tenement-house living must have found the prospect
of eradication of the past appalling. Surely it was necessary to
keep some contact with what had been. And so, despite the
advice, the church or the little synagogue in the new American
neighborhood was more than a place of worship: it was a center
where the old tongue and the familiar faces were everywhere in
evidence. The foreign-language newspapers—of which there
were about a thousand in 1914, with 140 of them published
daily—were also bridges back to the identity formed in another
clime, even if what they usually *said* in Italian or Hungarian was
that Americanization should be pursued as rapidly as possible.
The Polish grocery store, the Greek café, the formal association

178

for preserving the records and culture of the old country (the Polish National Alliance, for example), were all means of easing the shock of stepping out of one's native culture. There were, of course, impatient pilgrims who could not shed old styles fast enough, but most newcomers needed the reassurance of habit, the authority of custom in decision making, the support of the like-minded neighbor.

The creation of many local enclaves of particular "foreigners" in large cities gave them a spectacular heterogeneousness. A New York newspaperman, Jacob Riis—himself a Danish immigrant—wrote that in 1890 a colored map of New York with a different hue for each block that was dominated by a particular country's sons and daughters would present "more stripes than on the skin of a zebra, and more colors than any rainbow." Not only would there be solid areas for extensive Russian-Jewish, German, Irish, Italian, black, and Chinese neighborhoods, but also "dots and dashes of color here and there . . . where the Finnish sailors worship their *djumala,* the Greek pedlars the ancient name of their race, and the Swiss the goddess of thrift." Jane Addams, pathfinding social worker, described the neighborhood surrounding her settlement house in Chicago as the site of "three or four foreign colonies"—Italians (subdivided among Neapolitans, Sicilians, and Calabrians, with an occasional Lombard or Venetian), Germans, Polish and Russian Jews, and a Bohemian settlement "so vast that Chicago ranks as the third Bohemian city in the world." In an industrial town like Lawrence, Massachusetts, workers in the town's dominant industry, textile manufacture, spoke some forty-five languages or dialects and represented twenty-five nationalities. The organizers of a major strike there in 1912 had to be polylingual in their speeches.

Such a variety of human backgrounds in a single community created disturbing problems of adjustment, but it was, in its way, electric. Mass immigration, crossed with the rise of the city, created an urban culture that was distinctive in the modern world. The impact of the almost overnight transformation of whole neighborhoods was registered on a number of widely different institutions. For the political boss, the necessary adjustment might consist of adding *bar mitzvahs,* Pulaski Day parades, or soccer matches to the list of social obligations that already included wakes and communions; and what this meant in turn was that big-city politics not only spawned the ethnically balanced ticket but also developed a special breed of leader, sensitive to cultural diversity.

For the planners of public education, the effect was very likely to emphasize the "progressive" movement: teaching civic and social skills, the practical uses of education, and the routes to personal fulfillment. Confronted with a student body that spoke, ate, squabbled, dressed, played, daydreamed, and thought in half a dozen languages and cultural traditions, a principal could not assume a uniform level of preparation on which to base his academic curriculum. But a row of Chinese, Jewish, Greek, black, Italian, Bohemian, and Irish children stood on common ground when they were taught the Pledge of Allegiance, the principles of personal hygiene, and the creative joys of woodworking or dressmaking.

The thrust of the public schools toward Americanization was not merely a patriotic reflex. The schools were in any case only reinforcing what other agencies of popular education, such as the newspapers, were doing in the jingoistic era of Theodore Roosevelt. The schools, however, had a particularly portentous impact, since they caught the immigrants who were young and still malleable. "The public school," Mary Antin said, "has done its best for us foreigners . . . when it has made us into good Americans. . . . You should be glad to hear of it, you born Americans, for it is the story of the growth of your country; of the flocking of your brothers and sisters from the far ends of the earth to the flag you love; of the recruiting of your armies of workers, thinkers, and leaders."

The entire subject of immigrant culture is best examined in the context of what happened to it after its patterns stabilized slightly. That stabilization did not take place until the end of the mass migrations. Only then was it possible for scholars to study institutions without thousands of newcomers arriving almost monthly to disrupt those institutions. Then children and parents confronted each other across the gulf between those molded by Old World traditions and those reared in a crystallized mosaic of traditions. And it was then that the arguments over whether or not the immigrants could or could not be "assimilated," and at what cost, began to be settled (or at least limited) by the practical observation of what was actually happening. Predictions about the fate of the nation's adopted children could be tested against

180

their adult performance. Questions could be asked. Who among the foreigners had genuinely "made it"? Who had not? And why? And, for that matter, who decided the meaning of "making it"?

These puzzlers were formulated during a long period of strife which ended in legislation that shut the open gates. Clamorous public voices arose with the new century, claiming that the United States was—or was not—a "melting pot," that it could—or could not—"melt" whatever material was cast into it, that the net result of unlimited hospitality was—or was not—a national disaster. Statistics of immigrant pauperism and vice, and the records of immigrant achievement, became weapons in legislative battles. Politicians, social workers, teachers, scientists, editors, and ministers joined the combat.

Amid the thunder and the shouting, one fact was underplayed: the argument was almost entirely about the qualities of different clans of white Europeans. In that context, the use of the word "races," and the effort to give meaning to such terms as Nordic, Alpine, Saxon, Teuton, Slav, Celt, and Magyar, was confusing, even ludicrous. But there was one kind of crude racial classification that could be made by almost anyone, educated or not, who had a pair of eyes. That was the difference between those who were "white" and those who were "nonwhite."

The nation could argue, in 1920, about whether a white Pole might be as desirable an immigrant as a white Welshman. But so far as the views of whites about nonwhites were concerned, there was little conflict. A decision had been rendered already. Before the gates even began to swing shut on the "new" immigrants, some very special "old" immigrants—black, yellow, and red—had challenged the traditional American boast of one people out of many, and they had found it full of bitter inconsistency.

VIII
Red, Yellow, and Black

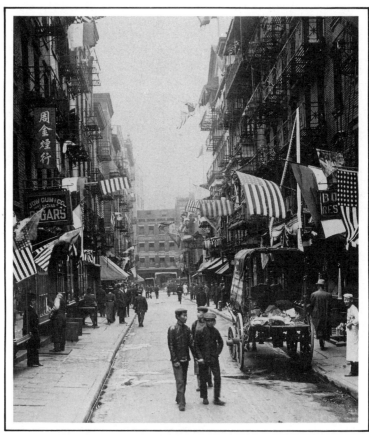

In a scene photographed about 1912, American
flags fly in New York City's Chinatown, where
ethnic cohesion coexisted with love of their new
country. *(Library of Congress)*

A prolonged national debate over immigration began in the 1880s, and it focused sharply on the question of what constituted an American. The country had been constantly redefining itself—by admitting newcomers to the land, by inviting fresh classes to participate in politics, and by spreading out across a continent hospitable to experiments in self-rule. There was a constant mixing of new and old, and no one could say quite what "*the* American" looked like or did for a living, what God he worshiped, or what learning was essential to his life. But there was a basic assumption: the true American was white.

The harshest inconsistency of the 1880s, while the Statue of Liberty was under construction, was that the United States firmly shut the door in the faces of all potential immigrants from China's teeming shore by the Chinese Exclusion Act of 1882. At about the same time, the nation was completing the virtual destruction of its remaining Indian population, killing many, psychologically and socially crippling the rest. And it was also abandoning its post–Civil War guarantees of equality to four million freed slaves.

The first Chinese to enter the United States, writes Betty Lee Sung, a historian of Chinese immigration, were three young men brought over by a missionary. One went on to become, in 1854, a graduate of Yale. Since then there have been many academically distinguished Chinese-Americans, including three Nobel Prize winners. But in his or her mind's eye, the average American until well into the twentieth century saw the "Chinaman" bent over an ironing board and chattering "No tickee, no shirtee" or pouring tea in a restaurant. Few stereotypes are more crude and unfair. When the "western barbarians" dwelt in Stygian ignorance, Chinese civilization, far older than Europe's, was full of achievements in art, pure science, philosophy, literature, cuisine, manners, education, and government. But in the nineteenth century, the "barbarians" mastered a technology that was the key to world rule. The Chinese Empire, sometimes referred to as the Celestial Kingdom, was an aloof and isolated realm in 1800. By 1900, Europe's major powers had carved it, like a cadaver in anatomy class, into spheres of influence. Although the empire was still territorially almost intact, its trade and commerce were controlled by privileged foreigners who were protected by their nations' fleets, and China's government was on the verge of collapse. While they walked down this road of humiliation, the Chinese people endured enough wars, uprisings, taxes, and oppressions to make emigration an attractive prospect for millions of them.

That was the situation in the 1850s in the hard-pressed agricultural hinterlands beyond Canton and Hong Kong, when sailors from the Yankee vessels taking on tea and silk there began relating astonishing tales. In a province of their country called California, they said, just across the great sea, were valleys and streams from which one might easily sift nuggets of gold; indeed, the entire region was a virtual mountain of gold. The message had the same meaning to a Chinese as to an American. A few years' work with pick and shovel, and a man could come home rich.

So the Chinese flocked to the ships. By 1852, an estimated 25,000 of them were in the mining camps. All were men; most were married; most, apparently, planned to return to families and farms in China. In their first decade and a half in the Mountain of Gold the Chinese arrivals found plenty of reasons to confirm their plans for early departure, and also a few enticements to remain.

The gold mining did not go well for them. From the beginning the pigtailed strangers were treated with hostility by white miners, who unceremoniously kicked them off the promising claims and forced them into poorer diggings. The California legislature, in the pride of new statehood, also made the Oriental's burden a heavy one. It imposed a miner's tax that somehow was collected only from the Chinese. Together, by 1875, the state of California and the city of San Francisco had also taxed Chinese fishermen, required special payments from shipmasters bringing in Chinese passengers (such payments of course were added to the fare), excluded Chinese from the San Francisco municipal hospital, banned their testimony in court, prohibited their naturalization and exercise of suffrage, and authorized segregated schools for their children. Though some of these measures were declared unconstitutional and others were repealed after a time, their chilly message was clear enough to the growing Chinese community.

B ut there were positive developments, too. Opportunities to make a living abounded. The Chinese discovered in the 1850s, for example, that the hungry and filthy miners who swarmed into San Francisco between prospecting expeditions were willing to part with cash in return for creature comforts. There were few women around to do the kinds of jobs normally handled in America by women. It was an easy thing to acquire soap and washboards, pots and pans, and Chinese social custom made it no disgrace for males to wash or cook. They began laundry and restaurant businesses and were soon earning some of the gold the white miners had monopolized.

Then another door opened in 1864. Work had begun on the Central Pacific Railroad, the western half of the first transcontinental rail line. As the railhead moved into the steep, forested canyons of the Sierra Nevada, the builders found themselves confronted by an acute labor shortage: hundreds of construction-gang huskies dropped out to try their luck in mining. Charles Crocker, one of the C.P.'s four owners, suggested to his superintendent, J. H. Strobridge, that they recruit some Chinese from San Francisco. Strobridge was skeptical. The Orientals were slender, frail-looking fellows; he thought they would never survive brutal days of grading, blasting, and hauling earth and rock up and down mountainsides. Crocker insisted on a trial run. A covey of Chinese hired hands was brought up to the railhead. On the first day they rose early, put in a grinding twelve-hour day without much hesitation or emotion, cooked themselves a meal of rice, tea, and dried cuttlefish, and went to bed.

Within months, thousands of Chinese were doggedly carrying basketloads of earth, wrestling and spiking ties and rails into place, clinging to the sides of sheer cliffs as they chipped out roadbeds, and hammering together snowsheds to shield the tracks from blizzards. Crocker got them to work on tunnels and aqueducts, too, and when Strobridge objected that masonry work was beyond the skill of "Chinamen," Crocker pointedly reminded him about the Great Wall of China. The new work force was cleanly, orderly, and perseverant. There were no epidemics, gun fights, or brawls in their camps. Eventually, six thousand of them helped to complete the coast-to-coast link, and then went on to build other Far Western lines.

When the railroad-building boom in the mountain states sub-sided, Chinese laborers found jobs on other construction pro-jects or on the giant-sized farms that were already a feature of the Far Western economy. In the cities, especially San Francisco, they created the framework of a Chinese community, complete with self-help organizations that grew out of the Chinese family pattern with its strong network of mutual protection, duty, and responsibility. The "invisible government" of the San Francisco Chinese was known as the Six Companies. It served as employ-ment and housing agency, legal-aid society, recreation and gam-bling center, mutual banking and insurance company, fraternal and burial lodge, lobby and union.

With the life-style successfully transplanted, with employ-ment and business prospects reasonably bright, thousands of Chinese were willing to reconsider their original plan of return. Some American public officials, reflecting on the Chinese contri-bution to the labor pool and to the tax revenues, were warmed with optimism and brotherhood. "Scarcely a ship arrives," wrote a San Francisco editor in 1852, "that does not bring an increase to this worthy integer of our population. The China boys will yet vote at the same polls, study at the same schools and bow at the same altar as our own countrymen." Another newspaperman watched two hundred "Celestials" step along in a Washington's Birthday parade, and beamed at the sight of "our most orderly and industrious citizens."

Such benedictions, however, ran counter to the exclusionary spirit of the latter half of the nineteenth century. In fact, the kindest words for the Chinese tended to come from businessmen to whom Chinese labor was a prime asset. In the depression of the 1870s, jobs became as valuable as pockets of pay dirt had been; once more, white men began to run the Chinese away from the best claims. In the middle of the decade, when bad harvests, declining yields of gold and silver, and the effects of a nationwide slump all hit the West Coast, "The Chinese must go!" suddenly became a demand of frightening power in Califor-nia politics.

The cry was raised by a variety of voices and was sustained by fictions that still stalk ghostlike through the textbooks. One of these fictions was based on the term "coolies," which to white Americans meant slaves, more or less; Chinese contractors were said to be importing workers wholesale and keeping back almost all of their meager earnings. In actuality, "coolie" is a Chinese word meaning to rent muscle or one who hires himself out as an unskilled laborer. Foreigners in nineteenth-century China used the term to describe gangs of Chinese who were sent out under contract for work in Cuba and Latin America. But almost all Chinese emigrants to the United States were individual volunteers. A number, certainly, did sign agreements with the Central Pacific line to borrow passage money and work it out on the railroad within seven months—an echo of the indenture system that had populated colonies in the East and South a century earlier. (The signing of workers to a contract before they arrived in America was finally forbidden by the Foran Act of 1885.)

Another word that lingers in the record of Chinese immigration is "hordes"—as used, for example, by the framers of the California state Democratic platform in 1869. They opposed any move—notably the Fifteenth Amendment to the Constitution, which guaranteed suffrage regardless of race—that would "ruin the white laboring men, by bringing untold hordes of pagan slaves (in all but name) into direct competition." The lurid picture of Chinese swarming ashore by the shipload to take over control of the labor market or of American local governments was hardly verified by what happened in the next ten years. Of the total population of some 865,000 in California in 1880, the Chinese numbered about 75,000, which was well under ten percent and not even a majority among the foreign-born residents of the state. And as early as 1865, they were contributing about fourteen million dollars annually to the economy, in the form of customs duties, fares, freight charges, taxes, and purchases.

But the Californians were unconcerned with that sort of facts. The state legislature "investigated" Chinese immigration in 1876, and in three hundred unsurprising pages denounced the Chinese as slaves, drug addicts, prostitutes, and heathens who drove honest American laborers from industrial and agrarian occupations. In a summary paragraph, the committee set down its definition of Americanization and its indictment of the Chinese for their failure to measure up:

> During their entire settlement in California they have never adapted themselves to our habits, mode of dress, or our educational system, have never learned the sanctity of an oath, never desired to become citizens, or to perform the duties of citizenship,

never discovered the difference between right and wrong, never ceased the worship of their idol gods, or advanced a step beyond the traditions of their native hive. Impregnable to all the influences of our Anglo-Saxon life, they remain the same stolid Asiatics that have floated on the rivers and slaved in the fields of China for thirty centuries of time.

Congress, with an eye to the California vote in the 1876 Presidential election, picked up the cue. Its own investigation resulted in twelve hundred pages of testimony and statistics but only a five-page published report, which was like that of California's solons.

While the legislative attacks multiplied, the Chinese had to face the more immediate threats of physical violence. During the depression winter of 1876–77, thousands of jobless workmen gathered in sandy vacant lots in San Francisco to listen to the inflammatory harangues of Denis Kearney, the founding father of California's Workingmen's Party. Kearney was an Irish merchant sailor who had graduated to independence as the middle-class proprietor of a cartage business, and its subsequent failure stung him into hatred of "the interests." He had the Irish gift for translating his wrath into oratory. Night after night he denounced the railroads and other great corporations, which, he declared, monopolized the best land, ground the faces of the poor by conspiring to skyrocket prices, and, worst of all, imported thousands of "filthy coolies" who would work for next to nothing, instead of hiring American laborers who demanded a white man's living wage.

The consequence of a Kearney performance was often a raid on a Chinese neighborhood by stirred-up whites; they would beat up whatever hapless residents were unlucky enough to be in the streets. In July of 1877, three days of anti-Chinese rioting rocked San Francisco.

Those Chinese who had dispersed from California to other locations in the Far West found no hiding place, either. "Every Saturday night," remembered one old-time mining-camp laundry operator, "we never knew whether we would live to see the light of day." Drunken miners would burst in, trample bundles of laundry, ransack the till, and break windows. In 1878 the whole Chinese population of Truckee, California, was driven

This cartoon exemplifies the "Great Fear of the Period," unrestricted immigration in the 1880s. In frame 1, an Irishman and a Chinaman devour Uncle Sam. In frame 2, Uncle Sam is completely eaten. Finally, in frame 3, the Chinaman swallows the Irishman, but only after first appropriating his hat. *(Library of Congress)*

from town; in 1880 an argument in a Chinese laundry in Denver led to a Walpurgis Night during which every Chinese business and home in the city was destroyed, the militia called out, and the whole Oriental population placed in jail for its own safety; in 1885, twenty-eight Chinese were massacred in Rock Springs, Wyoming. Only in faraway places like the Chinatowns of Chicago and New York and New Orleans was there some relative security of Chinese life and limb.

After the Workingmen's Party proved itself a strong political force in the state election of 1878, California redrafted its constitution to bar Chinese from employment on public and corporate construction. Then Congress in 1879 passed a bill prohibiting any ship from bringing in more than fifteen Chinese passengers. It was vetoed by President Hayes. Whatever else may have underlain his objection, the act was a flat violation of a treaty between the United States and China.

Negotiated in 1868, the Burlingame Treaty stipulated that the citizens of each nation residing in the other's territory should "enjoy the same privileges, immunities and exemptions" as the citizens of "the most favored nation." The Chinese could not give any country's merchants and missionaries better treatment than it gave America's. In turn, Chinese in the United States should be treated as well as nationals of a powerful state like Great Britain. Yet in 1879, with Pacific Coast Congressmen and labor unions breathing down his neck, Secretary of State William M. Evarts suggested to the American Minister at Peking, George Seward, who in turn suggested to the Imperial government, that China might consider restricting emigration to the United States, in view of the widespread opposition to Chinese entry.

The Chinese were willing to make some concessions, but they were understandably indignant. They had, as agreed, opened their gates; the United States was slamming shut its own.

But a righteous cause is no substitute for armed power. The Chinese could do nothing about harassment of their nationals in the United States, and it was clear that the American Congress might soon abrogate the Burlingame Treaty, even if it meant overriding a veto. China settled for what it could salvage by accepting a revision of the treaty in 1880. Under the new terms, whenever the United States government should decide that the entry of Chinese laborers would "endanger the good order of the said country or any locality within the territory thereof," such entry might be regulated, limited, or suspended. The revision did not say "prohibited," small comfort though that was. It also pledged the United States not to pass laws that would subject Chinese to "personal maltreatment or abuse," and to protect the freedom of travel of Chinese teachers, merchants, and tourists.

The ensuing years were a travesty on American good faith. Congress promptly passed the Chinese Exclusion Act of 1882, which suspended the immigration of Chinese laborers for a period of ten years. It was so effective that net Chinese immigration fell from 39,579 in 1882 to 22 in 1885. But in 1888, by the Scott Act, the United States specifically *prohibited* Chinese laborers from entering the country and denied reentry to those who had left—cutting off thousands of Chinese workers who had gone back home for visits. The Scott Act also redefined "Chinese" to include any member of the race, regardless of nationality. The Geary Act of 1892, besides renewing the exclusion of laborers for another ten years, required all Chinese to secure certificates of eligibility to remain in the United States. Subsequent legislation and treaty modifications between 1894 and 1917 hardened the pattern of rejection. And, in a particularly insulting gesture, after the United States had annexed Hawaii and the Philippines, the various anti-Chinese laws were made applicable in the islands, too.

Even those Chinese intellectuals, businessmen, and statesmen who were granted temporary entry faced harsh conditions. Under the pretext of preventing unscrupulous contractors from smuggling in coolies, immigration officials detained the Chinese in prisonlike quarters while their credentials were validated, and subjected the visitors to searches and interrogations as if they were pickpockets hauled before night court. The tone is best revealed by a set of instructions propounded for the Chinese exhibiting, by invitation, at the St. Louis World's Fair of 1904. All Chinese delegates were to be photographed and subjected to personal examination by the Bertillon system of identification, used on criminals. Each was to present evidence that he had no intention of remaining in the country, and to post a $500 bond to ensure his departure immediately after the fair closed. They were to proceed by direct and continuous travel from their entry point to the fair and afterward back to the same point, and to depart on the first available ship. None might leave the exposition grounds without a pass from the proper authorities, good for only forty-eight hours. If a Chinese stayed away longer than that, forfeiture of the bond and deportation could follow. No other country's nationals were subjected to the same conditions.

It was difficult to contrive further humiliation. The first-generation Chinese already in America were deprived of the power of political protest, since both judicial precedent and the Act of 1882 denied them naturalization—although their American-born children were automatically citizens. They were forced to accept employment in a limited number of occupations, such as cook, houseboy, and laundryman, and they drew together in Chinatowns where they beckoned tourists into curio shops and spurious "temples," and occasionally regaled reporters with exaggerated tales of tong wars, opium dens, and other images designed to freeze the blood of half-educated readers. Many boosted their children up the ladder of higher education; but the great majority—many of them perpetual bachelors, cut off from the possibility of returning for or importing brides—lived within their cultural enclaves, only voicing among themselves, in their clubs and newspapers, the bitterness they felt.

There was an ironic sequel to the story of the ostracized Chinese. When the closed-door policy cut off the supply of "yellow" farm workers from China, the Japanese took up the slack. By 1900 there were more than 24,000 Japanese in the United States; by 1910 the number had risen above 67,000. Like the Chinese, the Japanese exemplified the Calvinistic virtues that Americans claimed as indispensable to character. They bathed frequently, saved their money, acquired property, and set a high value on schooling, family life, and participation in community affairs. It is sad and almost superfluous to record that their behavior did not protect them in the least from the hostility of most Americans, and especially of Californians. The Golden State, spurred on by such organizations as the Native Sons of the Golden West and the Asiatic Exclusion League, had written into its statute books by 1913 a series of measures that barred "aliens" from landownership, forbade the issuance to the Japanese of licenses for commercial fishing, and in other ways closed avenues of legitimate economic self-improvement to them.

In 1906, the city of San Francisco brought matters to a head by an attempt to segregate Japanese children in separate schools.

The Japanese government protested vehemently—and Japan was not, like China, a helpless, dismembered dragon but a major naval power. President Theodore Roosevelt was worried enough to write to his son Kermit, "The infernal fools in California and especially San Francisco insult the Japanese recklessly and in the event of war, it will be the nation as a whole which will bear the consequences." In the end, the Japanese accepted a face-saving device. They concluded with the United States a "Gentleman's Agreement" in 1908, in which Tokyo agreed not to issue passports to laborers, skilled or unskilled, except those who were former residents of the United States and their parents, wives, and children. Japanese immigration thereafter declined. Meanwhile San Francisco, under Federal prodding, dropped its barriers to the entry of Oriental children into "white" schools.

Both the Japanese and Chinese were to endure further insults in 1924. The major immigration restriction act of that year set a top limit on total entries and assigned quotas to various nationalities. No quota at all was allowed to China or Japan.

Nativism had scored its first long-term, palpable victory over the Orientals. The pain of it touched author Robert Louis Stevenson. Describing a transcontinental train journey in his *Across the Plains,* published in 1892, he noted that the whites aboard showed a blind anger at the Chinese and "seemed never to have looked at them, listened to them, or thought of them, but hated them *a priori.*" Stevenson mused further:

> Awhile ago it was the Irish, now it is the Chinese that must go. Such is the cry. It seems, after all, that no country is bound to submit to immigration any more than to invasion. . . . Yet we may regret the free tradition of the republic, which loved to depict herself with open arms, welcoming all unfortunates. And certainly, as a man who believes that he loves freedom, I may be excused some bitterness when I find her sacred name misused in the contention....

The "sacred name" was not honored when it came to Indians, either. Their fate furnishes another example of how race, culture, and color created limits to the acceptability of particular groups within the basic American fabric. The Chinese came across the sea of their own free will, yet were not welcomed as pioneers.

Defeated and demoralized, Indians were put on reservations, such as the Sioux' Pine Ridge Reservation in South Dakota, photographed in 1891. Allowed to leave only with passes, they had become prisoners of a country no longer interested in them. *(Library of Congress)*

The blacks came involuntarily, but hostility toward them was not mitigated by the consideration that their "offensive" presence was scarcely their own fault. And the Indians were not immigrants at all (unless one counts the prehistoric migration from Siberia) and so were hardly guilty of intrusion. Yet they too were to suffer, and it was especially ironic. For as the original possessors and proprietors of the continent they had a legitimate claim to equal participation in the society planted on it. As white civilization swept across the remaining open spaces west of the Mississippi after the Civil War, Americans faced a fresh test of how much diversity they would allow. Would the national experiment in mutual accommodation allow for patterns of group living, worship, and expectation different from those of the dominant white culture? If the Indian put aside his implements of war, would there be a place for him, as an Indian and as an equal, in the American tapestry? One eloquent Indian, Chief Joseph of the Nez Perces, asked this of the country in 1879:

> If the white man wants to live in peace with the Indian he can live in peace. . . . Treat all men alike. Give them all the same law. Give them all an even chance to live and grow. All men were made by the same Great Spirit Chief. They are all brothers. The earth is the mother of all people, and all people should have equal rights upon it. . . . Let me be a free man, free to travel, free to stop, free to work, free to trade, where I choose, free to choose my own teacher, free to follow the religion of my fathers, free to think and talk and act for myself—and I will obey every law, or submit to the penalty.

Unfortunately, the chief's formula had already been rejected. He spoke at the end of a decade whose keynote, so far as Indian relations were concerned, had been sounded by a Wyoming editor in 1870: "The same inscrutable Arbiter that decreed the downfall of Rome, has pronounced the doom of extinction upon the red men of America. To attempt to defer this result by mawkish sentimentalism . . . is unworthy of the age." The Gilded Age was indeed mawkishly sentimental; but then, as always, sentimentality was not incompatible with cruelty. And compassion and restraint in dealing with Indians had never been an American trademark; the Wyoming editor only asked that the nation hew to established patterns and not be "unworthy" of its Indian-hating tradition.

In May of 1830, President Andrew Jackson had signed a Removal Bill providing for the "exchange" by Eastern tribes of their ancestral lands in return for "guaranteed" spacious hunting grounds in the West. But even before the Civil War, railroads were tracking out across the Mississippi, and the war had not been over more than a few years before the shining rails had bridged the continent. Suddenly, pioneer ranchers, farmers, miners, lumberjacks, and townspeople were spreading over the prairie and mountain tracts that had been solemnly pledged to the Indians as inviolable refuges. The inexorable process of new agreements and new removals began again, repeated with such frequency that one Sioux chief, Spotted Tail, remarked bitterly: "Why does not the Great Father put his red children on wheels, so he can move them as he will?" The story of the last Indian wars in the Far West, from the 1862 Sioux uprising in Minnesota and the Dakotas to the massacre of some three hundred Sioux at Wounded Knee, South Dakota, in 1890, is neither pleasant nor absolutely necessary to a full understanding of the American self-image at the time. It is sufficient to say that one by one tribes were forced onto reservations and overwhelmed by firepower when they offered resistance. The Modocs and the Nez Perces, the Cheyennes and the Kiowas, the Navahos and the Apaches, the Utes and the Comanches—one after another were reduced nearly to the condition of the buffalo herds on which they had once depended. At such places as Canyon de Chelly, Arizona, where the Navahos saw their flocks and herds, gardens and orchards, destroyed before their eyes, or at Sand Creek, where Colorado militiamen, under a bloodthirsty Methodist preacher-colonel named John Chivington, slaughtered Cheyenne children with the cry "Nits make lice," America showed the ugliest aspect of its celebrated westward march.

But the slow death on the reservations was almost as bad as outright massacre. Once confined to an area, a tribe depended on the government for the furnishing of rations (to replace the game that was no longer available), for protection of Indian property against marauders, and for assistance, instruction, and support in whatever new activities the tribes undertook for a livelihood. The Indian's link to the Great White Father in Washington was the Indian agent—a political appointee and, in all too many cases, a grafter embodying the frontier philosophy that an Indian had no rights a white person was bound to respect. In instance after instance, agents pilfered and sold rations destined for hungry Indians, or permitted whites (in return for generous bribes) to help themselves to Indian land, timber, and minerals. And contracting to provision the Indians was a profitable enterprise for businessmen who persuaded agents—for a consideration—to accept " 'steel spades' made of sheet iron; . . . 'best brogans' with paper soles; [and] 'blankets' made of shoddy and glue which came to shreds the first time they were wet."

S hortly after President Grant took office in 1869, a new policy was inaugurated in response to criticisms of the agency system. This was to apportion the nomination of agents and the direction of Indian "educational" activities among various religious denominations. Inasmuch as the misdeeds of scoundrelly agents often provoked the Indians to resistance, the new dispensation, which was supposed to cure the situation, was referred to as the Peace Policy. But it brought little tranquility. For one thing, even the worthiest boards of Catholics, Quakers, Episcopalians, Baptists, and Methodists were far removed from the reservations, and many of the agents they chose in good faith turned out to be no better than their less sanctified predecessors; this was at least partly due to the fact that the salaries offered by the government were unattractively low. The religious groups were expected to help the government finance the Indian schools, and both sources persistently skimped on that end of their activities.

But above all, the assumption behind the entire program was that Christianity was the answer to the Indian "problem" and that increasing the missionaries' influence would soothe the savage breast and guide the aboriginal foot in the paths of peace. In general, the Indians were having none of it. They had seen too much Christian charity at places like Sand Creek to be impressed. Moreover, the multiplicity of Christian denominations caused them to doubt the white gospel; if the preachers could not agree among themselves on divinity, what should the Indian believe? As Chief Joseph put it, "They will teach us to quarrel about God as the Catholics and Protestants do on the reservation. . . . We may quarrel with men sometimes about things on this earth, but we never quarrel about God."

After a short while, the plan of church-guided Indian acculturation was dropped. The Indians still at large were still hunted, and those on the reservations continued to starve, to freeze, and to undergo the slow decay of the spirit that overtakes people when the basis of their culture disintegrates. The clamor of white reformers, however, led to a fresh evaluation in the early 1880s, and to a new avenue of approach. The Indian would never join the mainstream of national life, it was now argued, so long as he clung to his blanket, his tepee, and his chieftains. Progress would come when he was converted into an independent landholder, separated from dependence on the rigid, outmoded patterns of the tribe.

Both those who simply wished to see the Indians canceled as a Federal problem and those who were benignly disposed toward them were enthusiastic about the potential of detribalization. It was, after all, America's crowning boast that each man, given education, the means of livelihood, and the ballot, could make himself a lord of creation if he had any ability. Inspired by these visions, the Congress passed, in 1887, the Dawes General Allotment, or Severalty, Act. Under its provisions for "severalty" (separation of land from common ownership), the government expanded a practice, already begun piecemeal, of assigning individual tracts of up to 160 acres to Indian heads of households. Most of the lands that were then reservations were to be disposed of in this way, or go on the open market. Titles to the individual allotments would be held in trust by the government for twenty-five years, after which the Indians would become the outright owners. Full citizenship accompanied landownership.

President Grover Cleveland, although he signed the act, remarked wryly that the "hunger and thirst of the white man for the Indian's land is almost equal to his hunger and thirst after righteousness." Indeed, white grafters moved in quickly; Indians were persuaded to adopt white "guardians" for their tracts, and these guardians would rob them of the fruits of the land or of the land itself. A modification of the Dawes Act, the Burke Act of 1906, tried, not wholly successfully, to deal with this problem. Moreover, even if making red hunters and warriors into farmers would guarantee them decent treatment (and past Indian experience did not hold out much encouragement there), the process was not a simple one. In the 1880s and 1890s on the Great Plains, well-established white farmers were being driven to economic desperation and political revolt by droughts, locusts, falling prices, rising interest rates and transportation charges, and an assortment of other calamities. The Indian trying to make a start at agriculture needed long-term credit, tools, stock, seed, and, above all, instruction and sympathetic consideration—absolutely none of which was forthcoming from whites whose major notion of helping the Indian was to take his children into boarding schools where they were taught to cut their hair, sing hymns, and work at trades that were nonexistent on the reservations to which they would return.

The Dawes Act approach was a failure. In 1887 some 138 million acres were held by Indians; by 1932, forty-five years after the act was passed, about 90 million of those acres had found their way into white hands. One Oklahoman observed, "If they don't learn the value of property and how to adjust themselves to surroundings, they will be 'grafted' out of it—that is one of the unchangeable laws of God and the constitution of man." In short, they were to be sheep among wolves so long as they clung to their own culture. The concept of America's openness to different kinds of humanity did not extend to the Indians, North America's first arrivals from the Asian mainland, any more than to the Chinese and Japanese, the latest comers from Asia.

Africa's offspring, too, entered modern American life with uprooting and pain; they too encountered the face of irrational hatred; they too were the subjects of debate between whites over their needs and capacities, as if their only function in life was to demonstrate their fitness in eyes other than their own. In a sense, each generation of American blacks became "immigrants." Their forebears had been brought over, a few hundred at a time, year by year, in the nightmarish stink of the slave ships. In 1865, by the grace of the Thirteenth Amendment, blacks became free men and women and were confronted by new responsibilities. The Fourteenth and Fifteenth Amendments, officially adopted in 1868 and 1870, defined them as citizens and forbade states to deny black men the vote on the basis of color. But the weight of color—or rather, of white prejudice against color—was a crushing handicap. The Radical Republican designers of Reconstruction, early in the 1870s, operated under the same theory as the reformers who advocated Indian detribalization in the 1880s. Land, schooling, and the vote would be the materials out of which free, good "colored" citizens were fashioned.

But as it happened, the freed black was not given land. Extravagant plans, proposed by a passionate hater of slaveholders, Pennsylvania's Thaddeus Stevens, for confiscating rebel estates and redistributing them to freed blacks were never implemented. And the ex-slaves had no money to buy the acres that some planters had to put up for sale after the war. In the end they went to work either for their old masters or for those shrewd men, Northern and Southern, who survived war and Reconstruction with profits in their pockets and became planters. Some blacks worked for wages; most landowners, however, found it more convenient to slice their holdings into small segments, each occupied by a renter who paid his way with a share of the crop he produced. Loan money for stock, tools, seed, and supplies was often raised by pledging the cotton yield of the coming year as security. The system encouraged a maximum of irresponsibility on the part of both tenant and landlord and a dependence on one crop—cotton—often produced in such a glut that it drove prices far below the cost of production.

Twenty years after freedom, a former slave was apt to be a black peasant, apathetically scratching a crop out of exhausted soil not his own, with scrawny mules and rusted plows and hoes that he had neither the incentive nor the means to improve. He was deeply in debt, lived on a subsistence diet—mainly molasses, cornbread, and hog fat—and gave the name "home" to a decaying cabin that was not much of an improvement, if any, over the slave quarters. And although some poor white "Southrons" were little better off, that did not in the least alleviate certain other major problems of his existence as a black.

In 1877 the North almost completely abandoned the postwar effort to compel Southerners to treat the blacks fairly. Reliance was now placed on the goodwill and sense of justice of the "best" Southerners, of whom there were simply not enough to carry the burden. White "conservatives," sometimes legitimately, sometimes by fraud, and sometimes by using the Ku Klux Klan and other terrorist gangs to frighten blacks from the polls, reestablished white control. They gave full rein to what one Freedmen's Bureau official referred to as "that pride of race which has marked all distinguished peoples. . . ." In so doing, they shut off one by one the blacks' routes of escape from degradation. The few pioneer factories for making textiles and processing tobacco, established in the South in the 1880s and 1890s in an

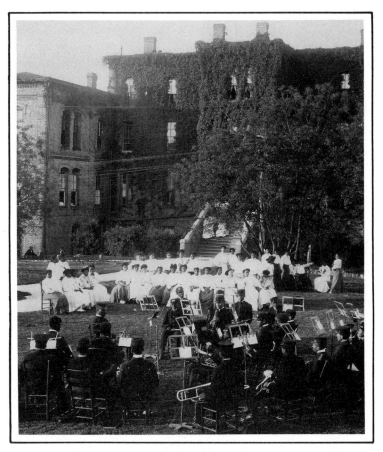

Students play in a concert at Tuskegee Institute in 1903. Begun in 1881 on an abandoned Alabama plantation by a former slave, Booker T. Washington, the school was, at first, no more than "a brokendown shanty and an old henhouse." But by the time its founder died in 1915, it owned almost thirty thousand acres and one hundred buildings, and offered classes for thiry-eight trades and professions. *(Library of Congress)*

attempt to create an economic balance, barred black men from all but the most menial jobs. The Yankee schoolteachers who had traveled South after Appomattox to teach the freedmen their ABCs and elementary hygiene were mostly gone; time and social ostracism had swept them away. A few Northern philanthropists had set up funds for financing black education, but their resources were in no way equal to the problem. A handful of black academies like Howard, Fisk, Hampton, and Tuskegee, founded between 1866 and 1881, were training blacks for useful vocations and even for the learned professions. But before a stream of potential black lawyers, educators, doctors, ministers, scientists—or even masons and dietitians—could enter their doors, elementary schooling had to be provided. The white governments of the Southern states after Reconstruction were little disposed to finance *any* schools, not to mention those which proposed to try the foolish experiment of giving "niggers" educations that, it was said, they could neither absorb nor put to use, and that would give them impossible hopes of rising above their stations. Most black public schools remained wretched and understandably ill-attended.

In the South, the black could as a rule use his ballot only to vote for a choice of Democratic white candidates, and even this choice of an unappetizing menu was taken from him around the turn of the century as the Southern states one after another enacted measures to evade the Fifteenth Amendment, by establishing poll taxes and literacy tests that were enforced against blacks but not whites and "grandfather clauses" that turned away from the polls those classes of people who had not voted before 1860—to wit, almost all blacks. "The negro as a political force," wrote Atlanta editor Henry W. Grady in 1889, with satisfaction, "has dropped out of serious consideration." What was more, if blacks tried, individually or in concert, to raise any protest, they were likely to be whipped, beaten, or arrested on trumped-up charges and almost certainly sent to prison. Jail might well be a steppingstone to a place where black labor *was* welcome—a work gang on a road or a railroad, in a lumber or turpentine camp in the woods, or in a coal or iron mine: the convicted black was liable to be leased out by the state. In such employment, his chances of being starved to death, worked to death, tortured to death, or shot while trying to escape were excellent. And even if the "uppity" black stayed out of jail and escaped all these perils, the threat of rope and burning remained. Between 1882 (when such compilations first were kept) and 1900 the number of recorded lynchings in the South never fell below 100 annually and reached a high of 235 in 1892. Most victims were blacks. Some might have been guilty of crimes, but they never came to the trials due them. And many, there is no doubt, were executed simply for didactic reasons: the strange fruit hanging from Southern trees was intended as a warning to all blacks to remember their condition.

This condition, at the turn of the twentieth century, was accepted as a fate that black Americans either deserved or could not evade. Majority white opinion viewed racial discrimination as a necessary evil at worst. Reconstruction Congresses had passed the Ku Klux Klan Acts of 1870 and 1871 and a Civil Rights Act of 1875, specifying Federal penalties for forcible denial of equal rights or accommodations to blacks. In a series of decisions from 1876 to 1883, the Supreme Court gutted these measures by interpretations that held the national government not bound to interfere, under the Fourteenth Amendment, when the offensive acts were those of individuals and not of state governments. Then a majority of the justices declared, in *Plessy* v. *Ferguson,* in 1896, that "separate but equal" railroad accommodations on interstate trains did not violate the Fourteenth Amendment either.

In 1890, in an effort to revive the Republican Party in the South, Massachusetts Representative Henry Cabot Lodge introduced a measure providing for Federal supervision of elections when violations of voting rights were evident. This so-called Force Bill was beaten down. In another approach, New Hampshire's Senator Henry Blair had earlier sponsored a measure for Federal aid to education in the states, to be given proportionally on the basis of poverty and illiteracy. Southern states, which stood to get the most money, professed themselves deeply insulted—and saw in the legislation the camel's nose under the tent; if the nation could undertake to improve the educational facilities afforded Southern blacks (even when whites shared in the benefits), it might move on to restore the entire Reconstruction atmosphere. "If you would allow us to work out our own salvation," Mississippi's Senator James Z. George told his Yankee colleagues, "without your external, and, I might add, infernal intermeddling, we might at last work out something."

Itself not committed to racial equality, the North accepted this view. The Blair Bill was defeated. And in 1906, the Yale sociologist William Graham Sumner wrote that in the matter of race relations, it was "evidently impossible for anyone to interfere. We are like spectators at a great natural convulsion. The results will be such as the facts and forces call for. We cannot foresee them. They do not depend on ethical views any more than the volcanic eruption on Martinique contained an ethical element." It was all very laissez-faire and offered very little hope to the blacks.

Intelligent black leaders understood well the import of these events. The court's decisions in the civil rights cases made them feel, said one of them, editor T. Thomas Fortune, as if they had been "baptized in ice water."

The question was, what redress should be sought, and various voices offered conflicting counsel. In 1879, officials of several black churches encouraged emigration from the South. Some forty thousand blacks, it is estimated, moved to Kansas and other Western states, but found little improvement in conditions there. There were also efforts at mass departures to Oklahoma in the 1880s and 1890s, which met both Indian and white hostility. Another abortive attempt was made to plant colonies of American blacks in Mexico in 1895 and again in Hawaii in 1897, but both came to nothing. Not until World War I would Southern blacks break off in considerable numbers and move, on the currents of job opportunities, to other parts of the country.

In 1895, one of the most interesting of the century's black voices spoke up for a new approach—temporary abandonment of any significant drive for black equality and political rights, in return for vocational and agricultural education, jobs, and assistance in establishing black businesses. Booker T. Washington was born in 1856 and spent his early childhood as a slave on a Virginia plantation. At the end of the Civil War, he was put to work in a salt mine in West Virginia by his freedman stepfather. Ablaze with intelligence and ambition, Washington somehow managed to acquire elementary learning in his few leisure hours. When he was about seventeen years old he walked several hundred miles, broke and hungry, to apply for entrance into Hampton Institute, a school in Virginia that had been founded in 1868. He put himself through the school by working as a janitor, wearing clothes rummaged from barrels of castoffs sent down

South by Northern churchgoers. From Hampton's superintendent General Samuel C. Armstrong, the Hawaii-born son of Yankee missionaries, Washington absorbed a complete faith in America's respect for hard work and the dollar.

In 1881, Washington took over the superintendency of Tuskegee Institute, then a school only on paper; it had been authorized by the Alabama state legislature, but was without funds, buildings, or teachers. In less than fifteen years, the driving and energetic Washington had converted it into a model agricultural and technical institute, sustained in good part by Northern capitalists' donations. Tuskegee produced its own electric power, food, clothing, and essential services of all kinds—laundries and kitchens, foundries and animal hospitals. Though critics have since complained that Tuskegee trained its people for skills already obsolete in an industrial society (such as brickmaking by hand and harness repair), its experimental farms and neat shops, all black-run, were marveled at by hundreds of distinguished white visitors, including Presidents of the United States. And at the same time, Washington was busy organizing black landowners and small businessmen into mutual self-help societies and turning out a stream of publicity for black self-improvement.

Called on to deliver an address at the Cotton States Exposition in Atlanta in 1895, he proposed the "Atlanta Compromise," which offered the white South a faithful and patient labor supply in return for a genuine mobilization of capital for upgrading the rundown cotton economy and an open door to blacks in technical schools, factories, and shops. "In all things that are purely social," he said to whites, "we can be as separate as the fingers, yet one as the hand in all things essential to mutual progress." He also declared that blacks must begin life at the bottom and not at the top, scorned the idea of blacks patronizing opera houses, and eschewed "artificial forcing." The white world applauded his speech, made him the most honored black spokesman of his day—and by and large never delivered what he asked for.

B ooker Washington has since been condemned as an acquiescent Uncle Tom, selling the black birthright for a mess of pottage—low-grade jobs and proprietorships in a segregated society. Within a few years after the Atlanta address, young black militants—W. E. B. DuBois and Monroe Trotter among them—

were rejecting his leadership and walking down the road of legal and propaganda combat that led to the founding in 1909 of the National Association for the Advancement of Colored People, of which Washington himself was not a member. Still, the principal of Tuskegee claimed never to have advocated anything but a truce with inequality; in fact, in his last years (he died in 1915), he covertly supported suits contesting disfranchisement and segregation, and he became more outspokenly critical of white failures to render justice to black brothers. The essential premise behind his strategy, however, was that the whites really meant what they said when they protested that the doors of acceptance were opened by achievement, regardless of the achiever's race, national origin, or creed. In his best-selling autobiography, *Up from Slavery,* written mostly as a self-conscious appeal to white intelligence and reason, Washington said:

> I believe it is the duty of the Negro—as the greater part of the race is already doing—to deport himself modestly in regard to political claims, depending upon the slow but sure influences that proceed from the possession of property, intelligence, and high character for the full recognition of his political rights.

Washington's mistake may have been in taking this Yankee shibboleth—"property, intelligence, and high character"—too seriously. Frederick Douglass, the fiery black abolitionist (and an ex-slave himself) who was about forty years Washington's senior and who died in the year of the Atlanta Exposition, would have disagreed with him strenuously. In 1892 Douglass noted that it was precisely the *successful* black who provoked jealousy. "The Jew is hated in Russia," said Douglass in a national magazine, "because he is thrifty. The Chinaman is hated in California because he is industrious and successful. The Negro meets no resistance when on a downward course. It is only when he rises in wealth, intelligence, and manly character that he brings upon himself the heavy hand of persecution." No saga of black achievement could appease a white Southerner who was capable of averring, as did Mississippi Congressman John Sharp Williams in 1898, that

> you could ship-wreck 10,000 illiterate white Americans on a desert island, and in three weeks they would have a fairly good

government, conceived and administered upon fairly democratic lines. You could ship-wreck 10,000 negroes, everyone of whom was a graduate of Harvard University, and in less than three years, they would have retrograded governmentally; half of the men would have been killed, and the other half would have two wives apiece.

Such a statement might represent only an extreme position, but on the whole the attitude was not sharply challenged by any significant portion of the elite that formed public opinion—the editors, ministers, professors, and politicians—even outside the South, in the first fifteen years of the twentieth century. That period, which saw the rising tide of Progressivism, has been described in one popular history after another as a testament to refreshed democratic vitality after the sordid materialism of the big industrial boom. But to nonwhites who know their history, such descriptions are an affront. All nonwhites felt the brunt of Social Darwinism (the scientific justification for "Anglo-Saxon" supremacy); all suffered from the arrogance of the light-complexioned. The dominant attitude was well expressed in an 1890 magazine article called "The Race Question in the United States."

By the destruction of the implacable Indian, we have possessed ourselves of his inheritance—the fairest and richest in the world. He would not be a slave, and we drove him out and filled his place with negroes, found in bondage in their native land, and imported as slaves. The patient, thrifty Chinaman was found to be depraved. He was invited to come here . . . When he became the successful rival to our laboring classes . . . we summarily decreed his banishment.

This, the author said, was an illustration of the English-speaking peoples' "unrelenting progress." He could not have chosen a more appropriate adjective.

IX

The Gates Close

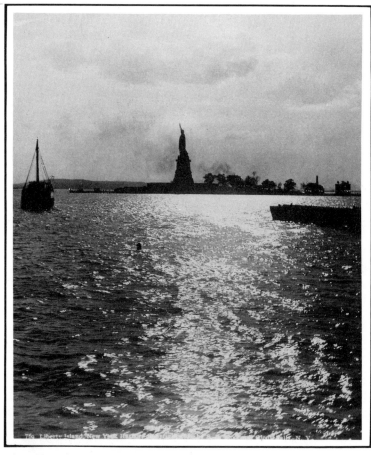

The Statue of Liberty as it looked in 1890 to
thousands of immigrants. "Give me your tired,
your poor", reads the poem inscribed in its
pedestal, "Your huddled masses yearning to
breathe free . . ." *(Library of Congress)*

In October of 1886 workmen wrestled the last huge bronze sections of the Statue of Liberty into place, and New York Harbor was thereafter the proud site of one of the country's most famous landmarks. The statue had been brought to completion by the spirited fund-raising campaign of Joseph Pulitzer's circulation-hungry New York *World*. Pulitzer, a Hungarian immigrant who became a millionaire, undoubtedly thought highly of Emma Lazarus's much-quoted lines, written in 1883 and, twenty years later, inscribed on the pedestal of Liberty:

> . . . *Give me your tired, your poor,*
> *Your huddled masses yearning to breathe free,*
> *The wretched refuse of your teeming shore.*
> *Send these, the homeless, tempest-tost to me,*
> *I lift my lamp beside the golden door.*

Like most of his fellow Americans, Pulitzer was not apt to worry over the note of condescension in the welcome. To say that the newcomers riding up the Narrows were "wretched refuse" was not entirely open-hearted: it was something like taking a newspaper advertisement to state that one had kindly volunteered to adopt an illegitimate, crippled, and penniless orphan. Ironically, that was the spirit of a long and generally negative national appraisal of immigration policy, which began at about the same time the Statue of Liberty was dedicated.

The appraisal of the open gate was part of a broad review of the quality and the promises of American life—a review that ultimately would be more or less formalized in the Progressive Era and would take on a liberal coloration. It was a period characterized, for example, by debates about government policy toward railroads, trusts, labor unions, courts, and political machines. There were heated national discussions of such matters as pacifism, progressivism in education, the future of science, the "new" woman, and emancipation of the arts from stifling conventions. In a way, the spirit of the time reached its apex in America's idealistic approach to the World War; and its last gasp might be said to have been Prohibition.

Since it was a time when liberal ideas were popular, it is not surprising that in the argument over immigration, some men were calling for a completely new concept of the nation's character. As stated in a magazine piece by Percy Stickney Grant, pastor of New York's Episcopal Church of the Ascension, it was a summons.

> We must construct a new picture of citizenship. If we do . . . we shall welcome the rugged strength of the peasant or the subtle thought of the man in the Ghetto in our reconsidered American ideals. . . . Let us rise to an eminence higher than that occupied by Washington or Lincoln, to a new Americanism which is not afraid of the blending in the western world of races seeking freedom.

Conservative alarm, however, had deepened with every boom period at Ellis Island. This alarm was concisely expressed by Henry Pratt Fairchild in a 1913 volume, which demanded "recognition of the fact that we are by no means prepared to accept the tremendous responsibility of admitting unlimited numbers of aliens whose entire future destiny depends upon the soundness of our political, social, and economic fabric."

Although the Reverend Dr. Grant's clarion call seemed much more in tune with the national chorus of welcome to "progress," Fairchild's voice more accurately reflected reality as Congress was to see it. In February 1917 a law was enacted over a Presidential veto restricting admission to America to those among the world's people who already knew how to read and write. In the early 1920s the grave of unlimited immigration was dug even deeper: the lawmakers decreed a series of cutbacks in the annual number of newcomers, aiming at an eventual ceiling of about 150,000 a year from outside the Western Hemisphere. Moreover, they applied to the "new" immigrants of Eastern and Southern Europe the sort of racist attitudes that already held down blacks and Indians and banned Orientals from entry. They created a quota system that froze the proportions of the intake according to the "national origins" of the American people as they were in 1920. The British, who had first come in 1607, had nearly twelve times as many descendants on the census rolls as the Italians, who had been coming in substantial numbers only since the 1880s; thus Britain's share of the annual total was twelve times that of Italy. There was a clear implication that a Briton was also twelve times as desirable a newcomer as an Italian. How the public mind arrived at a state of readiness to accept such a judgment, during a period of American history rich in liberalism, is a remarkable story. It involves labor leaders, intellectuals, patricians and proletarians, city dwellers and farmers, ministers of God and devil's disciples, and a constant interplay between hope and fear.

The story begins with the insecurity of the misnamed Gay Nineties: 1890 opened a decade that brought tremors of change and unease throughout the land, and before the ten years had passed there were bloody railroad and steel strikes, a brutal depression, a desperate political revolt by farmers that took the name of Populism, and the hotly debated leap into imperial responsibility that sent American young men to fight guerrillas in the Philippine jungles. New social problems seemed insoluble without the destruction of old and cherished values, and people were afraid; this fear attached itself to whatever was "alien"— including the genuine aliens who were entering in an apparently endless procession.

The climate of anxiety was reflected in a curious organization known as the American Protective Association. It was Midwestern in origin, founded in Clinton, Iowa, in 1887 by a Maryland-born lawyer named Henry F. Bowers. Members took an oath to use all their power to "strike the shackles and chains of blind obedience to the Roman Catholic Church" from men's minds, and "promote the interest of all Protestants. . . ." The Pope was the enemy still: papal agents, Irish politicians, were in control of the great cities; papal propagandists demanded tax moneys for parochial schools; the Pope even sent a delegate, Monsignor Satolli, to Washington in 1893 for purposes of secret and sinister intent, concealed behind a diplomatic façade. Thousands of Bowers's countrymen believed such distortions of fact. When the well-known printer and author Elbert Hubbard visited an Illinois friend in 1893, he asked his host if he intended to visit the Chicago World's Fair. The host gazed at him in shock. "Did I not know that the Catholics had been ordered by the Pope to burn the barns and houses of all heretics?" No Protestant dared leave his property untended for a moment.

Thus fantastic night riders—cloaked in papal purple— galloped through the nightmares of rural Protestant mid-America. The American Protective Association grew mainly where the corn grew, and when it affected cities at all, they were often part of the agrarian economic complex—Omaha, Kansas City, Duluth. Exactly how strong the group became is disputed; estimates of membership ranged from 100,000 to 2,500,000 people. In any case, neither major national party endorsed the APA, as both Republicans and Democrats knew the importance of the swelling urban vote—which contained important Catholic elements. The movement faded away soon after 1896.

New England was half a continent away from the heart of APA territory, but in the 1890s some of her most distinguished sons were gnawed by the same kinds of shadowy suspicion that beset the Middle West. In Boston and nearby Cambridge the enemy was not simply the Catholic but any freshly arrived foreigner of "new stock," and he was a dangerous type, even when not engaged in a plot, simply by virtue of being himself. "Wide open and unguarded stand our gates," warned Thomas Bailey Aldrich in 1892 in the *Atlantic Monthly,*

> *And through them presses a wild motley throng—*
> *Men from the Volga and the Tartar steppes,*
> *Featureless figures from the Hoang-Ho,*
> *Malayan, Scythian, Teuton, Kelt, and Slav,*
> *Flying the Old World's poverty and scorn;*
> *These bringing with them unknown gods and rites,*
> *Those, tiger passions, here to stretch their claws. . . .*

Aldrich had taken considerable poetic license. Migration from the "Hoang-Ho" had already been cut off by the Chinese Exclusion Act, and the Malayan and Scythian components of contemporary immigration, if they existed at all, were invisible to the keepers of records. Yet the sentiment behind Aldrich's imagery was common in the circles in which he moved. The descendants of the Puritan fathers were by and large gloomy, though there were exceptions among them. Politically speaking, they were losing control of—and to a great degree giving up—their inheritance. It was bad enough that the nation no longer looked to the Adams clan when seeking Presidents, and that no Daniel Webster bestrode the Senate like a colossus; but in addition the cities of southern New England were passing into the hands of the Irish. The established middle class was chiefly interested in business, and few "gentlemen" would lower themselves to compete for political power. In 1890, sixty-eight towns and cities in Massachusetts were controlled by Irish politicians. The sons of the wretched Popish peasants who had streamed ashore in the 1840s were making laws for townships laid out by Winthrops and Eliots.

New England's economic hegemony was on the decline, too. In shipping she had long ago lost primacy. Her bankers and investors and insurance companies had prudently put money into Western railroads, mines, and other ventures yielding incomes that tastefully supported the region's old families; but the really big industrial empires were not in New England hands, and the depression of 1893–97 confronted with ruin the thousands of Yankees who lived by clipping coupons. (Henry Adams wrote later that men died like flies under the strain.) New England's farms were largely exhausted. Furthermore, the factories that had produced clocks and sewing machines and guns and textiles, the factories that had made the names of Waterbury and Lowell and Hartford and Nashua and Providence famous, had grown old. Their aging machinery produced goods at smaller and smaller profit. In addition, those factories were worked by a labor force of French-Canadian, Irish, and other immigrant toilers whose social needs would clearly never be supplied by New England frugality.

Confronted by such a cheerless prospect of the present, old-stock New Englanders turned to a nostalgic, almost reverent re-examination of their past. A conviction grew among the elite families, particularly those rich in sons with Harvard degrees, that the institutions created by the English immigrants of the seventeenth and eighteenth centuries were incomparably great and, in fact, *the* essential foundations of American excellence.

This outlook was strengthened by an academic development, the rise of a "scientific" history that tried to apply Darwin's theories of evolution to social institutions. It was noted, for example, that certain kinds of political behavior had originated among particular "races," who carried them to new environments where they flourished or failed. If they did thrive, it was proof of the biological superiority of the initial stock. New England-born or New England-trained historians, such as Herbert Baxter Adams of Johns Hopkins or Albert Bushnell Hart of Harvard, taught that self-government had first been practiced among the Teutonic peoples in ancient days. The Saxons, one branch of the family, had taken the democratic passion with them when they invaded Britain at various times before the medieval era. The English settlers in North America, a mixture of "bloods" denominated Anglo-Saxon, had made the instinctive yearning for individual liberty their gift to the future United States. As Herbert Baxter Adams said, the purpose of his Hopkins seminar was "to show the continuity of English institutions in America." To understand the town meeting, one went back to the Magna Carta, and beyond that to tribal councils of war in the German forest.

This kind of Anglo-Saxonism was both comical and potentially sinister. Its Germanophilia contrasted oddly with the slighting popular image of the "Dutchman" in America as a beer guzzler with a droll accent; further, its adherents did not explain what had happened to that ingrained Teutonic love of liberty in Kaiser Wilhelm's day. It credited what clearly were acquired social traits to racial instinct. One found the statistician Richmond Mayo-Smith, for instance, insisting that good humor and a concern for the material comfort of the masses were qualities which came naturally *only* to descendants of pre-Revolutionary New England. This attitude of course included a kind of snobbery that was particularly brutal and unbeatable because it judged a man on "scientific grounds."

Since Anglo-Saxon blood was the seed of true Americanism, then the national future was in mortal jeopardy if Anglo-Saxons were becoming a minority in the land, overwhelmed by the descendants of the fecund immigrants. So in 1894 the Immigration Restriction League of Boston was founded, to carry on a vigorous campaign. Restrictionists in other localities quickly followed suit. The League's instruments were the usual ones of lobbyists and propagandists—letters, articles, leaflets, clubs, speeches, and forums. Though relatively few in number, its members were influential. They were soon found throughout the country, and they had ready access to the public ear. Eventually they included such men as Massachusetts Senator Henry Cabot Lodge, the popular author Owen Wister (who wrote *The Virginian,* the prototypal Western novel), and the social worker Robert A. Woods. There were also many academics in the League: historian John Fiske; economists John R. Commons, William Z. Ripley, and Thomas N. Carver; sociologist Edward Alsworth Ross; and university presidents, including Stanford's

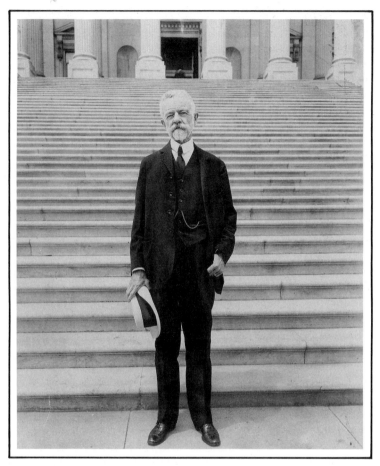

Respected men such as Massachusetts Senator
Henry Cabot Lodge joined the Immigration
Restriction League, which tried to limit the
numbers and kinds of immigrants allowed into
the country. Founded in 1894, it operated on the
arrogant and insidious premise that any heritage
other than the "biologically superior" Anglo-
Saxon line of the Founding Fathers would infect
and weaken the greatness and purity of America. *(Harris & Ewing)*

David Starr Jordan and Francis A. Walker of M.I.T. These men were the turn-of-the-century equivalents of Arthur M. Schlesinger, Jr., Jacques Barzun, Henry A. Kissinger, Eric Goldman, and John Kenneth Galbraith—educators whose words and works made headlines and who were sought out by men of power. When *they* talked about the problem of immigration with the apparent detachment of scientists discussing rock formations, they deployed a formidable power to influence public opinion against immigrants. It was a sign that even in 1901, at the start of immigration's biggest single decade, the concept of the open gate was in serious trouble.

In effect, the Immigration Restriction League purposefully cast suspicion upon the capacity of any immigrants, other than those from Northern Europe, to become Americanized. It was part and parcel of the anxious national argument over what "Americanization" meant.

Well, what did it mean? Was it successfully learning to cope with the problems of a new environment—securing housing, employment, schooling for the young or medicine for the sick and aged, without much dependence on influential outsiders? The immigrants were doing that in great numbers.

A study of Massachusetts in 1914 showed a strong pattern of mutual help among immigrant groups. The Greeks there, for example, did not let other Greeks wander alone through the labyrinth of urban life. Each sizable Greek community had an organization that was quasi-governmental in nature, going so far as to lay a tax of a cent on every loaf of bread sold to Greeks, with the income going toward support of the churches. The national Pan-Hellenic Union, which had twenty branches in Massachusetts, collected dues, paid sick and death benefits, and represented Greek immigrants in conflicts with loan sharks, landlords, and employers. Thirty-one consumer cooperatives in Massachusetts, organized around nationality groups, helped Italians, Finns, Swedes, French-Canadians, Poles, and others to stretch their dollars. Jews adrift in the cities that were like no *shtetl* they ever knew could find directions, counsel, loans, and interpreters at the offices of the Hebrew Immigrant Aid Society. The Lithuanians had sixty mutual benefit societies in the Commonwealth, while Poles had a National Alliance and a Catholic Alliance, as well as a Young Men's Alliance that provided reading rooms, classes in English and civics, and recreational facilities. The language might be that of Pulaski and the national spirit Polish, but the "foreigners" were doing much the same thing that the pious founders of the YMCA had undertaken in the 1850s when they provided a haven for American country boys who were in their own way "immigrating" into cities that were strewn with temptations and difficulties.

Curiously enough, many native Americans saw these ethnically based societies as evidence that the foreigners were clannishly resisting incorporation into the main currents of life in the United States. This was an attitude shared even by some immigrants, who made it their business to shed every vestige of "greenhorn" style as fast as possible. But there was another possible perspective. Self-reliance was said to be part of the American strain; so newcomers who divorced themselves as soon as possible from dependence on Anglo-Saxon charity were well on the way to useful citizenship. And for most people, self-reliance demanded a pride in self that was nourished by nationality identification. The Italian who felt despised by old Americans was apt to stand taller when his neighborhood Italian association reminded him that he was an heir of Garibaldi; such self-esteem prepared him for new American responsibilities and obligations. And the foreign-language newspaper, whose presence on the doorstep was taken by some to be a sign of the householder's slowness to give up the old ways, was often more insistent on the superiority of all things American than many an English-language newspaper.

Did Americanization mean succeeding in society by professional advancement and economic improvement? Of course, thousands of uncelebrated immigrants were quite successful on those terms, working their way up to become foremen and supervisors, independent businessmen, property owners—men who had good reason to say, as did one Italian immigrant, that in the adopted country "work was rewarded with abundance." Many a grandchild of the great 1900–1914 migration knows men and women now in their seventies and eighties who began life in America with no more than the clothes they stood up in and ended it with bank accounts, pleasant homes, college-educated children, and other sweets of life. These stories are deservedly commonplace whenever positive things are said about the promise of America. Then there are the rosters of immigrants who became exceptional figures in business, the arts, science, sports, and entertainment. Entire books have been filled with the doings of such worthies, who range in variety from John Jacob Astor and Andrew Carnegie to Victor Herbert and Charlie Chaplin.

But so much has been made of those who succeeded in this fashion that there is danger of forgetting the contributions of those who did not advance at all. The prism of nostalgia distorts the images of thousands upon thousands of immigrants who contributed their labor to the industrialization of America and received no more than calluses in return. One Slavic immigrant declared, *"My people do not live in America, they live underneath America. America goes on over their heads. America does not begin till a man is a workingman, till he is earning two dollars a day."* Some never reached that plateau. Restrictionists condemned these "failures" as biological inferiors. Even the ethnic historian, eager to refute the restrictionists by focusing on his group's highest achievements, has ignored them. Yet to ignore them—to suggest that only the economically successful in the United States are truly American—has disturbing implications.

Did Americanization involve bringing up children to embrace American styles of life? In that case, almost all immigrants were Americanized, even if only involuntarily. Except in communities tightly knit by some factor such as religion or by racial exclusion (a Chinatown, for example), it was impossible to keep youngsters properly deferential to parental authority and thus bound by old-country traditions. The schoolroom was the first separating force. "It is sad to notice," one commentator wrote, "the patronizing attitude that the child assumes toward his father and mother after a few months in the public school." And a New York district superintendent, Julia Richman, summed up the experience with this observation: "The parents remain foreign; the children become American. There is thus created an almost unbridgeable gulf between the two. Difference in taste, customs and language brings about domestic shipwreck." Half a century before it struck upper middle-class American families, the pain of the "generation gap" was an unhappy reality to the once close-knit, patriarchally led immigrant household. All successful parenthood must end in the loss of the child, but immigrant fathers and mothers, who saw their offspring move into a world of different gods and satisfactions and roles, lost them twice over.

What, then, was the genuine meaning of Americanization? While the newcomers struggled to find it in experience, those who were already "old" Americans ranged widely in their search for the answer.

Some seemed to believe that whatever the process might have been in the past, it would not work with the post-1900 mass arrivals, because the forces propelling earlier immigrants up the ladder of successful acculturation had burned out.

This conclusion was reached by several routes. Samuel Gompers, president of the American Federation of Labor, came to it as a result of his decision to build a labor movement around skilled workers. The success of the movement, in his eyes, required that there not be a large pool of unskilled workers from which employers could draw replacements when there were showdowns with the unions. And this, in turn, meant keeping out the impoverished new immigrant, an ironic attitude for Gompers, who in his childhood had emigrated from England. Yet his thin turtle mouth uttered speech after speech built around the idea that he expressed typically in a letter to a Congressman: ". . . both the intelligence and the prosperity of our working people are endangered by the present immigration. Cheap labor, ignorant labor, takes our jobs and cuts our wages." Interestingly, converting cheap and ignorant labor to well-paid and trained labor through organization and education was not on Gompers's agenda.

Edward Alsworth Ross thought that immigrants could never take intelligent part in the kind of "rational" politics—concerned with public health, conservation, control of trusts, and protection of the weak—that he and his progressive friends espoused. When he saw a billboard during a 1912 election campaign in Chicago listing candidates named Kelly, Cassidy, Alschuler, Pfaelzer, Romano, and Knitckoff, he did not find it heartening evidence of the flexibility of the American political order. Instead, he despaired of cleaning up corruption in a polyglot community. "The clashings that arise from the presence among us of many voters with medieval minds are sheer waste of energy," he wrote. How could great issues be explored by Cassidys and Romanos who preferred to fight over whose neighborhood would get new playgrounds? Sadly, he reflected that the "little homogeneous peoples are forging ahead of us . . . and learning

The shadows of their immigrant origins loom
over restrictionist American plutocrats in this
watercolor for a *Puck* cartoon of 1893. The
hypocrisy implicit in prorestrictive arguments
made itself easy prey for lampooning cartoonists
and writers, or anyone who honestly examined
his place in America. The tycoon himself would
not have risen to his heights without the opportunity made available to him as a poor
immigrant. *(Prints Division, New York Public
Library)*

220

to look pityingly upon us as a chaos rather than a people."

Even sympathetic social workers among the slum-trapped foreign-born poor sometimes despaired, as one of them revealed to Jacob Riis:

> They are down on the scrub level; there you find them and have to put them to such use as you can. They don't know anything else, and that is what makes it so hard to find work for them. Even when they go into a shop to sew, they come out mere machines, able to do only one thing, which is a small part of the whole they do not grasp. And thus, without the slightest training for the responsibilities of life, they marry and transmit their incapacity to another generation that is so much worse to start off with.

Behind even this well-meaning disparagement was the feeling that so large and varied a human swarm as the new immigrants could never be fused into the national whole. And that fusion was assumed to be indispensable to a healthy public life. Richmond Mayo-Smith wrote in 1890 that in order to have the "strength begotten of common national ideals and aspirations" there must be "one language, one political practice, one patriotism and one ideal of social development."

For Mayo-Smith, Ross, and many of their fellow social scientists, the single language had, naturally, to be English, and the single standard of social and political behavior to be "Anglo-Saxon." The immigrant should be "assimilated" into the dominant English-born culture, and if this were impossible, he should be turned away. But had it ever been possible? Anglo-Saxonism seemed to assume that it had been.

At the same time there were enthusiasts of America who thought the amalgamation did take place, but in a different way. In a 1908 play by an English Jew, Israel Zangwill, young David Quixano and his Gentile sweetheart, hand in hand, look out on New York and David says:

> There she lies, the great Melting Pot—listen! Can't you hear the roaring and the bubbling? There gapes her mouth—the harbour where a thousand mammoth feeders come from the ends of the world to pour in their human freight. Ah, what a stirring and a seething! Celt and Latin, Slav and Teuton, Greek and Syrian,—black and yellow—
> VERA: Jew and Gentile—

DAVID: Yes, East and West, and North and South, the palm and the pine, the pole and the equator, the crescent and the cross—how the great Alchemist melts and fuses them with his purging flame! Here shall they all unite to build the Republic of Man and the Kingdom of God.

But although the United States has been called a melting pot again and again by historians justly eager to celebrate American diversity, there has been no time when the nation's peoples have been on the verge of wholly losing their identities as Jew and Gentile, Celt and Teuton, or, most especially, white and red and black and yellow human beings. If the Great Alchemist has made much progress in creating a society blind to color, religion, and national origin, it is a secret to every political boss, every child who has fought in the schoolyard with or against some "minority group," every sociologist scanning an urban neighborhood population map, every employer and union organizer and teacher and social worker and minister who has dealt with large numbers of Americans.

In reality, few people in 1908 wanted a national immigration policy that would encourage such a fusion—any more than, sixty years later, they would support a definition of "integration" that meant a blending of races into indistinguishability. The inability, real or imagined, of immigrants to be amalgamated was simply an excuse not to accept them.

B ut there were Americans who wished to continue to accept the streams of immigrants, and they developed a concept of Americanization that offered a possibility of mating large-scale immigration with a consistent national character. Perhaps, they seemed to say, it was possible to thrive in a multilingual, multicultural society. Even at Harvard, the nursery of so many restrictionists, there were Yankees who felt disdain for those who wrung their hands over the supposed invasion. Harvard's president, Charles W. Eliot, noted that "the different races already in this country live beside each other, and all produce in time good citizens of the Republic." The philosopher Josiah Royce, commenting on the "scientific" sociology and history of some of his colleagues, wondered "whether a science which mainly devotes itself to proving that we ourselves are the salt of the earth, is after all so exact as it aims to be." William James, distinguished in both philosophy and psychology, privately wished that "the Anglo-Saxon race would drop its sniveling cant" about the white man's burden. A vigorous anti-imperialist, James rejected notions of racial superiority, and he was also impatient of religious bigotry. Once, when a hotel sent him an advertising circular that said that "applications from Hebrews cannot be considered," he fired back a one-line reply: "I propose to return the boycott."

A few young Americans from proper homes, already incubating the revolt against Main Street that would erupt in the 1920s, found the coarse vitality of the "foreign" neighborhoods exhilarating. A person could stand on New York's lower East Side and look around at surging life: peddlers bawling the contents of their pushcarts—hot chestnuts, chick-peas, sweet potatoes, pickles, watermelon, and corn; pots, pans, knives, scissors, and can openers; petticoats, shawls, stockings, and scarves. That person could hear Salvation Army Sallys wooing the bums home to Jesus with tambourine and trumpet, and Socialist orators lambasting the bourgeoisie in Russian, Italian, Yiddish, and English. On a saint's day, there might be processions winding through the streets, and booths with statuettes and pastries and ribbons for sale lining the sidewalk, and the popping of firecrackers. And on any day there would be children screeching in Chinese, Hungarian, Greek, and Rumanian, dodging wagons, playing hopscotch or jacks or marbles, jumping rope, fishing for coins through sidewalk gratings. The visitor could sample half a dozen cuisines in as many blocks or, like the writer Hutchins Hapgood, drop into a Yiddish theater and sit down next to "the sweat-shop woman with her baby, the day-laborer, the small . . . shopkeeper, the . . . Ghetto rabbi and scholar, the poet, the journalist."

In 1915, Horace M. Kallen, an educator and philosopher, proposed that rather than a homogeneous culture, there might be a "great and truly democratic commonwealth," whose form was

> . . . that of the Federal republic; its substance a democracy of nationalities, co-operating voluntarily and autonomously in the enterprise of self-realization. . . . The common language of the commonwealth, the language of its great political tradition, is English, but each nationality expresses its emotional and voluntary life in its own language, in its own inevitable aesthetic and intellectual forms. . . . an orchestration of mankind.

Four years later, the English-born leader of Chicago's Ethical Society, Horace J. Bridges, put it even more sharply in a book called *On Becoming an American*. Bridges declared that immigrants ought to glory in their own folkways rather than shedding them as they rose in the American economic hierarchy—the same message being beamed at educated young blacks today. There was "yet no fixed or final type" of American, said Bridges, nor could there ever be. Let the newcomers, he wrote,

> keep alive Italian and German music and literature, Balkan handicrafts, and the folk-lore and folk dances of the Old World;—not for the sake of the Old World, but as elements contributory to American culture. . . . There is no such thing as humanity-in-general, into which the definite, heterogeneous, living creature can be melted down. . . . The business of America is to get rid of mechanical uniformity.

But in 1919 the hour was late. In fact, the nation had already reached the climax of debate and had taken the first steps toward racially biased immigration restriction.

Even before 1900, the government had begun to shut out immigrants who it felt were likely to cause problems. From the beginning it mingled economic, moral, and medical judgments highhandedly. An act of 1891 denied entry to paupers, polygamists, and "persons suffering from loathsome and contagious diseases." In 1903, barriers were raised against epileptics, prostitutes, professional beggars, anarchists, and persons who believed in the overthrow by force of the government of the United States. These last two categories were in part a reaction to the assassination of President McKinley in 1901; though the murderer, Leon Czolgosz, was American, his parents were Polish, and he was an anarchist. In 1907 to the list of undesirables were added "imbeciles," tuberculosis victims, and those who had "committed a crime involving moral turpitude."

Restrictionists meanwhile pressed for a literacy test. True, it would not satisfy those who feared that the mere presence of too many aliens, literate or not, would water the nation's lifeblood; but it would tend to raise the economic level of incoming immigrants. Bills calling for such a test were introduced in Congress often. Versions were beaten in 1898, 1902, and 1906, presumably out of regard for the ethnic vote. One was passed in 1896 but was vetoed by President Cleveland; another that made its way through Congress in 1913 was vetoed by President Taft. President Wilson also vetoed one in 1915 in a message that got down to basics. Such requirements, he said, were not "tests of quality or of character or of personal fitness, but tests of opportunity. Those who come seeking an opportunity are not to be admitted unless they have already had one of the chief . . . opportunities they seek, the opportunity of education."

In 1906 President Theodore Roosevelt had decided to meet the immigration problem by a device that would simultaneously appease restrictionists, avoid any immediate affront to foreign-born voters and their children, and preserve the theory that his was a progressive administration governing only on the basis of intelligence marshaled by experts. He proposed that Congress create a commission to study the subject exhaustively, as a basis for future legislation. The enabling legislation was passed in 1907, setting up a nine-member body—three each chosen by the House and Senate's presiding officers, and three by the President; supposedly all were to be nonpartisan specialists.

The panel was known as the Dillingham Commission, after its chairman, William Paul Dillingham, a Senator from Vermont. Its impartiality was questionable, to begin with. The chief among its experts, a professor of political economy named Jeremiah Jenks, recalled a time in his life when he and his academic colleagues at Cornell were for the most part "proud . . . of being Anglo-Saxons," and thought that anyone "born in New England must be particularly good." He believed in restriction, and so did the secretary of the commission, Morton E. Crane, whom Theodore Roosevelt had chosen on the recommendation of his old friend Henry Cabot Lodge.

The Dillingham Commission hired a staff of three hundred, spent a million dollars, and labored over statistics and reports for three years. The end product was two volumes of summary and forty volumes of material, presented to Congress for adoption in 1910. It contained a *Dictionary of Races,* and long analyses of the laws governing migration, of economic conditions in Europe, and of the effects of immigration on literacy, charity, crime, vice, and insanity in the United States. As a document it seemed overpoweringly authoritative—but in its organization and conclusions, the report remorselessly stacked cards.

The *Dictionary of Races,* for example, purported to classify people on the basis of a language, but it deserted its own rules when necessary. On a linguistic basis, Yiddish-speaking Jews might theoretically have been classed with the Germans, since Yiddish is largely a German dialect, but they were not, any more than the English-speaking Irish were classed among the British stocks.

Time after time, data were compared for "old" and "new" immigrants as a whole, in ways that permitted misleading and adverse conclusions about the recent arrivals—conclusions that would have been different had the comparisons been made among specific nationality groups. As an instance, the commission matched arrivals for 1907 and departures for 1908. They found that the countries of the "old," pre-1890s, immigration furnished 22.7 percent of the 1907 ingathering but only 8.9 percent of those going back to Europe the following year. Those from the lands of the "new" immigration comprised 77.3 percent of the 1907 arrivals but a huge 91.1 percent of 1908's homeward-bound pilgrims. The implication was that the "new" immigrants furnished greater numbers of "birds of passage," who came to the United States to make a lot of money in a hurry and then get out. But when the figures were broken down by national origins, it turned out, of course, that each group was different in this respect. In 1908 the Italians and Croatians had high returnee rates. But more people of English, German, and Scandinavian stock per thousand left the country than was the case with the Armenians, "Hebrews," and Portuguese.

Crime rates were arranged in odd configurations; thus, "frequency of crime by type among different groups" supported the fraudulent notion that hot-blooded Italians committed more assaults than judicious native Americans. Much was made of literacy figures that proved "new" immigrants on the whole to be less literate than Americans; in the main body of the report such illiteracy was blamed on poverty, but in the summary it was blamed on "inherent racial tendencies." The commission found the conditions under which "new" immigrants worked usually deplorable, and asserted that this happened because the newcomers were "as a rule . . . tractable and easily managed." Yet a comparative investigation of the textile workers of the American South would have shown the proud descendants of the warlike Anglo-Saxons, native whites all, grinding away in circumstances

226

Adult naturalization classes such as this one
made available to future American citizens both
daytime and nighttime instruction. Students
were expected to gain a basic understanding of
civics and American history, to understand the
rudiments of democracy, and to possess a working knowledge of the English language. *(Library
of Congress)*

as wretched as those in any New York sweatshop. The summary bristled with negative judgments: the Serbo-Croatians had "savage manners," the Poles were "high-strung," the Italians had "not attained distinguished success as farmers."

The commission had, as directed, laid the basis for the immigration policy finally adopted, but its conclusions were not implemented for some ten years after its report was filed. In the interim the country was increasingly subjected to racist indoctrination. In 1915 *The Birth of a Nation* spread to millions of moviegoers the notion that blacks in the South during Reconstruction had been gorillalike despoilers of white women. As if on cue, Colonel William J. Simmons of Atlanta revived the Ku Klux Klan, to battle blacks, Jews, Catholics, and all foreigners who had, as one Klan leader put it, made the "Nordic American . . . a stranger in large parts of the land his fathers gave him." The Klan flourished in the South, the Midwest, and the Far West; it reached a strength of nearly four and a half million by 1924, and shook the Democratic Party as nothing had since the slavery issue.

In 1916 a distinguished New Yorker, Madison Grant, published an influential work called *The Passing of the Great Race.* Grant was a Yale graduate, an attorney, an amateur scientist, secretary of the New York Zoological Society, and a trustee of the Museum of Natural History. Said he: ". . . it has taken us fifty years to learn that speaking English, wearing good clothes, and going to school and to church, does not transform a negro into a white man. . . . We shall have a similar experience with the Polish Jew, whose dwarf stature, peculiar mentality, and ruthless concentration on self-interest are being engrafted upon the stock of the nation." The Jews, Grant declared, "adopt the language of the native American; they wear his clothes; they steal his name; and they are beginning to take his women, but they seldom adopt his religion or understand his ideals."

The whole nation was on the brink of a protracted frenzy. Its entry into the World War made hysteria respectable in a way, especially when it was aimed at foreigners. The logical objects of wartime xenophobia were two "old" immigrant groups, the German and the Irish; the latter group because it never developed any collective enthusiasm for the nation's British allies. But the popular fury that was unleashed against such representatives of evil as dachshunds and band conductors who unwisely programmed Wagner and against Irish speechmakers who damned King George V was not fully spent by the effort. Much of it naturally boiled over on other foreigners, especially the "dagos" and the "bohunks" who became involved with such left-wing organizations as the antiwar Socialist Party and Industrial Workers of the World. The public mind made persistent connection between foreigners—especially those with names ending in "-ski"—and militant radicalism. This linkage was strengthened enormously by the Russian Revolution, and in 1919 the usually urbane New York *Times* rebuked the Attorney General of the United States for advocating liberal immigration policies. These "ancient and outworn views," the paper said, were "not too pleasant to hear when, all over the country, alien or foreign-born agitators are carrying on in many languages . . . the Bolshevist and IWW propaganda for the overthrow of the Government." If the *Times* was so aroused, it was understandable that a Representative from Tennessee should say just a few years later: "We get the majority of the communists, the I.W.W.s, the dynamiters, and the assassins of public officers from the ranks of the present-day immigrant."

This, then, was the emotional environment: first, the ugly mood of a progressive nation girding itself up and battling for the millennium, then the country's disappointment and frustration in the peace, and the hangover of readjustment. Once the American involvement in the war began, it took only a few years to unhorse the advocates of unlimited asylum.

First came the passage of an act in 1917 that broadened the government's rights to keep out and expel undesirable aliens. The law also created a "barred zone" in the Southwest Pacific area, from which no immigrants could come—a measure to block any Orientals who might find a way through the existing barbed-wire entanglement of anti-Chinese and anti-Japanese policies. Finally, it required that, with a few exceptions, those desiring admission be able to read a short passage in English or some other language. It was the literacy test again, and again Wilson vetoed it. But this time it was repassed over his veto.

The war was scarcely ended when a tide of refugees from the battle-scarred and hungry nations of Europe began to flow westward. Even the literacy test could not keep the numbers significantly down. Between June 1920, and June 1921, for example, there were some 805,000 admissions, more than sixty-five percent of them from Central, Southern, and Eastern Europe; American consuls warned that thousands more would soon be following. In February of 1921 Ellis Island was so jammed that ships had to be diverted to Boston. Meanwhile, since the armistice, the nation had experienced a great Red scare, a brutal steel strike involving a work force that was largely foreign-born, and the start of the Sacco-Vanzetti case.

Congress had begun to react to all these stimuli. In April of 1920 the House Committee on Immigration and Naturalization employed Dr. Harry Laughlin, an expert in the study of human breeding, to dust off the Dillingham Commission report, analyze its data, and advise the country what should be done to protect its future generations. Dr. Laughlin did not render his verdict until late 1922: his tone is reflected in a key sentence that declared, "Making all logical allowances for environmental conditions, which may be unfavorable, . . . the recent immigrants as a whole, present a higher percentage of inborn socially inadequate qualities than do the older stocks."

The Senators and Representatives, however, did not wait those two and a half years before acting. In May 1921 they passed a law that limited "the number of aliens of any nationality who may be admitted . . . in any fiscal year . . . to 3 per centum of the number of foreign-born persons of such nationality resident in the United States as determined by the . . . census of 1910. . . ." The impact of this first Quota Act was to reduce the allowable figure for immigrants to about 357,000 per year. Originally scheduled to terminate after one year, the law was extended for two more years in the spring of 1922.

Then, in 1924, the temporary measures of 1921 and 1922 were replaced by a long-term plan, the Johnson-Reed Act, which went even further to satisfy the restrictionists. For the next three years quotas would be cut from three to two percent, dropping the total permitted admissions to some 164,000: moreover, the base year of calculation would be set back to 1890, when the countries of the "new" immigrants were represented by smaller fractions of the populace than in 1910. After 1927, the law said, total immigration from outside the American continent was to be held to 150,000, with each nation's share proportionate to its representation by birth or descent in the American people of 1920. There was a little leeway: the allowable quota could go higher by as many as one hundred newcomers from each country that had made only a minimal contribution, or none at all, to the American breed before 1920. And no limits were placed on immigration from Canada, Central and South America, and the Caribbean. On the other hand, this generosity did not apply to Orientals. They were shut out completely, without any quotas at all, because by law, unless an Oriental was born in the United States, he or she was ineligible for citizenship.

The national-origins formula was anything but scientific as a measuring rod. At best, determining the ancestry of fifth- and sixth-generation Americans was chancy. It had to be done by statistical projections, in which guesswork naturally played a major role. There were no firm guidelines for classifying a European forefather's nationality, and the creation of new nations only compounded the problem. Did a grandparent from Galicia—Austro-Hungarian in 1914, Polish in 1920—count with the Poles, the Austrians, or the Hungarians? That, apparently, was up to immigration officials.

Such niceties were not the basic point, however. The point was revealed when the first quotas went into effect in 1929: more than half of all spaces were reserved for residents of the British Isles, whereas only 5,802 Italians and 6,524 Poles could be admitted. And the bureaucracy could use the ambiguities of classification to tighten the valves on various pipelines still further. Restrictionism had won.

Possibly, however, its victory was not so complete as at first it appeared. From Canada, the Caribbean, and Central and South America would come a steady stream of immigrants, many not white, most of them poor, Catholic, and Latin. Nonwhites from various United States territories and possessions would also negotiate the corridors of entry. Total immigration sank only slowly at first—307,255 in 1928, 241,700 in 1930. Then the Great Depression succeeded for a time where the law had failed; in 1933 immigration dropped to a twentieth-century low of 23,068. But after World War II it began to rise again.

Nevertheless, 1924 was a turning point. Not only had a set of laws been written; a chapter of history had been closed, a certain spirit snuffed out. There would be more immigrants, more shiftings and mingling of peoples—spurred on by war, social upheaval, and the special needs of the United States. But after three hundred years, the awesome transoceanic migration was over.

X

Urban Promised Land

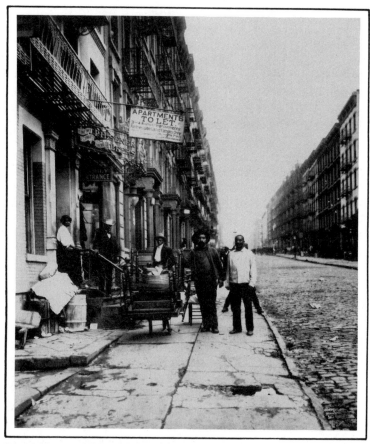

Seemingly peaceful before its population swelled
in the twenties, Harlem nurtured seeds of the
conflicts to come. *(Brown Brothers)*

And so the gates closed on the annual inward surge of European seekers of a new life, and absorption began its work. True, there was a continued influx from the Western Hemisphere, while American nationality itself remained an amalgam of many kinds of "foreign" clay, not yet molded, not yet hardened. But with the damming of the torrents of newcomers, there was space for native and immigrant alike to test, clarify, and reassess the meaning of their encounter.

Americanization, it was evident, was a process acted out largely by the young—the sons and daughters and grandsons and granddaughters of Polotzk and Molfetta and Ljubljana. They were the ones who blended their parents' gift of traditions with the staccato messages of the new environment. If, as many believe, the essence of human experience in the depersonalizing twentieth century is a search for identity, for ties to the past that will strengthen but not confine us, then the story of the second- and third-generation Americans is one of the central sagas of modern American history.

The bits and pieces of transplanted Europe hailed by the cultural pluralists (such as the Swedish newspaper, the Polish clubhouse, the Ukrainian-speaking parish) diminished as the foreign-born aged. The rate of this fading varied for different groups and so set dissimilar styles for each nationality's children. Contrasting patterns of assimilation, moreover, preserved variations in the quality and tone of life among immigrant groups, and kept America a land of noticeable ethnic diversity and color. The offspring of Marco and Isaac and Stefan all did learn to do the same properly American things—to revere the flag, pay taxes promptly, pray in English, save their money, buy homes and insurance, and keep their own young in school. But where they lived and worked and voted—and how—continued to depend in some measure on Old World backgrounds.

One thing was certain: almost all of them were part of the ceaseless swelling of the cities. Furthermore, they were being affected by cultural revolutions of unsuspected scope. During the booming twenties, hungry thirties, war-torn forties, and tense fifties, the whole structure of American social values was under heavy assault. The automobile, the movies, television, Freud, Keynes, suburbia, and all other aspects of an age of tech-

233

nology, leisure, and abundance challenged and upset the moods of respectability and responsibility dominant in 1914, at immigration's high tide. And by the time the newcomers were successful on, say, Calvin Coolidge's terms, many of the terms were obsolete.

Meanwhile, a second part of the story was developing. There was a steady and fateful internal migration of America's black peasantry to the urban frontier. As millions of black Americans, after 1910, sought the real and imagined opportunities of the industrial North, they created yet another "new" immigration. This one was not funneled through Ellis Island or blessed by the Statue of Liberty—or suspended in 1924. Like its predecessors, it flowed into the jobs and neighborhoods at the lowest levels of desirability and displaced their former occupants upward. Black bodies twisted and sweated in the coarse-labor jobs that the Irish and the Italians had held in their turn. Black faces peered from tenement windows vacated by Jewish peddlers. In time, it was hoped, they too would move to better things.

But the black "invaders" soon encountered the seemingly permanent force of racism, both as a barrier imposed by whites to their advance and as the source of crippling social damage and inadequacies in black society itself. The hoped-for upward movement of black youngsters into professions and property ownership took place either at a heartbreakingly slow rate or not at all. By 1955, black leaders (and white liberals) were straining against the brakes on integration. By 1965, some angry and desperate blacks had given up on integration and were issuing calls for black separatism.

Either way, the black men and women fighting for change found themselves on a collision course with white immigrants' descendants. Irish, Italians, Poles, and Jews held the approaches to the stairway upward. They owned the small businesses and were foremen and union leaders in industry; they were teachers and principals in the school system; they were officers and supervisors in the police and fire and sanitation departments and other branches of the civil service; they dominated the neighborhoods adjacent to the slums. They occupied the strong points that advancing black pride would need to possess and fortify. It was an old pattern, except that this time the advance was black against white. The American social stage was set for disturbing confrontations in the 1970s.

Every immigrant group has its own body of "up from Ellis Island" legends, lovingly preserved by ethnic historical societies. The operative word is "up." The values binding American society together in the days of Andrew Jackson, Abraham Lincoln, and Horatio Alger had not changed much in the 1920s, when the former Commissioner of Immigration in New York, Frederic C. Howe, wrote a piece for a symposium entitled *Civilization in America*. Discontent with the status quo, said Howe approvingly, was the power plant of progress for the immigrant as for the old-timer:

> The newcomer speedily acquires the wants of those with whom he associates. He becomes dissatisfied with his shack. He demands more and better food and clothes. He almost always wants his children to have a schooling and to rise in the scale, which to him means getting out of the hod-carrying, day-labour, or even artisan class. And the next generation does rise. It rises only less rapidly than did the early immigrant.

The extent and consequences of the upward escalator ride differed according to the culture of each foreign-born community. Boundaries between nationalities in the new land were blurred but not erased. As a perceptive black activist, the Reverend Jesse Jackson, noted in 1969, "There is talk about it [America] being a melting pot. But it really is more like vegetable soup. There are separate pieces of corn, meat, and so on, each with its own identity." The special talents and traditions of each nationality dictated that some would merge almost totally into American society, as the Germans have since the two wars against the homeland, or remain highly visible on ceremonial occasions, like the Irish on March 17 each year. America's Italians and Jews—both basically elements in the "new" immigration—offer other interesting examples of contrast.

More than three million Italians landed on American shores between 1900 and 1914. By 1980, 12,184,000 Americans reported that they were of Italian ancestry. Fifty-seven percent of these lived in the Northeast, and 1,471,000 people over eighteen reported that they still spoke Italian at home.

Italian neighborhoods were quickly formed, duplicating in a few square blocks the supportive closeness of the village. Inevitably these communities were known as "Little Italys." Despite relative prosperity, Italians tended to remain in their original localities. Jewish, Irish, black, and Puerto Rican neighbors might come and go, but the Italians tended to stay on, undismayed by a shabby external appearance in the area, so long as the interiors of their own homes were pleasant.

Some Italians went into truck farming in the Northeast, and a few ventured to till the soil of the Far West. Others undertook entrepreneurship and became *prominenti,* neighborhood leaders. In New York alone, such names as La Rosa and Ronzoni in macaroni products and Santini in moving and storage testify to just how successful some were in their chosen lines. And although Italian-Americans are understandably sensitive about it, the presence of many Italian names on the top-level rosters of organized crime also reflects success of a kind.

Below these major figures were the thousands of Italians who operated barbershops, drugstores, restaurants, bakeries, butcher shops, and, in the old days of iceboxes and coal furnaces, ice and coal dealerships. The realities of the hardworking world of the Italian laborers or shopkeepers were reflected in some of the commonly used words of the Italianized English that served the new immigrants and that are sometimes fondly recollected by their children. Among them are *scioppa,* shop; *storo,* store; *giobba,* job; *grosseria,* grocery; and *bosso,* boss.

Italian clan spirit helped to launch business careers, but it was also a potential handicap to the Italian-American children. The strong dependence on paternal authority made them vulnerable to the peasant concept that education is not of vital import, that intellectual achievement is disloyalty to the past. Large numbers of Italian boys and girls were not encouraged to hold ambitions for academic achievement beyond the high-school diploma, and some drew frowns even for that limited aspiration. Many a dropout of the 1920s bore an Italian name. Working-class Italians, used to the authority of *padroni,* seemed less aggressive unionists than the Irish or the Jews, despite the records of firebrand radicals like Carlo Tresca, Arturo Giovannitti, and Joseph Ettor, not to mention Nicola Sacco and Bartolomeo Vanzetti. Therefore, few of them achieved positions of authority in the national labor movement. In the church, they found the Irish in unyielding command and were not moved in any great numbers to undertake the studies required for the priesthood.

With the passing years, many Italians did enter the ranks of skilled craftsmen (such as electricians and plumbers) through their connections with the building trades. Others enlisted in the civil service's corps of technicians and administrators. But an occupational census of New York City in 1950, for example, showed that among sons of Italian immigrants surveyed, thirty-three percent were in professional, technical, clerical, and sales fields or were managers, officials, and proprietors. The comparable figure for the Irish was forty-seven percent; for the male children of Russian (and therefore, in New York, primarily Jewish) immigrants it was seventy-four percent. More Italian girls than boys had "made it"; forty percent were in the clerical and sales area alone.

Yet by the 1960s the Italians had moved a considerable distance from a living standard sustained by the shovel and were justly proud. In neighborhoods where TV antennas sprouted like denuded trees from the ridgepoles and tomorrow's pizza was stored in a late-model freezer, they congratulated themselves on what they had achieved "without help"—a phrase they sometimes used to disparage the blacks' need for public assistance. And on vacation, at places like the Villagio Italia in the Catskills, where strolling minstrels caroled "O Sole Mio" in the Stella Alpina Lounge, they showed that one ethnic group could be quite Americanized in certain ways but also quite "unmelted."

Both the Italians and the Russian-Polish Jews reached the shores of opportunity in America at about the same time. The Jews, too, after half a century or so, remained a discernibly separate group. Yet in some ways, not shared by other elements of the mighty 1890–1914 migration, they had been successfully joined to contemporary America—to such an extent that their communal and religious leaders worried over Judaism's possible loss in America of the hardy virtues acquired during centuries of persecution. Or even, thoroughly unlikely as it might appear, of American Jewry's disappearance into the lonely crowd of mass society.

Like the Italians, the Jews had a strong sense of family. But they also traditionally placed a formidable premium on intellectual achievement, especially for males. If this outlook tormented generations of Jewish boys who did not glitter in the classroom, it was a tremendous asset to those offspring of the *shtetl* in whom natural ability was fertilized as well by their own hunger for success. Thousands of boys from New York's lower East Side and other Jewish urban neighborhoods pushed their way through schools of accountancy, pharmacy, education, law, and medicine in the 1920s and 1930s, when those seemed the professions most open to Jews. Often they were financed by a combination of a student's part-time job and parental sacrifice. Their own children and grandchildren attended colleges and graduate schools in record numbers.

Even armed with diplomas, Jews were not able to pry open every door closed by historic prejudice. But in the post-1945 industrial and scientific booms, great numbers of Jewish engineers and research specialists found their way onto corporate and government payrolls. In entertainment, journalism, literature, and the performing arts the efflorescence of Jews was universally noted. And professorships, formerly the near-monopoly of old-stock Americans, became increasingly available to aspiring Jewish youth. Overall, by 1980 Jews remained heavily involved in wholesale and retail trades and exceeded the national average for self-employment. The image of the American Jew as a basically middle-class type was justified by the facts. But some were still blue-collar workers, especially in New York City, where half of the country's Jews lived and accounted for a fourth of the city's population. Most of the rest were concentrated in some nine other major metropolitan areas in the country. In New York, Jews still worked in garment factories, drove taxis, wore police uniforms, and served as house painters, plumbers, and carpenters. Thousands of others were in white-collar occupations whose incomes probably did not exceed those of skilled laborers—for example, teaching. Half of New York City's teachers in 1970 were Jewish; and every year schools closed on the High Holidays out of sheer necessity as well as deference to the ethnic vote. This predominance produced an ominous conflict in 1968 between teachers' demands for job security and the clamor of many blacks and Puerto Ricans for control of their neighborhood schools; a bitter strike resulted. It was disturbing for New York's future that blacks had traditionally known Jews only as "superiors"—landlords, shopkeepers, social workers, doctors, lawyers, and employers.

Rich or poor, the Jews retained their visibility. Most of those in New York had long since moved out of their bastions on the East Side, but they created identifiable neighborhoods in Bensonhurst, the West Bronx, and Washington Heights in the 1920s and 1930s and in suburban towns on Long Island, in New Jersey, and in Westchester after World War II—communities with counterparts around other large cities. In suburbia, their synagogues, designed by expensive architects, rose amid landscaped parking lots—a far cry from the storefront *shuls* of urban Jewry forty years before. Alleged Jewish ostentation, vulgarity, and lack of genuine piety had been assailed, not least by Jewish intellectuals themselves. Rabbis, commentators, and novelists asked whether Professor Goldstein, with his summer home, sailboat, hi-fi, son at Harvard Law, and daughter in the Peace Corps, was as whole and as self-aware as his pants-pressing grandfather.

But the question itself implied a curious tribute to the United States. The descendants of the Russian pants presser might agonize over whether they still needed his specifically Judaic faith and folkways, whether they were being disloyal to Grandfather by substituting the purchase of Israel bonds for the multitude of religious observances that once concerned him. But their "problem" arose from a society that took the pants presser from the *shtetl* and gave his children a chance. That they used it so effectively said something complimentary about them and about America.

Ethnic groups of all kinds continued to exist on the national scene. Most occupied the middle ground—somewhere between totally divorcing themselves from their Old World customs and clinging to them so rigidly as to become isolated from any meaningful participation in modern life—like the Amish. In the industrial cities where the immigrants gathered years ago, Polish, Italian, Hungarian, and other "unassimilated" neighborhoods still stood, complete with their own grocery stores and churches. Though they, too, were changing, one key to identifying those that changed most slowly was the persistence of the foreign-language paper. The immigrant press had been in decline since its zenith in 1914. There were then some 1,300 foreign-language newspapers and periodicals published in the continental United States, forty percent of them in German. Between 1914 and 1940 the number diminished by a fourth and then plummeted. And yet as late as 1982 the *Ayer Directory of Publications* still listed eight pages of periodicals in the U.S. and Canada printed wholly or partly in foreign languages, including Arabic, Armenian, Bulgarian, Chinese, Croatian, Czeck, Finnish,

Greek, Hungarian, Japanese, Polish, Swedish, Ukranian, Vietnamese, and Yiddish.

Nowhere could one get so strong a sense of ethnic persistence as in New York—where groceries might change nationalities and aromas every few blocks. Oriental youngsters from Chinatown ate pizza in the adjoining Italian neighborhood along Mulberry Street. Puerto Ricans, Haitians, Dominicans, and Cubans clustered on the West Side, mingling with Koreans and Japanese in the same neighborhoods. Ukrainians patronized the Akra Discount Store for "native" clothing and feasted on pigs' feet and mushroom dumplings at the Odessa Restaurant.

Thus in the great metropolis, the peasants who came from a dozen cultures sixty and seventy years before and helped make the United States a modern nation had left enduring legacies. American children sprung from their loins carried their inheritance forward, conscious of that past as well as what they might become. American social institutions, still malleable, were being shaped as much by the presence of those immigrants' children as by anything that happened on the frontier or in the "Saxon" past.

One arena in which the process was most apparent, naturally, was the political. Partisan politics in the United States specialized in mediating among diverse groups, often groups with really conflicting interests. Immigrants have been among the most readily identifiable of groups, and therefore American urban politics developed what is known as the ethnic ticket. In New York, for example, ward bosses still spoke in the 1970s of "the Three-I League"—Israel, Ireland, and Italy—and took it seriously, as they did in 1965, when the regular Democratic candidates for the offices of mayor, president of the city council, and controller were Abe Beame, Frank O'Connor, and Mario Procaccino.

At first glimpse, such ethnic back scratching might have seemed foolish and trivial. But more than a quarter of a century had elapsed since the New Deal drew a deep dividing line across American political history. As the political analyst Samuel Lubell pointed out, the 1930s were just about the time when the children of the new immigration came of voting age. Two great forces, the city and the immigrant, made it inevitable that the national political center of gravity would settle amid an electorate that was largely urban and non-Protestant. It would be the Irish story again, in one sense, but far wider in scope and impact, as the nation of the 1930s was far more complex than that of the 1890s. Those who were most sensitive to the needs of the new voting masses would have ready-made majorities at their command.

Lubell discovered this pattern in scrutinizing the Presidential votes of the country's twelve largest cities. In 1920 they gave the Republicans a plurality of 1,540,000. But eight years later, they gave the losing candidate, Alfred E. Smith, a 210,000 plurality. "What Smith really embodied," Lubell wrote, "was the revolt of the underdog, urban immigrant against the top dog of 'old American' stock." His Catholicism lost him crucial rural votes, but his religion was an essential element in that revolt. Brown-derbied, speaking with an accent unabashedly New York, he was quintessentially urban. He was a genuinely productive and pro-gressive governor in Albany, but the heart of his appeal to the voters was symbolized when the band struck up his theme song, "The Sidewalks of New York." He pushed the Democratic Party away from one of its historic bases—the Bible-thumping crossroads towns beloved of William Jennings Bryan—and this momentum endured. The key metropolitan areas included in Lubell's investigation gave Franklin D. Roosevelt a 3,479,000 plurality in 1936 and later piled up victory margins for John F. Kennedy and Lyndon B. Johnson.

Under the lash of depression, Roosevelt and his aides formu-lated programs of public assistance to the aged, the jobless, the unorganized, the untrained, and the ill-cared-for—programs that met the basic needs of a new generation of city-bred Ameri-cans disenchanted with unrestricted free enterprise. The quarter-decks of state and local Democratic organizations were fortified at the beginning of this movement by old-timers from the re-form establishment and by a few machine veterans. But it was only a question of time before the rising young public leaders of the second-generation immigrant communities would aspire to visible and prestigious roles. And it was inevitable that they should achieve these roles, especially after many returned with honorable records from World War II service.

The story of Rhode Island's John Pastore is highly illustrative. When he was born, in 1907, one of a tailor's five children, Ital-ians constituted one thirteenth of his state's population. They

At a Talmud school, Jewish boys study the
Talmud, the ancient Rabbinical writings embodying the religious authority for traditional
Judaism. Jewish immigrants insisted on religious
instruction, not only to educate the boys in
their faith, but also to preserve Judaism in
pluralistic American. *(The Jacob A. Riis Collection, Museum of the City of New York)*

voted for the Republican Party, the supposed provider of prosperity and the full dinner pail, but got little by way of political reward. In 1910 Providence had only one schoolteacher, one policeman, and one fireman of Italian descent. In 1912 the Republicans named Antonio A. Capotosto as assistant to the state attorney general, and that completed the Italian patronage list.

If the Pastore family, for one, felt any resentment at such sights, it was overshadowed by personal tragedy in 1916, when John's father died suddenly. Mrs. Pastore went to work full-time as a seamstress, never permitting her children to stray from the path of respectability, even when it demanded the utmost from her, such as ironing twenty shirts a week so that her boys would never appear at school without a fresh one.

Young John worked his way through night law school. When he passed the state bar examinations, in 1932, only four or five Italian-Americans a year were doing so. Also in 1932 FDR was elected. The ethnic urban vote was noticed. The Italians were suddenly, visibly more important, and by 1938 every fifth Rhode Island voter was of their stock. The Democrats moved in and showed themselves ready to improve on Republican parsimony by sharing the spoils more liberally. And so, one Sunday, John Pastore waited outside St. Bartholomew's Church for Tommy Testa, the Democratic boss of his ward, and gave his oath of allegiance. By 1944 Pastore's credentials were so good that he was given a spot on the state Democratic ticket—candidate for lieutenant governor. The ticket won, and when Governor J. Howard McGrath resigned to take a federal post, John Pastore was governor. He ran for another term in 1946 and won. Then, in 1950, a proven vote getter, John Pastore became the first Italian-American to sit in the United States Senate.

It was also in the 1950s that Foster Furcolo became the governor of Massachusetts, Abraham Ribicoff the first Jewish governor of Connecticut, and Edmund Sixtus Muskie, Polish-American, the governor of Maine. The 1950s were the decade of arrival. At the outset of that decade, New York City saw a three-way race for its mayoralty, often considered the second most important and trying political job in the United States, in which all the candidates—Vincent Impellitteri, Edward Corsi, and Ferdinand Pecora—were Italian, as was the boss of Tammany, Carmine De Sapio. As the next decade began, a Catholic heir of Irish immigrants in Massachusetts won the Presidential office that Al

Smith had vainly tried to reach. Part of the explanation for all this could be found in the words of a Buffalo Polish ward leader in 1940 predicting the ultimate election of a Polish mayor (which happened in 1949): "Out in ritzy Humboldt Park they get two voters to a family. I get six out of my house. I got neighbors who give me eight." But there was something else, too—a change of attitude, a softening of heart, since the days of the restrictionist crusade.

By no means had the millennium of universal tolerance arrived. As the 1970s began, there were still underrepresented minority groups, mostly nonwhite, and their urgent pressure for admission to the feast of office was mercilessly straining the joints of the traditional New Deal alliance. The 1960s had witnessed the election of black mayors in Gary, Indiana, Cleveland, Ohio, and Fayette, Mississippi, but also a great backlash and the nationalizing of the appeal of demagogic conservatives. Moreover, to win office is not necessarily to find a path into such major strongholds of social and economic power as banks, corporations, and communications networks and universities—all of which at the end of the 1960s had few directors from the "new" immigration's offspring. And finally, the Italian or Polish or Jewish or black mayor or governor could stay in office only by spreading favors with reasonable evenhandedness. He could not offer much to his own ethnic group that he did not offer to others, except perhaps the honor inherent in his election.

Yet people live by such symbols as honor, and in the long run the symbolic meaning of an election can be as influential as its immediate impact on parties. The election of John Kennedy as President was a genuine landmark, but little notice has been given to the sequel. Only eight years later the two vice-presidential candidates were of recent East European roots. Spiro Agnew did not parade his Greek background; on the other hand, the fact that his original family name was Anagnostopoulos caused him no embarrassment. As for Edmund Muskie, his father's surname in Poland had been Marciszewski; it was changed by an Ellis Island official in 1903 who found it too much to spell. Agnew is an Episcopalian, but Muskie's middle name, Sixtus, is proudly that of five popes.

During the campaign, everyone was aware that the Vice-

Presidency was an important office. Of the five most recent Presidents, two had died in office—one by assassination, one had been the intended victim of an assassination attempt, and one had been seriously ill several times. Yet there was no major outcry over the prospect of putting a second-generation American a heartbeat away from the most powerful office in the world. The bodies of the old Klan, the American Protective Association, and the Immigration Restriction League may have turned over in their graves, but if so, that caused no earthquakes. Society had, in fact, come a long way in seventy years.

While the offspring of the steamship immigrants were working their ways into American life, black families were moving northward. Their journey was not unique. Everywhere in developing nations, rural people pricked up their ears at the sound of the factory whistle. And the nearly nine million American blacks who lived in the South in 1910 (and made up ninety percent of the nation's total black population) were predominantly a peasantry, living on farms, confronting permanent tenantry, poverty, ignorance, and disease. A government commission studying farm labor crisply summarized their plight that year: "There is absolutely nothing before them on the farm . . . no prospect . . . but to continue until they die." From this desperation they began to flee, in a movement that still continued in the 1970s. By 1920, fifteen percent of the nation's blacks lived outside the South. By 1940 it was twenty-three percent, by 1960 forty percent, and by 1980 between fifty and sixty percent of black America lived outside what might well be called their "old country."

They came to the cities by train in the early days, pouring onto the platforms with their bundles and their boxes, looking around, filling their eyes with the sights of Mecca. They came in response to letters and messages from relatives—sometimes in response to nothing more than ads clipped from the Pittsburgh *Courier*, the *Amsterdam News*, the Baltimore *Afro-American*, or the Chicago *Defender*, that said things like "3000 laborers to work on railroad. Factory hires all race help. More positions open than men for them." It was very encouraging. True, the unions would not easily accept black men, so the factory jobs turned out many times to be the hardest, the dirtiest, the ones offering the smallest promise of advancement. Or else they were for strike-breakers, which was a dangerous way to earn a living. Even a scab's work was not always available, so black men and women had to do the traditional chores of their people in America: cooking, cleaning, fetching, and grooming for whites.

Still, it was the North. Schools were better than what the South offered. The coarser humiliations of legalized segregation were somewhat muted. Voting was possible, and there might be a future for the young. There was an air of promise. Some black men in the cities, members of Booker T. Washington's National Negro Business League, were making money as owners of their own barbershops, funeral parlors, and livery stables. Washington's well-known antagonist, W.E.B. DuBois, was talking about a "talented tenth" of the Negro race, which would save its future. In 1909, DuBois and other black leaders had helped to found the National Association for the Advancement of Colored People, then a "radical" force fighting courtroom battles for black rights. At their side were sympathetic and brilliant whites like Mary White Ovington, Joel Spingarn, Oswald Garrison Villard, and Moorfield Storey. In 1910 the National Urban League was founded to set about opening job opportunities for blacks. A new day did seem on the way.

There were drawbacks, of course. Living quarters were scarce. Northern whites would seldom accept black neighbors except perhaps along the alleys behind their houses; so old black districts, cramped for expansion, grew desperately crowded. The poet Langston Hughes, born in 1902, remembered that his family in Cleveland always seemed to inhabit attics or basements and to pay a lot for them. When white people did finally rent to blacks, they would cut up their houses into five or six apartments and charge gold-rush prices for each—and for garages and sheds, too.

But a Northern city offered a little acceptance to black people. Hughes went to Central High School. Once it had taught the children of proper Clevelanders; by 1916 it was full of the children of the foreign-born, divided mainly between mutually suspicious Jews and Catholics. When elections were held for class officers, Hughes often won as the "compromise candidate," having apparently the advantage of being considered neither Jew nor Gentile. On a summer vacation he visited Chicago, which was exciting. South State Street was "in its glory" in 1918, "a teeming Negro street with crowded theaters, restaurants and cabarets. And excitement from noon to noon. Midnight was like day. The street was full of workers and gamblers, prostitutes and pimps, church folks and sinners. The tenements on either side were very congested. For neither love nor money could you find a decent place to live."

More attractive than Chicago for many a bright young black was a place that had once been a quiet Manhattan suburb, "the rural retreat of the aristocratic New Yorker"—a place called Harlem. After 1900 black real-estate operators began to buy buildings there, hoping to open the ownership of tidy homes to worthy blacks. They undoubtedly had profits in mind, but they also hoped to avoid the creation in New York of a "Nigger-town," a "Buzzard's Alley," a "Bronzeville," as black slums were already called in other cities. And, though New York's black population began to increase markedly after 1910, they seemed for a while to be succeeding. White residents, unsurprisingly, fled before the migrants, who were described by one newspaper as "black hordes . . . eating through the very heart of Harlem." But they left behind a Harlem that suddenly became a magnet for black artists and intellectuals, who made it their cultural capital.

Young whites reveled in Mencken, Eliot, Pound, Hemingway, Stravinsky, Cubism, and Dadaism, while black poets and writers like James Weldon Johnson and Claude McKay and Countee Cullen, black scholars like Carter G. Woodson, Alain Locke, and E. Franklin Frazier, and black musicians like Bessie Smith and Duke Ellington sang their various lyrics of emancipation. Not all of them lived in Harlem, but for most it was at least their spiritual home. Langston Hughes spoke for a whole black generation when he described how it was to come up from the subway under Harlem after a long absence: "I stood there, dropped my bags, took a deep breath and felt happy again."

And yet there was another side to Harlem in the 1920s. It might float the mirage of a "new Negro" before the eyes of intellectuals—who, even so, quickly perceived that New York was a place where good jobs for blacks were scarce and pay skimpy. But when, between 1920 and 1930, the city's black population rose by another 115 percent, goodwill and hope collasped. Black and white slumlords found that milking decayed buildings for a few years was more profitable than longtime investments in repairs, and so black Harlemites endured falling plaster, exposed wiring, malfunctioning plumbing and heating systems, and rats and roaches. Disease flourished in Harlem.

Black death rates from rickets, tuberculosis, childbed fever, venereal disease, and respiratory infections climbed and stayed high. Doctors were few and expensive; folk remedies and charlatanry were relied on. The white visitors who taxied to Harlem to listen to jazz at the Cotton Club neither saw nor wanted to see this Harlem. They wanted to see the black as an exotic, who could laugh and dance spontaneously in a land "flowing with Socony and Bryan and pristine Rotary purity." If they sensed black agony, they made it part of a fashionable Negrophilia. Carl Van Vechten, author of a best-selling 1926 novel, *Nigger Heaven,* wrote that the "squalor of Negro life, the vice of Negro life, offer a wealth of . . . picturesque materials to the artist." That had a familiar ring: the Noble Savage now lived in a tenement instead of a jungle.

But the squalor of black life was scarcely "picturesque" to those who endured it. They sought everywhere for escape. A few turned to political radicalism; more to red-hot religion—Christianity melted in the crucible of memory and pain. Sometimes they pursued the anodyne of hope by gambling on a "hit" in the numbers game. Sometimes they clutched the transient solace of liquor or drugs. Each night the squeals and swoops of jazz mingled with the exhortations of preachers in store-front churches, while the pushers and the whores and the gamblers—black themselves—separated other blacks from what cash the grocer and landlord had left them.

And, slowly, many of the children whose parents had moved north to give them a second chance died spiritually. Small dark wraiths wandered the streets with keys on strings around their necks, while fathers who had given up the fight drifted, somewhere, and mothers scrubbed kitchens in white people's homes. Those black youngsters who made it to school were bowed by psychological burdens that few white teachers understood. If they were recent "immigrants," they also suffered from the inadequacy of Southern preparation.

Despite the glamor of the "Harlem Renaissance," the nation's best-known black community had become by 1930 what it would remain for fifty years at least—a place of enmity between police officer and community, where many local business people were outsiders and enemies. It was a pit of dilapidation and fury, often turned inward by blacks to become self-destruction, a center of narcotics traffic and crime. The crash and the Depression

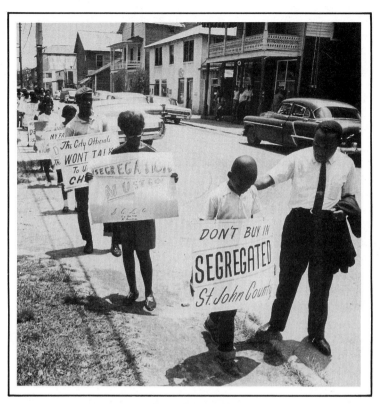

Dr. Martin Luther King gives a boy a pat on the back as a group of young people picket against segregation in St. Augustine, Florida, on June 10, 1964. "For years now, I have heard the word, 'Wait!,'" King once said. "When you are forever fighting a degenerating sense of 'nobodiness'—then you will understand why we find it difficult to wait." *(Wide World)*

merely sealed its fate. For blacks the hard times had started early. As Langston Hughes put it, "The Depression brought everybody down a peg or two. And the Negroes had but few pegs to fall."

Behind the immediate crisis of black poverty lay a question that ran deeper. Newly urbanized blacks raised as sharecroppers faced the same problem as their grandparents just out of slavery. How could they take a comfortable and dignified place in a rejecting society? Would the task require that they transform themselves? If so, what would be the cost, if any, to their sense of identity? These were questions that every immigrant group faced, but the issues were bitterly complicated for blacks not only by the unchangeable fact of their color but also by the passionate intensity of the feelings that race provoked. Could any metamorphosis of black life take place without massive white help, and would that help be encumbered by impossible reservations and conditions? Was it worth it? Would any such improvement really overcome white fears and open the way to a livable common future for both races in America?

Thinking blacks weighed such questions, and their answers took either of two general directions. One was toward black separatism, and in Harlem in the 1920s, separatism raised up a prophet in the stout figure of Marcus Garvey. Born in the West Indies in 1887, he had been trained in youth as a printer, a trade congenial to the upsetters of applecarts long before Benjamin Franklin's time. He drifted around the Caribbean and then to London, where he met rebellious "colored" students from various parts of the British Empire. Back in Jamaica, Garvey founded the Universal Negro Improvement and Conservation Association and African Communities League. There was a steady, economically motivated West Indian migration to the United States, and in 1916 he joined it. In Harlem he founded a paper, the *Negro World,* to bring redemption to his people.

Garvey was the first to take up the cause that black is beautiful. "Up, you mighty race!" *Negro World* exhorted. "You can accomplish what you will." And Garvey also told them: "When Europe was inhabited by a race of cannibals, a race of savages, naked men, heathens and pagans, Africa was peopled with a race of cultured black men, who were masters in arts, science and literature, men who were cultured and refined; men who, it was said, were like the gods."

By 1919 the black community was more than ready for his message. In that so-called Red Summer, as the pressure of the black migration increased and black servicemen returned from France more impatient than ever with the old ways, race riots tore half a dozen cities. In Washington, troops had to be called out. In Chicago, street fighting lasted more than a week, leaving twenty-two blacks and sixteen whites dead, and five hundred injured. Black emotions surged high, and Garvey fed some of their needs with pageants. He decked himself in gaudy uniforms. He devised a flag—a black star on a red and green background: black for the race, red for its blood, green for its hopes. He collected, mostly from the poor, ten million dollars for a Back to Africa movement. Blacks who were working toward improving conditions in America, such as the fiery union leader A. Philip Randolph of the Pullman Car Porters, denounced Garvey as a fool and a fraud, but Garvey stirred a pot that still boils. His organization founded a Black Star Line of ships to carry the pilgrims back to the homeland, as well as a Negro Factories Corporation, an African Orthodox Church and Court of Ethiopia, a Universal Black Cross Nurses association, a Black Eagle Flying Corps, an African Legion. None of this got beyond the paper stage except for the Black Star Line, whose first ship nearly sank off Newport News on its maiden voyage. Yet despite white snickers, this was much more than minstrel-show foolery. National flags and national histories and institutions and insignia were part of the paraphernalia that buttressed white self-confidence. For blacks they had to be rediscovered and even invented.

Garvey distrusted integrationists and mulattoes (whom he called "hybrids of the Negro race"), and he was even baited into kind words about Klansmen for their comparative "honesty" about racial feelings. Conservative blacks believed he was milking the community for his own aggrandizement. In time, leading Harlemites took up the slogan Garvey Must Go. Finally, Garvey went—in shackles—to a federal penitentiary on a charge of using the mails to defraud. In 1927 he was pardoned and deported to Jamaica; he died in London in 1940.

Was Garvey a charlatan and a false Messiah? Many blacks came to believe that he was a groundbreaker for the militants of the 1960s who demanded black economic self-sufficiency, black control of black institutions, black pride, black power. In any case, Garveyism was moribund by 1930. At that point, the curtain rose on a period of some thirty-five years during which black Americans appeared to take the alternative road, away from black isolation. They used a combination of legal argument, moral suasion, economic pressure, and political influence to quicken white America's conscience. They walked the path of coalition and integration.

The compass needle of black policy swung in that direction as a result of historic paradox. The Democratic Party, ancient bastion of Southern segregationism, became the sponsor of the New Deal, whose programs for public relief, employment, and housing did not discriminate. The federal government under Franklin Roosevelt did not bring blacks into the Promised Land, but it did feed them some manna in the wilderness. In 1933 more than 2 million blacks were receiving some form of public aid. In 1935 the figure ran to 3.5 million. About a third of the 120,000 dwelling units built by the United States Housing Administration up to 1941 were for blacks. Ten percent of the Civilian Conservation Corps' youthful membership was black. The Works Progress Administration (WPA) had a marked effect on black employment rates.

So the black was swept into the New Deal coalition, along with white farmers, workers, homeowners, and small-business owners, and gave thanks at the voting machine for AAA, TVA, homeowners' loans, bank-deposit insurance, Social Security, and the Wagner Labor Relations Act. Then World War II and postwar prosperity opened economic doors wider. Between 1940 and 1950 the number of black males in nonfarm labor went from 1.8 million to 2.8 million; ten years later it had risen to more than 3.5 million. In those twenty years the number of blacks in white-collar occupations rose from 149,000 to more than half a million, in skilled workers' and foremen's slots from 130,000 to 407,000. In 1950 only 0.3 percent of black families earned more than $6,000 a year. By 1960 that had risen to 13.9 percent. In 1940, 4.5 percent of blacks finished high school and 1.3 percent completed college. Twenty years later those percentages had nearly tripled. Blacks might see some of these figures—legitimately—as puny, but forward movement was visible.

Meanwhile, legal and political victories made the headlines—integration of the armed forces during and after the Korean War, the Supreme Court's school-desegregation decision of 1954, the bus boycotts and the lunch-counter sit-ins and the freedom rides of the 1950s and 1960s, the breaking of a Senate filibuster to pass the Federal Civil Rights Act of 1964, and the historic Voting Rights Act as a legislative climax in 1965. The continued shift of blacks to the cities began to produce, in the customary way of immigrant groups, black faces in city government. In seven of the twelve most populous cities in the United States in 1960, blacks formed more than twenty percent of the population. After 1962 five such cities were sending black Congressmen and -women—all Democrats—to Washington. In the mid-1960s, one black, Robert Weaver, was appointed Secretary of Housing and Urban Development, and another, Thurgood Marshall, was named to a Supreme Court seat. Black voting strength was receiving traditional forms of recognition.

Yet by that time the picture was not at all rosy. Blacks had made definite gains in an absolute sense, but relatively they were well behind the rest of the society. A white youngster was much more likely to go to college than a black. Black professional, managerial, and clerical workers had median incomes of $3,700 in 1965, with a figure of $5,400 for comparable whites. Only one black high-school graduate in three landed a skilled or white-collar job, while two out of three white graduates did. The likelihood that a white college graduate would become a manager or an official or a proprietor was three times greater than it was for a college-educated black. And at the base of the economic pyramid black unemployment, especially among young males, always far exceeded that of whites—as it still does today. Civil rights or no civil rights, it was still Depression time for millions of black Americans.

The black person, in short, was getting a smaller slice of a growing pie. The frustration of the black masses seemed to melt very slowly in the intermittent sunshine of white "benevolence." Impatience fed on aroused expectations. "It is precisely because this is a period of high mobility that it is a period of high tension," said historian Oscar Handlin.

Heartsick blacks were reaching a crossroad. At best, integration had a faint suggestion that for blacks redemption could be found only by a change of skin. "Nobody demanded of the Irish, Italians or Jews," said Handlin, ". . . that they become a vanishing element." So once more the appeal of separation was sounded in the streets, by Black Muslims and Black Panthers. Yet it was hard to know if a black community that isolated itself from the major tides of surrounding American society would fare any better psychologically or economically than it had in the "integrated," underdog role.

In a sense the situation presented separate problems for blacks and whites; blacks had to achieve some unity to develop a solution to their dilemma, and whites had to make their accommodation to the undying reality of black aspiration. Yet it was also a crisis for the nation as a whole, and it was, once again, an ethnic conflict presenting a familiar pattern. The union workers, the low-income homeowners on the margins of the black inner cities, the people who would literally have to move over to make room for oncoming blacks, were by and large of recent immigrant stock. They were now the "native Americans," confronting the barbarians at the gate. Many of them felt resentful. They were asked to bear, in taxes, a burden of reparation for an original sin—enslavement—that was not of their making. They were asked to commit their children to a new order that, even if they were being unreasonable, they desperately feared. They were asked to rework their values on behalf of people who appeared to lag far behind them in the cleanly and parsimonious virtues of good Americanism—and people moreover that they disliked as if by instinct and who were now sufficiently self-aware to return the dislike openly. In many ways, particularly economically, these whites were closer as a class to poor blacks than they were to the affluent liberals who preached racial equality at them; this seemed only to deepen their sense of betrayal.

It had happened before. But the circumstances were more dangerous in 1970 than they had been in 1910. There was a steadily contracting market for unskilled labor, little room for growth within the major cities, a huge public budget that kept much of the individual's surplus revenue from being used in entrepreneurial activities. In short, there was no frontier—literally, less room for maneuver and, it seemed, less time to maneuver in. There seemed to be no consensus of social values to which newcomer and old-timer could both conform. It was a violent, anxious era. The nation was fused in a way by mass media but not cohesive in beliefs—performers and audience, not a community. The prospects seemed ominous.

254

Yet despair is always slow to see the first edge of sunlight on the morning horizon. Solving the dilemmas of human diversity had been a task the American people had met reasonably well during a long period of unrestricted immigration. There was no reason to think that the assets the nation then had brought to the work had somehow disappeared. The restrictionists of the 1920s had been foolish to believe that by barring the doors they would solve the problems brought on by ethnic variety. It might be equally foolish for crowded America a half century later to believe that the problems could not be solved at all.

XI
Brain Drain

The rise of Nazism in Europe forced one of history's most creative intellects, Albert Einstein, and countless other talented foreigners to flee to America. *(Zionist Archives)*

In the 1930s Walter W. S. Cook, then director of New York University's Institute of Fine Arts, delivered an apparently insane judgment: "Hitler is my best friend." Before his listeners could explode, Cook added: "He shakes the tree, and I collect the apples," meaning that the institute had grown into an important center of art studies, thanks to the work of European refugee scholars. In that respect Hitler was all America's "friend." First the movement that brought him to power and then his regime uprooted tens of thousands of Europe's best thinkers and forced them to flee and serve the brainpower needs of other countries, notably the United States. It was a mistake made by other totalitarian governments. Laura Fermi, wife of a Nobel Prize-winning physicist who left Mussolini's Italy, compared the 1930s to "the fifteenth century, when the learned men of the dying Byzantine empire, fleeing from the barbarian invasion, sowed seeds of the old Hellenistic culture in European centers."

On a May morning in 1933 England's *Manchester Guardian Weekly* ran a story headlined NAZI 'PURGE' OF THE UNIVERSITIES. More than three columns of small type listed dismissals of professors between April 13 and May 4, including such luminaries as the philosopher and theologian Paul Tillich, the artist Paul Klee, and Fritz Haber, a chemist and inventor of the synthetic-ammonia manufacturing process on which Germany had depended for nitrates to produce explosives in the First World War. By April of 1936 more than sixteen hundred persons had been fired from universities and scientific institutions. They were a *Who's Who* of German intellect. They included Jews, Socialists, and a variety of hard-to-herd intellectuals. Some were migrants to Germany from other European countries. Some were among the artists and the thinkers who had given Germany's postwar Weimar Republic an outstanding cultural life, and so many were promising scientists that the Hungarian-born mathematician John Von Neumann wrote to a friend, speaking of the Nazis, that "if these boys continue for only two more years ... they will ruin German science for a generation—at least." Self-mutilation was one of Joseph Paul Goebbels's first gifts to the homeland.

British intellectuals, at the onset of Nazism, in 1933, had quickly created an Academic Assistance Council to try to place some of the ousted scholars in university posts. On the American side of the Atlantic, a similar organization, the Emergency Committee in Aid of Displaced German [later Foreign] Scholars, was founded by Stephen Duggan, then director of the Institute of International Education.

One of the Emergency Committee's wheelhorses was a scholar-journalist then nearly sixty years of age, a friend of Duggan's named Alvin Saunders Johnson. Johnson was a Westerner, born in 1874 to Danish settlers in northeastern Nebraska. As a boy he had more or less taught himself Greek and Latin. He had planned to be a doctor, but the grind of memorizing muscle names and doing laboratory work was not enough food for his restless spirit. Johnson quit college to fight in the Spanish-American War, then settled down to graduate study in economics. He took his doctorate at Columbia University in 1901.

For sixteen years he lived the peripatetic life of a professor— Bryn Mawr, Columbia, Nebraska, Cornell, Chicago, Stanford—while writing crisply and successfully on a variety of public issues. He became an editor of *The New Republic* in 1917 and of the *Encyclopedia of the Social Sciences* in the 1920s, when he was also appointed director of New York's New School for Social Research, which specialized in offering advanced study to adults. In 1933 he was intellectually alive, tough, adventurous, and full of a prairie individualist's anger at any kind of forced orthodoxy. His reaction to reading the list of dismissed German professors was that it contained "the names of nearly all the social scientists who had any creative spirit in them."

Quickly, Johnson emerged as a major formulator of plans for bringing these creative spirits to America. He had more than a touch of the academic impresario about him and delighted in assembling a star array of minds. His first impulse was to bid for a single refugee economist, but that gave way to a much more ambitious idea. In the United States it was easier to get money for a large project than for a small one. On April 24, 1933, Johnson wrote to a number of friends, proposing to hire fifteen men for two years at $4,000 a year each and assign them as graduate faculty at the New School. He would call them the University in Exile. "I want to make what return I can," he said "for liberties I have enjoyed." A benefactor, Hiram Halle, offered to guarantee the required funds for two years, and Johnson was promptly off to London to assemble his faculty. By the beginning of summer they were "arriving ship by ship," and he was meeting them at the gangplank. Meanwhile he continued his labors with the Emergency Committee in Aid of Displaced Foreign Scholars. Working with him were Walter Cook of N.Y.U.'s Institute of Fine Arts and Abraham Flexner, head of Princeton's new Institute for Advanced Study. As the 1930s—and Nazism—advanced, Johnson, Cook, and Flexner with a number of museum directors, major librarians, and university presidents rescued group after group of scholars, scientists, artists, writers, and musicians from under the shadow of the swastika as it fell over Austria, Czechoslovakia, Poland, Norway, Denmark, Holland, Belgium, and France. Committees and conferences proliferated to handle the flow of refugees—not only academics but those from every walk of life. The Joint Distribution Committee, the National Council of Jewish Women, the American Friends Service Committee, the Hebrew Sheltering and Immigrant Aid Society, the War Relief Services of the National Catholic Welfare Conference, and the Emergency Committee in Aid of Foreign Physicians were a few of the names on a lengthy roster of such agencies. Their inevitable overlaps and conflicts were partially harmonized by a National Coordinating Committee, ultimately called the United Service for New Americans.

Of all the organizations for dealing with refugees, perhaps none had annals so full of dramas as those of the Emergency Rescue Committee, created in 1940 to face the situation brought about when the Germans subjugated France in six weeks.

One condition of the Franco-German armistice was that the Vichy government surrender on demand all antifascist refugees wanted by the Gestapo. Thousands of Hitler's enemies, chased from all parts of Central Europe, had found a temporary haven in France. The speed of her collapse now trapped them. The Emergency Rescue Committee was formed to save as many of them as possible.

The committee soon learned from contacts in the German underground that it would need an agent in Marseilles. The man whom the directors named to the job was Varian Fry, a young scholar and an editor of the Foreign Policy Association. Fry had a month's vacation due him. He agreed, at the committee's urging, to spend it in France organizing rescue work under the cover of operating a Centre Américain de Secours, a free food-distribution center for needy refugees.

Varian Fry's one month stretched into thirteen, each as taut as any spy-novel aficionado could wish. He and his assistants first had to locate those on the Nazi "wanted" list. Many were in hiding; rescue teams had to find them. Some were in French detention camps; their releases had to be secured. Finally, they had to be smuggled to the coast and onto outgoing ships. The academically oriented Fry became adept at dealing with the grubby underworld of a Mediterranean port—where he found, for example, forgers of passports and visas; he learned to trace men living under aliases in cheap hotels, to bluster and lie to Vichy bureaucrats.

Fry and his associates were tailed, spied on, raided by the police, and harassed by Marshal Henri Pétain's collaborationist government. But they had the help of other agencies such as the American Friends Service Committee and the Unitarian Service Committee. Before Fry was expelled by the Vichy government, in September of 1941, he had aided in almost fifteen hundred departures. A successor added another three hundred before the committee ended its French operation in June 1942.

Not all the escapees went to the United States. Yet Fry's work must have made an impression, even beyond the *Scarlet Pimpernel* heroics of the mission. Hans Sahl, a refugee writer, put it in moving terms. Sahl had been in concentration camps, been marched out of Paris to southern France, ducked Nazi bombs and strafings, been in jail for a while in Marseilles and then let out, but believed that he was at a dead end there. Sitting despondently in a café, he was approached by someone who whispered the name of a Mr. Fry, Hôtel Splendide. Sahl went there. He wrote:

> Imagine the situation: the borders closed; you are caught in a trap, might be arrested again at any moment; life is as good as over—and suddenly a young American in shirt sleeves is stuffing your pockets full of money, putting his arm around your shoulders, and whispering with the conspiratorial expression of a ham actor: "Oh there are ways to get you out of here," while, damn it all, the tears were streaming down my face, actual tears, big, round, and wet; and that pleasant fellow ... takes a silk handkerchief from his jacket and says: "Here, have this. Sorry it isn't cleaner." You know, since that day I have loved America.

For the United States those years of Hitlerism marked new beginnings in immigration policy. Nineteen thirty-three was only the fourth year after the national-origins quota system had gone into full effect. Almost from the start, events had a more powerful effect on the actual flow of immigrants than the fine print in the lawbooks. As soon as the Depression set in, immigration dwindled. There was, therefore, a chance to see what actually happened when virtually no immigrants were arriving—to think afresh about laws whose basic pattern had been set in the martial atmosphere of 1917 and the "Red scare" of 1919–21. The arrival of the European refugees spurred further reflections on what a truly wise and modern immigration-control policy should be.

The refugees were far different in number and kind from the peasants and villagers of the earlier waves at the beginning of the century. Not even determined disparagers, for one thing, could describe them as "hordes." Less than half the 580,000 visas issued to persons from Germany and German-held areas between 1933 and 1943 were actually used to come to the United States. Immigration to America *from all countries* in that period was 528,549. Less than seventeen percent of the total European quota was taken up, and only in 1939 and 1940 was the generous German quota near full utilization. Moreover, an extraordinary percentage of the more than a quarter million refugees consisted of professionals and self-employed men who had had from eight to fourteen years of education. They were cosmopolites and heads of families, multilingual and cultivated—the kind of successful people who in America would be found at PTA meetings, in political caucuses, and on the advisory committees of churches and charity drives. They were inclined to remain in cities, where openings for them were comparatively plentiful, and surprising numbers (after the fumbling confusion of readjustment) found their way back into their fields of specialization.

Maurice R. Davie, director of the study *Refugees in America,* recorded that managers, bankers, architects, and lawyers had hard times in finding jobs like those they had left. But eventually more than three fourths of the chemists, dentists, and physicians surveyed reentered their professions. So did some seventy-two percent of the clergymen, sixty-eight percent of the musicians, sixty-one percent of the professors and teachers, and fifty-five percent of the engineers. In Davie's sample of more than eleven thousand refugees, about half the artists and a third of the writers were back at their old occupations by 1944. The same was true of about two thirds of those described as "skilled workers." Often there was an upward climb in the best American Horatio Alger rhythm. A bookkeeper might begin as a stock clerk and, as he acquired English, get back into his calling. A female dressmaker might "graduate" from domestic service to a sales job as she mastered the new tongue, and from there return to couture. Hundreds of refugee scholars were placed in colleges and universities scattered throughout the country. Interesting things happened in small college towns— where, outside of the faculty, sophistication usually reached its peak in *vin rosé* for dinner and the "1812 Overture" at a band concert and where intellectuals were generally regarded as "men who wouldn't be able to make a living if they didn't find someone willing to pay them for talking." Authentic philosophers, musicians, and scientists, speaking the language of Kant and Beethoven and Roentgen, appeared at grocery stores and garages, still wearing clothes tailored in Berlin or shoes made in Munich. They inevitably made friends and learned their way around. At Winston-Salem and at Erskine and at the University of Kansas City aristocratic European males learned to play (or at least to watch) softball, while their wives taught white neighbors and black cooks the secret of thin strudel dough and, in turn, were initiated into corn bread.

Not all encounters of native and alien were warm. Some refugees were stiff-necked and demanding and had a hard time suppressing an ingrained contempt for America. Some American professionals consistently depreciated their European colleagues. Yet the fugitives remained and, as had so often happened before, adjusted to the American scene. By 1970 their children were grown and their grandchildren doubtless found the story of the 1930s as remote as tales of the potato famine must have been to the youngest Kennedys.

Thousands of men and women in the refugee migration were ordinary souls. But there were among them some truly outstanding figures: in music and the musical arts, Darius Milhaud, Béla Bartók, Arnold Schönberg, Igor Stravinsky, Bruno Walter, Otto Klemperer, George Szell, and Lotte Lenya; in art and art history, Willem de Kooning, Paul Klee, Erwin J. Panofsky, Mar-

When Enrico Fermi, here receiving the Nobel
Prize in 1938, realized that he could no longer
remain in his native Italy, he let a hint drop to
four American universities that he would be
willing to accept an invitation; he received re-
plies from five. In 1942 he produced history's
first self-sustaining nuclear chain reaction. The
coded telegram to Washington read, "The Italian
navigator has just entered the new world."
(Agence France-Presse)

cel Duchamp, Marc Chagall, George Grosz, and Vasili Kandinski; in architecture, Ludwig Mies van der Rohe and Walter Gropius; in literature, Heinrich and Thomas Mann, Bertolt Brecht, Stefan Zweig; in philosophy, history, music, and the social sciences, Ernst Cassirer, Werner Jaeger, Joseph Schumpeter, Hannah Arendt, Hans J. Morgenthau.

In the sciences, and particularly in the field of psychoanalysis, the honor roll would run to vast length, its names recognized primarily by specialists. But one story of émigré scientists is of absolutely overpowering significance. Essentially it was a handful of refugee physicists who gave to the United States the tip-off to the possibility of the atomic bomb and who thereby started the nation on the road to Hiroshima.

European physicists had been drifting to the United States for nearly a decade before World War II. Some were in flight from dictators; some, trained by Europe's outstanding theoreticians, needed to use the high-powered and high-priced experimental machinery available here. In the United States at the beginning of 1939 were Russia's George Gamow; the German Hans A. Bethe; three Hungarians, Edward Teller, Leo Szilard, and Eugene P. Wigner; and the Roman-born Enrico Fermi, who by then already had a Nobel Prize. They had come to stay. The American physicist J. Robert Oppenheimer later recalled that "they were all very good and yet wonderfully adaptable ... they genuinely came to this country not as a temporary and resented alternative but as something that could be lived with and enjoyed."

In January 1939 the Danish physicist Niels Bohr, on a visit to New York, sat down for a round of professional gossip with his friend Fermi, then at Columbia. Among his bits of news was an account of an experiment by two German scientists who had bombarded uranium with neutrons—the noncharged particles in the nucleus of the atom—and produced a lighter element, barium. Bohr's information came from one of the Germans' former associates, Lise Meitner, who was brilliant but Jewish and therefore in exile in Sweden. She interpreted the result to mean that the neutrons had actually split the unstable uranium atom to produce the barium, with its different atomic weight.

Fermi drew the same conclusion and was thunderstruck. If such a reaction had taken place, he reasoned, then the tremendous energy binding the particles of the nucleus together had been liberated. And if, in this "nuclear fission," additional neutrons were released to split other atoms, liberating more neutrons to split still more atoms, a chain reaction could result that would free incredible amounts of energy. In harness it could perform prodigious work—or create devastating explosives. Fermi quickly revealed his apprehensions to scientific friends, including Leo Szilard, who was between teaching appointments and was visiting with Wigner at Princeton.

Szilard, too, was alarmed. In Berlin, in 1933, he had kept two bags packed in his living quarters, and within a few weeks of Hitler's accession to power, he had picked them up and fled first to Austria, then to England. Szilard and Fermi, though differing on many matters, were both haunted by what Laura Fermi described as "this vision of Hitler with an atomic bomb in his hand." Szilard joined Fermi at Columbia University (without benefit of an academic appointment) to study the theoretical foundations and possibilities of chain reactions. By the summer of 1939 Frédéric Joliot-Curie was already on the trail in France; German physicists—even those certified one hundred percent pure by the Nazis—would not be far behind. Hitler now held the uranium mines of Czechoslovakia and had just forbidden exports of the material. Did he know something?

Fermi was away for the summer. Szilard and Wigner, worrying at their problem, suddenly devised a plan. The world's most distinguished refugee scientist, Albert Einstein, who came to the United States in 1933 and had been a member of the Institute for Advanced Study since that year, was much admired by the dowager Queen Elisabeth of the Belgians. The Belgian Congo had large deposits of uranium. Perhaps he could write to her, warning of the danger of letting uranium fall into Nazi hands. Impulsively the two scientists jumped into Wigner's car and drove out to Peconic, Long Island, where Einstein was vacationing in the cottage of a friend. Once on the rural roads around Peconic, they realized that they had no idea of the cottage's exact location. It was fortunate that Albert Einstein's sunburst of white hair and swoop of moustache were unforgettable. Wigner and Szilard spied a boy alongside the road and asked if he knew where Dr. Einstein lived. They immediately got directions.

Einstein was willing to cooperate; he fully understood the possible horror. But there was still the problem of arousing the United States. Szilard took it to an influential friend, Alexander Sachs, an economist with the Lehman Brothers banking firm.

Sachs had access to President Roosevelt through his Lehman connections (it was Herbert H. Lehman who succeeded Roosevelt as New York's Democratic governor); he promptly advised Szilard to forget the Belgian Queen. If Einstein would sign his prestigious name to a letter explaining the peril, Sachs would deliver it personally to the President. So, after a drafting conference (which by now included Edward Teller), the letter was prepared. It described the concept of nuclear energy's release and warned that it could lead to the manufacture of bombs so powerful that a single one, "exploded in a port, might very well destroy the whole port together with some of the surrounding territory." The President was asked to take steps to secure a uranium supply for the United States and money for further experimentation.

The immediate action initiated by the letter was minimal. An Advisory Committee on Uranium was appointed, and the tiny sum of six thousand dollars was allotted for research. Not until 1940 was the pace accelerated appreciably; not until after Pearl Harbor was the basic decision taken to proceed with the bomb and the financing provided to enter the race in earnest.

In the end, there really was no race. The Germans had not worked intensively on nuclear explosives. Hitler died in his bunker while the atomic bomb was still two and a half months away from its first test at Alamogordo, New Mexico. Japan endured the fury of the bomb in August 1945, by which time some of the weapon's fathers were regretting their work and trying to persuade the United States to forgo its use and further development. But they had, in Oppenheimer's brilliant phrase, "known sin," and the consequences were to be as inexorable as when Adam made the same mistake. Yet they had begun with the intention of sparing mankind horror, through trusting the United States with their knowledge. It was in a way their repayment to the land of their liberation.

Pearl Harbor opened a period of nearly four years when practically all transoceanic travelers wore uniforms. Yet new developments were in the making. The war, which allied us with one Asian nation and against another, led to contradictory steps on the home front. On the one hand, there was a savage anti-Oriental outburst when, early in 1942, approximately 112,000 Japanese-Americans from the West Coast were summarily hustled into bleak, remote "relocation centers" that were, in fact, prison camps. Those born in the United States as well as those born abroad were uprooted and detained, sometimes for years before release. The excuse was that the government had to protect California against spies and saboteurs in the event of a Japanese naval attack, yet Americans of German and Italian extraction were not treated in the same way—confined wholesale merely on the basis of race. But the American tradition of civil liberties was always wobbly where nonwhites were concerned.

In the next year, Congress opened a door that had been slammed shut by the Chinese Exclusion Acts. But just a crack. Sending Americans to fight alongside "yellow" people who were not allowed to enter the United States was an incongruity obvious even to West Coast legislators, and Representative Warren G. Magnuson of Washington State sponsored a repeal bill. But the act scarcely spread open arms to the Chinese. It gave them an annual quota of 105—105 members of "the Chinese race" from the entire world. Moreover, it reserved half of the entry visas for those with skills needed in the United States. Still, it was a first step; and later the Chinese, like other nationalities, were allowed to take advantage of various ways of getting around the official quotas, so that between 1944 and 1965 the total number of Chinese entering the United States was 52,959. One such method was embodied in the War Brides Act of 1945, under which Congress allowed returned soldiers who had married foreign women to bring their wives and children into the country without regard to quotas. More than 5,000 Chinese women and infants entered in this way—as did 9,046 brides and babies from Italy, 14,175 from Germany, and 36,390 from the United Kingdom.

The commonsense compassion that permitted overseas wartime romances to continue happily ever after in the United States was also one reason for the Displaced Persons Act of 1948. Refugees were a problem of the entire world community, and the United Nations took responsibility for feeding, sheltering, and otherwise caring for millions of homeless and jobless families. But three years after the war, the problem was still acute. It was clear that the unscarred and wealthy United States should fulfill its United Nations obligations in this situation not only with cash—which it had been doing—but with refuge.

The response of Congress was something less than wholehearted. It authorized a four-year quota credit plan to accommodate the overflow of visa-seeking applicants. During that period a country could "borrow" extra visas and later "repay" the loan by accepting reductions of up to half its future quotas. In this way enormous waiting lists of applicants (773,465 long in 1951) were pared down. Of course the greatest need was precisely in devastated Eastern Europe, against which the national-origins policy had been aimed in the first place. War-torn Poland had an annual quota of only 6,524. Because of the many thousands of Poles admitted during the life of the Displaced Persons Act, subsequent Polish quotas were diminished by half and would remain at half quota until the year 2000. Tiny Latvia, with a quota of 236, had been in the track of both Soviet and Nazi armies. Its half-quota mortgage was supposed to run until the year 2274. But it had been swallowed up by the Soviet Union, and American consuls simply charged visas issued to its nationals against its hypothetical account. These "mortgages" became irrelevant in 1965, when a change in the law abolished the national-origins quota system. In hindsight, these bookkeeping devices, in which the columns represented suffering human beings, were simple-minded and repugnant. Even so, some 400,000 refugees were taken into the United States under the law—a rescue that drew heroic efforts from American assistance agencies, which had to find jobs and housing for the immigrants before entries could be authorized. Congress measured out its hospitality by the teaspoon.

The game of quota stretching continued beyond 1952. Special enactments measured the spread of global disaster, natural and artificial. In 1953—the year of an unsuccessful East German uprising against the Russians and four years after the Communist triumph in China—a Refugee Relief Act authorized the issuance, beyond quotas, of 205,000 temporary visas to "refugees, escapees, and expellees." It was expected that the "temporary" visa period would probably never be terminated while the immigrant was on his good behavior. In effect, he was on parole and was sometimes even referred to as a "parolee."

In 1957 and 1958 two new acts allowed provisional entry to about 39,000 of the nearly 179,000 people who fled Hungary after the failure of the October 1956 revolt against the Stalinist government in Budapest. Still other legislation between 1958 and 1962 opened the doors to victims of earthquakes in the Azores; to Dutch settlers dislocated by purges of "colonialists" following Indonesia's independence; to 15,000 Greek, Italian, Japanese, and Korean orphans adopted by Americans; and to 15,000 fugitives from Communist China who had been crammed into British Hong Kong. There was also the matter of the hundreds of thousands of Cubans who had left Castro's island by 1965. As Western Hemisphere immigrants they were not restricted by quotas, but special bills committed the Federal government to help with their transportation and resettlement in the United States.

Total immigration did not rise spectacularly in the first two decades after the war. The publicity given to some over-subscribed quotas obscured the fact that many countries, such as England, were not utilizing theirs to anywhere near the full. Between 1945 and 1965 some 4,800,000 immigrants, all told, were admitted. The biggest single year was 1957, with 326,867. The total number for the period 1951–60 was 2,515,479; excluding the 1940s, when the world was at war, that was the smallest decade's ingathering since the 1860s.

Nevertheless, the old fear of inundating hordes existed throughout that period, and it certainly underlay the McCarran-Walter Immigration and Nationality Act of 1952. There was indeed a need for an overhaul of the patched and red-taped immigration system, but it was unfortunate that the overhaul should be done in the middle of one of the periodic national fits of xenophobic anxiety. The McCarran-Walter measure was not only intended as a tightening and unifying of legislation; it was aimed at insulating the United States from the dangers of the post-1945 revolutions in world order.

The national-origins quotas were preserved at the old levels. Countries in the Asia-Pacific triangle did receive small quotas, but all persons with even one Asian parent, no matter where they were born or lived, went on an Asian quota. (A Cambodian's son, for example, might have been born in Paris and gone to school there and never left; still, if he chose to resettle in the United States he was not counted on the French annual quota of more than three thousand but rather against Cambodia's one hundred.) Further, whereas immigration from all Western Hemisphere countries had in the past always been free, now colonial dependencies in the Western Hemisphere were given subquotas of their "parent" nations. The effect was to curtail the immigra-

These Hungarian refugees posed for this photograph after disembarking at McGuire Air Force Base, in New Jersey. Restrictive immigration laws provided visas immediately for only five thousand of the Hungarians who fled their country following the ill-fated revolution in 1956. But President Eisenhower intervened and issued invitations to thirty thousand others, who were thus able to enter as provisional immigrants. *(Wide World)*

tion of nonwhite people from such places as the British West Indies. The law was also loaded with harassments for aliens who were suspected subversives. There would be a series of inquiries. Did the alien have a criminal record? That might even mean a record incurred by resistance to a dictator's police or by some childhood misdemeanor long forgotten. Had the alien ever been a member of a Communist party? It did not matter that such membership was virtually obligatory in some Iron Curtain countries: a Communist is a Communist is a Communist. If all these barriers were overcome and the alien was admitted, he or she might still be deported virtually without a hearing if deemed by the U.S. Attorney General to be engaged in activities "prejudicial to the public interest." (The Alien Act, in 1798, had contained a similar provision, but the phrasing was "dangerous to the peace and safety of the United States.") Even foreign-born persons who had achieved citizenship were vulnerable to this arbitrary denaturalization.

The McCarran-Walter bill also proposed the creation of a Congressional Committee on Immigration and Naturalization Policy, which was to keep a suspicious eye on the State and Justice departments to make sure that the Executive branch was sufficiently zealous in enforcement of the law. This provision in particular was a clear challenge to the White House, whose occupant, Harry Truman, was no man to let a flung gauntlet lie at his feet. He vetoed the bill on June 25, 1952, with a message that denounced the national-origins idea as "utterly unworthy of our traditions and our ideals.... It repudiates our basic religious concepts, our belief in the brotherhood of man.... It is a slur on the patriotism, the capacity and the decency of a large part of our citizenry."

Senator Pat McCarran of Nevada, a vigorous conservative who was the bill's public defender as well as its cosponsor, had his way as Congress quickly overrode the veto. But the long-run tide was against the McCarran principles. His measure would stand up for only thirteen years.

Consider what had happened since the passage of the Johnson-Reed Act, which had closed the doors in 1924. The German "Aryan" racial-superiority myth had been blasted by a war; that put American exponents of race superiority on the defensive. Furthermore, the high economic and intellectual quality of the refugees of that war suggested that some immigrants could be as valuable as gold to a nation and that national-origins quotas that took no account of special skills and talents demonstrated not only poor ethics but poor sense. This became increasingly a factor as the age turned to nuclear and jet power, transistors, computers, rockets, satellites, wonder drugs, and miracle synthetics. Advanced industrial nations found that they needed now not just muscle power but alert, trained minds to program, to devise, to measure. A talent hunt swept the world's laboratories, and rich America started with a big advantage.

Simultaneously a black, brown, and yellow Third World emerged from the wreckage of Europe's Asian and African empires and was wooed by Soviet and American foreign offices. This diplomatic courtship helped further to undercut racist thought in the United States. The concepts of Anglo-Saxon or Northern European "superiority," so firmly lodged in 1910, were almost entirely discarded by the educated community of half a century later. Gradually, therefore, America's immigration laws were reworked.

A Truman-appointed immigration study commission dug zestfully into the national statistics. Between 1924 and 1951, while the total population went from 114 million to 154 million, the gross national product of the United States had soared from $140 billion to $329 billion, based on the value of the dollar in 1951. The labor force had increased from 41.2 million in 1920 to 66 million in 1951. More hands and minds than ever were required on the production line. In the nation's first modern industrial boom, from 1880 to 1920, the labor pool had been fed by the massive European migrations. In the quarter century after the restriction act of 1924, the slack in the labor market had been taken up by rural migration to the cities and by nonquota Western Hemisphere immigration. When these streams failed to fill certain needs for manpower, temporary immigration programs had been set up. For example, in wartime 135,283 Mexican nationals had been admitted to sweat on the railroads at substandard wages. In 1951 another 191,000 or so were allowed, supposedly temporarily, to come in for agricultural work—at substandard wages. (Thousands more entered illegally, swimming the Rio Grande, thereby earning the name "wetbacks.") Special legislation in 1951 also admitted 10,000 Canadian woodsmen.

Loophole making could take time, and there was now a fast-growing demand for the superskills of engineers, designers, and research scientists. One basic reason for liberalizing immigration policy was expressed to the commission by Dr. Alan T. Waterman, director of the National Science Foundation, who said that visa delays had "a seriously detrimental effect on the strength of science in this country."

The national need, the commission decided, was for a policy that would regard immigration not as a problem but as a potential resource to be utilized judiciously, humanely, and with an eye to self-interest. America had been approaching the problem of control from the wrong end. As Dr. Vannevar Bush, a former scientific adviser to President Roosevelt, put it, "Instead of placing our emphasis on the desirability of attracting the right individuals, most of our emphasis has been on the problem of keeping the wrong ones out."

The commission therefore developed a set of recommendations that would completely overturn the McCarran–Walter Act. (Senator McCarran sputtered that the report resembled "the current series of articles attacking the Act in the Communist *Daily Worker.*") It was proposed that a total annual immigration ceiling be set at one sixth of one percent of the entire American population as of the most recent census. At the time, the existing legal limit was based only on the white population and only as of the 1920 census. Also suggested were mechanisms for streamlining application procedures, coordinating various agencies' work, and providing avenues for immigrants to appeal deportation orders.

The Eisenhower administration did not push immigration reform, but John F. Kennedy had new legislation introduced in July of 1963. That year, Congress allowed the measure to die, but Lyndon Johnson, in January of 1965, resumed the work of reform and succeeded. On October 3, 1965, a liberalized Immigration Act became law, providing a new framework in which the United States could continue its centuries-old history of accommodating some of the world's wanderers. With his eye for the conjunctions of history, politics, and public relations, President Johnson chose to sign it at the base of the Statue of Liberty.

The foremost novelty lay in the abandonment of the national-origins quota system. It is not coincidental that the year of the act marked the peak of a legislative assault on racism. That assault also produced the Voting Rights Act of 1965. A lid remained on immigration: 170,000 a year from outside the Western Hemisphere. Furthermore, as of July 1, 1968, immigration from Western Hemisphere countries was limited to 120,000 a year until a special study of the impact of immigration from the Americas was completed. But gone at last were the mortgaged quotas of the Cold War and the knotty questions of assigning nationality. The only reservation was that no more than 20,000 might be admitted from a single country in a given year.

There were official ranks of preferability—a continuation of practices already long formalized and written into pre-1965 laws. First preference went to unmarried grown sons and daughters of United States citizens (spouses, minor children, and parents were already permitted entry without quota). Second, fourth, and fifth preferences went to other relatives of citizens and resident aliens; seventy-four percent of visas were initially reserved for such kinfolk. But third on the list of preferences were members of professions and persons with exceptional ability in the sciences or the arts, who received ten percent. Sixth on the list and also permitted ten percent was "skilled labor in great demand." Seventh in preference were specially designated refugees for whom six percent of the spaces were saved. There was, therefore, room each year for at least 34,000 engineers, teachers, doctors, nurses, performers, craftsmen, and their families. There would be more when higher-preference categories went unfilled, because the 1965 act permitted unused visas from high-preference categories to be transferred downward. The potential newcomers still were required to pass many tests of economic self-sufficiency and moral character as official America defined these qualities. Western Hemisphere immigrants coming to the United States to take work, for instance, had to secure certificates stating that their specialties were genuinely needed and that they would neither displace American workers nor affect wages and working conditions adversely. Yet these demands were at least capable of fulfillment, where under previous law a person might irrevocably be doomed to exclusion because he could not change his or her birthplace.

After only two full fiscal years had elapsed since the act took effect, the statistics for July 1, 1967, to June 30, 1968, hinted at an interesting profile of new Americans in the 1970s.

Fiscal 1968 had produced 454,448 "immigrants." Not all of them arrived at sea- and airports; the number, by a convention of immigration figures, included 130,455 who were already in the United States and had their temporary status adjusted by the Immigration and Naturalization Service of the Department of Justice. That is, instead of visitors they became settlers.

More than 105,000 of the newcomers were natives of Western Hemisphere countries—with 41,290 from Mexico, 27,018 from Canada, and 17,414 from Jamaica leading the list. Those people entering the United States from Puerto Rico, of course, did not count as immigrants.

From countries outside the Western Hemisphere came 156,212 immigrants, who were subject to the numerical limitations of the law; 8,153 were professional people, scientists, and artists, and 7,940 workers came to fill needed jobs and brought spouses and children with them.

The proportion of skilled people in the total may seem small, but a study of the 102,726 persons *naturalized* in 1967–68 adds some highlights to the picture. Of these new citizens most had come from Germany, Italy, Great Britain, Canada, Cuba, or Mexico. About 45,000 of them were men—roughly 11,000 professionals, 20,000 skilled craftsmen and technicians, 4,000 managers and foremen, 11,000 sales and service workers. Only 3,379 were classed as laborers, 948 as household workers, and 487 as farmers or farm laborers. It was a long way from the days of the steerage.

Specific nationality-group examples multiplied. Of the Hungarian refugees to the United States after 1956 about three quarters were well educated and possessed skills or professional background. Chinese arrivals from Formosa and Hong Kong between 1956 and 1965 totaled about 46,000; the 20,000 men included 6,000 professionals and technicians; an approximately equal number were officials, proprietors, and service workers; very few were laborers. The "coolie" was gone with the buffalo, a legend of the Far Western past.

In August 1968 a pair of events—the Soviet invasion of Czechoslovakia and a fresh wave of anti-Semitism in Poland—led to a rush of petitions by Czech, Polish, and other Eastern European scientists and artists for immigration visas to the United States, Canada, and Australia. Many of them had been "involuntary

Communists," who needed—and got—special waivers for entry to America. In one month American officials in Vienna processed 1,500 prospective immigrants, including Ida Kaminska, former director of the famous Warsaw Yiddish Theater; János Kende, conductor of the Košice Symphony Orchestra in Czechoslovakia; Rumanian opera singer Yolanda Malanescu and her husband, Sandu Stern, first violinist of the Bucharest Symphony Orchestra; and Dr. Jan Kemplenyi, a Czech heart specialist.

There might have been surviving restrictionists who continued to have bad dreams of an immigrant inundation. But by the late 1960s the rest of the world worried that America and other growing modern countries were taking the cream of the world's talent. A study printed in 1966 showed that 2.2 million of the 4.7 million immigrants to the United States between 1947 and 1965 had work experience and were in the prime productive years. Other nations had borne the expense of raising and educating them; America would get the finished products. Seventeen percent of these occupational veterans had been professionals, one in six a craftsman, one in five a clerical, sales, or managerial employee. Between 1956 and 1965 nearly 7,000 chemists were admitted, along with more than 35,000 engineers, almost 38,000 nurses, and more than 18,000 physicians. They came to sharpen and use their skills, as Americans.

The brain drain problem was an old one, going back to at least as far as the Ptolemaic dynasty in Egypt; the Ptolemies enticed scholars to Egypt from all over the Hellenistic world. But the losing countries took little comfort from historical perspective. In Scotland, birthplace of the steam engine and the Industrial Revolution, a newspaper complained in 1967 that red tape and wage-and-spending freezes were driving intelligent Scots to Canada, South Africa, and the United States in record numbers. At least 47,000 had left the country in the preceding two years. Between 1952 and 1961 Great Britain lost sixteen percent of its Ph.D.s down the brain drain; half of those who left went to the United States. Between 1955 and 1960 an average of 483 British medical doctors emigrated each year, with one sixth going to the United States.

If the problem was serious for sophisticated Britain, it could be life and death for underdeveloped nations. A cultural attaché in a Middle Eastern embassy estimated in 1966 that only half of Iran's six thousand students in the United States would return to

Iran; the rest would inevitably be drawn to the greater opportunities of the Western world. In 1961 the United States "absorbed" nearly a third of the medical graduates of Greece; five years later it was taking more than a fifth of the Greek crop of engineers. Such figures haunted the thoughts of ministers of education in the capitals of many a country.

Such emigration was a surprising footnote to history and a trend that would continue on through the century and involve all developing nations that had more skilled people than they could employ at home.

XII
The Spaniard's Children

Robert Kennedy shared bread with Cesar
Chavez as the Mexican-American leader of the
grape pickers ended a fast in 1968. Chavez
always preached nonviolence, using techniques
such as fasts and peaceful mass marches in his
strike against the grape growers. *(UPI/
Bettmann)*

In the early morning hours of July 3, 1898, bugles rang out across the harbor of Santiago de Cuba. They sounded from the deck of the Spanish battle cruiser *Infanta María Teresa,* one of six warships penned up by a United States blockading squadron; they summoned the Spaniards to a brave but ill-fated dash for the open sea, in a climactic and decisive moment in the Spanish-American War. Within four weeks Madrid would sue for the peace that stripped her of her last New World possessions. The *María Teresa's* captain, Victor M. Concas y Palau, later wrote mournfully that his buglers' notes were "the signal that the history of four centuries of grandeur was at an end. . . ."

Yet it was not the end of Spain in the Americas, only of her jurisdiction there. A nation's power may die, but its imprint on history survives. In four centuries Spain and Portugal had stamped an Iberian image on the greater part of the Western Hemisphere. From Cape Horn all the way up to the southern tips of Texas and Florida at the twenty-fifth parallel of north latitude, mountains, jungles, lakes, rivers, seas, and islands are part of what we still call Latin America. Most of its people and place names are a blend of the Indian and the Hispanic, with a strong infusion, particularly in the Caribbean region, of the African strain created by the importation of slaves.

Hundreds of thousands of the children of this Latin culture formed the backbone of one of the twentieth century's great migrations into the continental United States. By 1970 they and their sons and daughters constituted a bloc of perhaps fifteen million Americans of Hispanic origin. The descendants of the conquistadors were thus encountering and modifying the folkways of the nation to the north that grew from seeds planted by England, Spain's mortal enemy when she was at the height of her glory in the 1500s. Long after the armor had rusted and the flags faded, heavily modified remnants of the two nations' traditions still confronted each other, as if some historical cycle beyond our comprehension had to be fulfilled.

The greatest numbers of these latest Hispanic settlers in the United States came from Mexico, which won independence from Spain in 1821, and from Puerto Rico and Cuba, both of which Spain lost in 1898. It is ironic that these generally poor and undereducated dark-complexioned Catholic immigrants arrived mostly after the passage of the laws of the 1920s that had the aim, among others, of reducing the inflow of poor, undereducated, dark-complexioned Catholics. But Congress did not foresee the increasing demand for cheap labor in the fields and orchards of the Southwest, which acted as a magnet for Mexicans. It did not anticipate that hundreds of thousands of Puerto Ricans, already under the American flag on their home island, would move without restraint or red tape to seek new opportunities on the mainland of the United States. Nor did it forecast a revolution in Cuba, sixty years after the Spanish left, that would fill certain neighborhoods in Miami with refugees from Communism.

The migrations that resulted furnish the occasion for a summarizing scrutiny of America's role as world asylum, and for some analysis and speculation concerning the future. For these latest immigrants came, in good measure, from unusually "primitive" localities to a modernized United States. They came to a nation more powerful than it had ever been, more richly endowed with miraculous inventions—and more self-conscious, divided, and hamstrung by its problems than at any time in its history. Inevitably, this affected the reception accorded the Latin-Americans, their prospects, and their hopes for themselves. In one way, they could not avoid reexperiencing what the Germans, Irish, Swedes, Italians, Africans, Poles, and others who came before them experienced. But they would do so in a radically different setting. Old theories might not apply to them; repetition of earlier immigration behavior on their part might have no value. In any event, they would test, under new conditions, what had been said by exclusionists, assimilators, pluralists, Anglo-Saxonizers, those who still denounced the American past as ever flawed by racism, and those who insisted that meritorious men of every race and tongue had always prospered in the United States, given a little time. In the end Spain's children might show Americans where the nation had been and where it was going. At least as far as the next bend in the road.

The first "Mexicans" to live within the boundaries of the United States were not immigrants at all but members of old Spanish-descended families in the territories taken from Mexico by conquest—the future states of Texas, California, Nevada, Utah, and parts of Arizona, New Mexico, and Colorado. These sons and daughters of the Spaniard were good copy for writers of romantic fiction, among them Helen Hunt Jackson, whose *Ramona* (in 1884) glamorized the *Californios* and their world of missions, horseflesh, wine, and hospitality. There were also the distant vanguard of less aristocratic legions who began to trek northward from Mexico around 1900.

As always, jobs were the attraction. The Southwest pulsed with booms in mining and railroad construction from 1880 onward; then, in 1910, as the region's cattle-based agrarian economy was being broadened with the help of irrigation to include large-scale general farming, there was a revolution in Mexico. In the Southwest hands were needed to plant and to pick cotton, beans, lettuce, beets, artichokes, grapefruit, oranges, spinach, grapes, tomatoes, and melons. Native American "hoboes," "bindle stiffs," "fruit tramps," and other picturesquely named migrant workers furnished much of the necessary labor, but the Mexicans fleeing their homeland were hired, too. World War I and the industrial expansion of the 1920s drew many American workers to army camps, factories, and cities—and created an even more urgent demand for Mexicans to fill the vacated places.

The true dimensions of Mexican immigration are hard to draw. The border was long and ineffectively patrolled, and thousands slipped back and forth unrecorded by statisticians. The official figures alone, however, showed a Mexican influx of 185,000 in the period 1910 through 1919, and nearly 500,000 from 1920 through 1929. Even the Mexican who reported himself to United States officials, furthermore, and intended to remain in his new homeland, did not quite fit the category of the uprooted. His journey might be only a few miles in length; the cactus-strewn deserts and mountainous horizons around Santa Fe or Los Angeles were like what he had left behind; he moved in what one writer on Mexicans in the United States has called "an environment that was geographically, culturally, and historically familiar."

What he sought and found in the United States was, first of all, freedom from the uncertainties and dangers of internal warfare that plagued Mexico during the long period of revolutionary upheaval that began in 1910; and, secondly, a wage that was higher than any he could command on his native ground: in the 1920s, for example, it was about $105 a month in the United

States and $18 in Mexico. A popular *corrido,* or ballad, about a Mexican youth who emigrated caught the essence of things.

Vámanos, madre, que allá está el dollar
y mucho, juro, que he de ganar.
(Let's go, Mother, over there is the dollar,
And I swear I am going to earn a lot of them.)

The dollars did not come easily, however. The work was brutally hard. Cesar Chavez, who in 1969 was leading the United Farm Workers Organizing Committee in the fourth year of a strike against California grape growers, recalled for a reporter his own boyhood as a sugar-beet harvester in the 1930s. "That was work for an animal, not a man. Stooping and digging all day. And the beets are *heavy.* Oh, that's brutal work. . . . *That* is how a man is crucified. *Crucified.*" And the camps in which the farm laborers were put up were often horrible collections of unshaded tents and shacks, inadequately supplied with water and open-ditch latrines. Moving from one such camp to another in boxcars, trucks, or rusted jalopies piled high with bedsprings, chicken coops, and children, the Mexicans knew they were in no Promised Land. This was particularly so after the Depression began, when wages plummeted to as low as fifty-six cents a day; when families of four, with every member working, toiled to earn cash incomes that averaged $340 a year for the family; when a Mexican father spoke for thousands when he cried, "It is work or starve for my children"; and when, in the off seasons, sheriffs' deputies, state troopers, and the border patrol would round up and deport Mexicans by the hundreds to save relief costs.

Along with economic exploitation—which the white migrant farmer also endured, especially in the Depression era—went anti-Mexican prejudice. All the traditional charges that had been leveled at immigrants in the past were sounded anew. Typical remarks were those of the Archbishop of San Francisco, Edward J. Hanna, who declared that the Mexicans "drain our charities," formed "a large part of our jail population," and were of "low mentality."

"You can Americanize the man from the southeastern and southern Europe," said another Catholic clergyman, before a Rotary Club audience, "but can't Americanize a Mexican."

Yet while labor unions and civic boosters in Texas and California denounced the policy of allowing unchecked Mexican immigration, the growers, who held the Southwest's highest political cards, saw to it that the supply of cheap and manageable Mexican labor was not reduced. During World War II, when there was a generally acute labor shortage, the United States government entered into an agreement with Mexico for the temporary admission of workers called *braceros,* who were trucked across the border during harvest months and trucked back later. Thus the restriction-minded Americans who had denounced Southern and Eastern European immigrants twenty-five years earlier for allegedly being "birds of passage" were treated to the sight of their own government providing Mexican "birds" with temporary nests and grain. The *bracero* program, a testimony to the strength of the Southwestern farm lobby, was supplemented during the 1950s as unregistered workers slipped into the country by—among other methods—swimming the Rio Grande. No one knows how many of them came and went before the border patrols were tightened, but as many as 447,000 *braceros* were imported in 1959. In 1964 the utilization of *braceros* ended, but in the late 1960s it was still possible, under a clause of the McCarran-Walter Act, for individual foreigners to retain their foreign citizenship while entering the United States for periods of temporary work. In one form or another such flexible arrangements have continued to the present day.

A good many Mexicans, then, had never considered themselves, or ever been considered, immigrants in the ordinary sense. Yet as the decades rolled by, more and more of them remained in the towns and cities intermittently between farming jobs, and some of them settled into industrial or service work or small businesses. Somewhat more than seven decades after 1910, when the heavy Mexican surge northward had begun, there were at least ten million Americans of Mexican birth or parentage in the Southwest, adding color to the national demographic patchwork and creating fresh data for the students of assimilation patterns.

They were an almost unknown minority, in one sense. They were crowded into *barrios* (literally, "neighborhoods") in major cities, in squalor bearing the usual marks and scars of poverty—broken homes, high rates of infant mortality, frequent arrests, much disease, a tendency toward narcotics addiction, a staggering school dropout rate—and, with all these discouragements, a birth rate as much as fifty percent higher than that of the general population. Yet the Mexicans had not attracted the kind of anxious attention from domestic critics of America's shortcomings that other minority groups had. One student of the problem went so far as to say, "For the Mexican-American, there are no liberals."

Part of the reason for this state of affairs might have been found in the fact that the Mexicans, while eager as any other people for a decent livelihood, had not sought much help from non-Mexicans, or shown any eagerness to adopt American lifestyles as part of breaking poverty's grip. They did not practice the self-rejection implicit in some of the earlier immigrant groups' struggles to "Americanize." There was in them a kind of Indian stoicism and Spanish pride, expressed in Cesar Chavez's reply to the question *cómo está,* namely, *batallando con la vida:* "I am still struggling with life."

The Mexican sometimes struggled with life by singing in the face of adversity, confirming in hostile minds the stereotype of the "lazy, happy greaser." Sometimes he sought strength for the struggle in wine or in marijuana or in intense religious exercises, to the neglect of what the Puritan-based national culture called "useful work." Sometimes he struck an aggressive "I am myself" pose, and suffered for it. That happened, for instance, to some Mexican youths in Los Angeles during World War II. They called themselves *pachucos*—roughly "regular guys," or "swingers"—trying to maintain their treasured masculinity and arrogant freedom, *machismo,* despite their impoverished minority status. They adopted as a uniform the "zoot suit," a costume consisting of broad-brimmed hat, finger-length jacket, and billowing pants pinched tight at the ankles—a costume that cried, "Hey, look at me," just as did the beaded chaps and gorgeous leather boots of the Mexican cowboy. But American servicemen in Los Angeles, despite the fact that thousands of Mexican-Americans were in service, regarded the zoot-suiters as draft dodgers and delinquents. Young arrogance met young self-righteousness; insults were traded; fights broke out, and finally, from June 3 to June 8, 1943, thousands of sailors and soldiers rampaged through the Mexican *barrio* of Los Angeles, beating up and stripping zoot-suit wearers, often with the amiable acquiescence of the police.

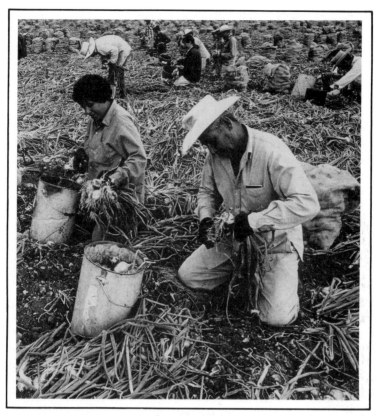

Working under conditions not much changed from those in the 1930s, Mexican migrant workers in 1968 harvest onions in New Mexico. "That was work for an animal, not a man," said Cesar Chavez, recalling his own boyhood toiling in the fields. "Stooping and digging all day . . . oh, that's brutal work . . . that is how a man is crucified. Crucified." *(Library of Congress, Marcia Keegan)*

D ecades later the sons and nephews of some of the Mexican-Americans involved in those riots were still attempting to find a comfortable place in the national life. Again the paths they sought might not be the same as those trodden by the "newcomers" from Europe in the first half of the twentieth century. Those older immigrants had fought their way upward by successful performance in the schools, by group involvement in American party politics, and by individual adaptation to the prevalent social demand for success in business and the professions. But Mexican-American children, to begin with, seemed unwilling to meet a school's demands if they perceived in those demands a threat to Hispanic identity. Often the teacher's first requirement was that pupils abandon the speaking of Spanish during school hours. Unlike earlier "foreign" children, the young Mexicans found that this change set up an unacceptable tension between themselves and their families. To follow the rule was to turn their backs on their own. Yet to reject it was to be punished. "It's always my parents telling me to be proud I'm Mexican and the school telling me to be American," one junior high boy complained. Often the dilemma was solved by dropping out—which elicited harsh reactions of the sort expressed by one Los Angeles high school principal: "They don't belong here anyway—they belong in the fields." Ultimately both child and society were losers in that sort of battle.

In the emotionally charged liberal atmosphere of the late 1960s, when minority groups were generally asserting their ethnicity, this pride in Hispanic folkways became a public rallying point for many Mexicans in America. Dr. Manuel Guerra, an educator of Mexican background, made a plea for bilingual instruction and raised the familiar flag of cultural pluralism. "We do not want," he said, "to give up the Spanish language, pray to God in English, substitute mashed potatoes for *frijoles* or 'junk' our *piñatas*. Rather we want to bring all of these values to American society as our contribution to the diversity and wealth of our country. Rather than the melting pot, we believe in the heterogeneity of American society, including the give and take with other peoples and other cultures."

Even setting aside the language question, the schools might also have failed to make contact with large parts of the Mexican-American community because the educators focused on the preparation of youngsters for a middle-class status, which few of them desired. In the late 1960s, for example, in the entire Southwest, there were only thirty thousand Mexican-Americans—a very small percentage of their population—who were in "professional, technical and similar work": doctors, lawyers, teachers, accountants, engineers, draftsmen, and the like. Only modest increases in the total took place in the succeeding two decades. That might have been due to lack of opportunity and preparation, but it was also possible that Mexican-Americans by and large were not eager to accept the constraints on dress and behavior, the rigid time schedules, the emphasis on such symbols of security as insurance policies, bank accounts, expensive automobiles, homes, gadgets, and vacations—in short, all the appurtenances of a life-style that even successful middle-class Americans term a "rat race."

Moreover, Mexican-Americans did not pursue the quest for advancement through bloc voting power as assiduously as had other groups, such as the Irish or the Italians. They elected modest numbers of representatives to the legislatures of the Southwestern states where they were concentrated, and sent a few of their political leaders to the House of Representatives and the Senate. Some Mexican-Americans sat on the judicial benches of Arizona and Texas, and there was a slow but noticeable increase in the number of appointees of Mexican origin to high federal posts by presidents Nixon, Ford, Carter, and Reagan. In addition, Mexican-Americans sat in increasing numbers on city councils and boards of education in urban areas where their presence was heavy. Time might well bring more and more Mexican names onto party slates. Yet even minority-group officeholders under modern political conditions must undertake expensive campaigns, make numerous concessions, and worry about their public images in order to win elections; once in office they must make compromises to secure even marginal gains. It is a basically conservative system that may work best in a smaller and simpler society.

Young Mexican-Americans who were convinced that traditional political practices were irrelevant might see the way out for them in other action. One possible variety of it is suggested by the career of Cesar Chavez.

Chavez was born in 1927, the grandson of a successful Mexican immigrant who owned substantial property in Arizona. But his parents lost everything in the Depression, and Chavez spent his youth in the movable hell of the migrant camps. In 1952 he was an apricot picker, living in the Mexican *barrio* of San Jose that was grimly named *Sal Si Puedes,* "Escape If You Can." While there he was recruited into the Community Service Organization, a grass-roots pressure-and-action group of and for the poor, started under the leadership of Saul Alinsky, a Chicago-based self-styled radical who specialized in such work. Through the CSO, Chavez rose to leadership. Chavez in the 1960s was not a politician in the ordinary sense, and he would even have denied that he was particularly a leader of Mexicans; his constituency was agricultural labor. Yet the bulk of his followers were Mexican-born or of Mexican parentage. And if politics is the art of securing group objectives in a pluralistic society through persuasive leadership, then politics was the primary gift of Chavez. He had organized the grape pickers, whose earlier brave attempts at unionization had been ignored by established labor organizations—and been broken with ease by the growers. Chavez had earned national attention, publicity, and donations, and had inspired a nationwide liberal boycott of table grapes. He had gradually begun to win concessions from the growers.

Despite the influence of the tough world in which he grew up, Chavez preached nonviolence and adopted Gandhi-like techniques, including fasts, peaceful mass pilgrimages to legislative halls, and constant exhortations to his followers to practice love and brotherhood. His career bore a clear resemblance to that of Martin Luther King, Jr.

Chavez deplored radical talk exalting *la raza,* "the race." "Today," he warned in 1969, "it's anti-gringo, tomorrow it will be anti-Negro, and the day after it will be anti-Filipino, anti-Puerto Rican. And then it will be anti-poor Mexican, and anti-darker-skinned Mexican." And yet Chavez himself, with his contemplative withdrawals, stubborn individualism as a leader, and strangely contrasting appeals to the mystique of community spirit, seemed quintessentially Mexican. He shared with many black leaders the goal of autonomy for the ghettos, and with young Indian activists, too, the demand that the government stop trying to impose on the minority poor the cultural values of the majority; thus money for improvement should be spent as the affected groups saw fit. All such spokesmen reflecting the mood of the sixties preached the worth of the minority group; all aimed to bring their people into the sunlight by strengthening, not discarding, the customs that made them different. For Chavez the cultivation of such group consciousness among Mexican-Americans was only a first step toward a larger concept of brotherhood. In time this mood was to soften somewhat.

Many of the problems and responses visible among the Hispanic-Americans of the Southwest were strikingly similar to, almost duplicated by, the next largest Spanish-speaking group in contemporary America, the Puerto Ricans, who were primarily in and of New York.

The Puerto Rican migration began, like so many others, with the modernization of the homeland. In 1940 the island was impoverished, its economy wrecked by long years of heavy dependence on sugar and tobacco cultivation. Then the government undertook a series of development programs to bring diversified industries to the land, resettle impoverished farmers, increase cash incomes, encourage tourism, modernize cities, and raise the level of literacy and of public health. The programs were remarkably successful, but one consequence was a population boom. In 1968 some 2,700,000 Puerto Ricans were clustered on their island—an average of close to 800 per square mile—making Puerto Rico one of the world's most crowded areas. This furnished one stimulus for emigration. Another was added not by the poverty that survived in the midst of progress but by the improvement in national living standards. The phenomenon of rising expectations set in. "Even in the 'thirties," a Puerto Rican explained to a reporter, "many of the basic commodities were imported from the mainland. The people began to yearn first for a radio, then for an automobile, and eventually for a TV set. . . . Their desires were aroused; cash became more and more important to them, and New York was the place to get it."

New York did offer attractions after World War II, primarily jobs that paid an average of thirty-five or forty dollars a week, almost twice as much as island jobs did, with unionization, health benefits, pensions, and Social Security sometimes included. Moreover, New York was easy to reach. There were no problems of immigration visas. Puerto Ricans had been American citizens ever since the Jones Act of 1917 created the framework of government for the Caribbean colony. They retained that status when Puerto Rico became an almost completely independent self-governing commonwealth in 1952. And, just as the

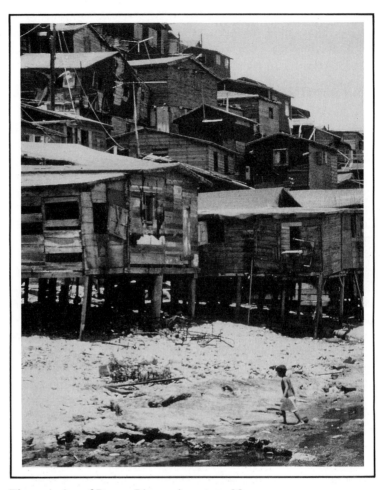

The majority of Puerto Rican migrants to New
York at one time lived in a San Juan slum.
Shown here is La Perla, typical of the squalid
settings from which they tried to escape. But
for most of the Puerto Ricans who uprooted
themselves, chronic poverty, the language barrier, and the burden of large families relegated
them to equally oppressive conditions in the
northern slums of mainland American cities.
(Library of Congress, Marcia Keegan)

transatlantic steamer of the 1890s offered the European migrant cheap passage to the Promised Land, the postwar transport plane furnished the same to the hopeful Puerto Rican. Price wars among major carriers and a number of nonscheduled lines reduced fares to as little as $35 per person, and the aircraft flying at 250 miles an hour ate up 1,600 air miles in no time. A family could board a "thrift flight" at San Juan at eleven at night, carrying coats to put on over their light clothing when they got off in the northern climate, and be deposited at Idlewild (now Kennedy) air terminal when dawn was silhouetting the New York skyline. So the steerage had become airborne. Thousands of Puerto Ricans made the journey. Some were "birds of passage" and did not stay long, but by 1953 the average net gain was about forty thousand a year, with the flow swelling or diminishing in response to business conditions in the United States.

Not many of the newest immigrants were *jíbaros,* cane-field peasants. They were already partially urbanized. A 1950 sociological study of a sample group of Puerto Ricans in New York showed that they were on the whole older, better educated, and more likely to be skilled than those who had stayed behind. About eight out of ten went to work immediately upon their arrival, in jobs overwhelmingly concentrated in the light manufacturing and service occupations. The men became "pressers and floor boys in garment factories, dishwashers, bus boys, pantrymen, laundry workers, [and] porters"; the women were likely to end up as "domestics, in hospitals, and in laundries . . . as hand sewers, floor girls, cleaners, [and] sewing-machine operators."

In some cases the Puerto Ricans actually lost job status, though gaining in salary, as a result of migration. An experienced machine operator unable to understand complicated instructions given in a new language might at first have to accept a job pushing a hand truck between departments in a plant. In many cases the lost ground was made up, occasionally with the help of the unions, particularly in the garment industry. Puerto Ricans were not readily accepted, however, into the skilled-labor unions like those of the painters, carpenters, electricians, and bricklayers. Not many, therefore, were able to attain such employment. At the same time, few moved into the white-collar classes. Even those who qualified for that sociological label were apt to be owners of marginal small businesses—operating barbershops, cleaning establishments, lunch counters, beauty parlors, radio repair shops, and groceries. Like the owners of "Mom and Pop" candy stores and delicatessens in older ethnic neighborhoods of New York, they fended off bankruptcy only by using their families as unpaid and overworked help.

Some Puerto Ricans were placed by the Migrant Division of the Commonwealth of Puerto Rico's Department of Labor in jobs as far to the northwest as Milwaukee. But the overwhelming concentration was in the low-wage brackets in New York. That was the mecca, though a tarnished one. The Puerto Ricans hit the city in the early years of what was to become an apparently permanent shortage of low-income housing. The median income of $36.28 a week for a Puerto Rican family in 1950 bought little in the way of residential space. Most of the newcomers were confined to a few neighborhoods. They lived in Brooklyn, in a district known as Morrisania in the Bronx, or, most of them, in East Harlem. Also known as Spanish Harlem, or simply *El Barrio* to the Puerto Ricans, East Harlem ran from 100th Street northward, bounded on one side by the East River and on the other (roughly) by central, or black, Harlem. The quality of accommodation offered in these Hispanic enclaves was reflected when, in the early 1950s, a church group in East Harlem circulated a questionnaire among 1,000 tenants asking them to list their housing problems. There were 721 cases of defective wiring, 612 of inadequate plumbing, 571 of broken windows, 895 of rats in the building, 696 of gas leaks, 778 of no heat, 553 of no hot water, and 308 of leaks in the roof. It went without saying that the victims of these housing-code violations, lacking political influence, lacking command of English, without money for lawyers, and having no comprehension of bureaucratic byways, were almost powerless to compel landlords to make repairs.

Life had not been any more gracious in the slums of San Juan, it was true. And yet in familiar surroundings, misery had perhaps been less threatening. A Puerto Rican named Piri Thomas grew up in *El Barrio,* experiencing early in his life poverty, drug addiction, and prison. In a deeply moving memoir entitled *Down These Mean Streets,* he recalled his mother comparing the lot of the lowly in two cultures:

. . . in Puerto Rico those around you share *la pobreza* with you and they love you, because only poor people can understand poor people. I like *los Estados Unidos*, but it's sometimes a cold place to live—not because of the winter and the landlord not giving heat but because of the snow in the hearts of the people.

Similar observations by Puerto Ricans are plentiful in *La Vida,* a study by the anthropologist Oscar Lewis of the culture of poverty in San Juan and New York.

Puerto Ricans in the United States also found themselves coping with a problem that was relatively new to them, racial discrimination. Some of the islanders were quite "white," many were dark-skinned like the majority of Mexicans, but about twenty-five percent were *negritos* and *grifos,* blacks and mulattoes, descended from slaves brought in by the Spaniards. In a general way, social and economic advancement in Puerto Rico, as in the United States, came more quickly and easily to the light-skinned. But black Puerto Ricans, and especially those with only a few "negroid" characteristics, were unprepared for the shock of being taken for "niggers" in the United States and treated accordingly. For them, the choices were agonizing. They might deny their blackness, assume the white man's attitude of hostility to blacks (often thoroughly reciprocated by American blacks), and live in a twilight zone between the races. Or they might seek cooperation with blacks, individually or in organizations, and even positively accept their own color and define their own loyalties by it. Very few made this choice. Piri Thomas did, and it imposed on him the ache of a painful separation from his father, who was likewise black but who cried out to his son: "I don't like feeling to be a black man. Can you understand it's a pride to me being a Puerto Rican?" To which Piri replied with cruel honesty, "What kind, Poppa, black or white?"

For some Puerto Ricans, the escape from this and other traps was a return flight to San Juan. But thousands stayed to rear families, and each child born in the United States was a tie to the new land. By 1980 the Puerto Rican community of New York City had grown to nearly two million. According to the census of that year, the unfortunate truth was that most of New York's Puerto Ricans remained at the bottom of the economic and educational heap.

The children often suffered the same initial linguistic problem in the schools as did the Mexican-American youngsters. A majority of Puerto Rican parents might want their children to attend college; a survey in 1950 indicated this ambition. But it was a vain hope for most of them. Puerto Rican children had a high dropout rate in the 1950s and 1960s. Bewildered by the strange tongue, the first- and second-graders would drop behind the class, would sometimes be labeled "uncooperative" or "stupid," would retreat into fantasy, aggression, or truancy, and would begin a long downward slide. To combat this sequence, some teachers in the New York City system suggested a new approach: that the Puerto Rican beginner be taught in Spanish and gradually introduced to bilingualism. It was assumed that whatever benefits this might produce, an improvement in the child's competence in Spanish was itself a worthwhile educational goal.

Such an approach, of course, would set the pupils marching to a different drumbeat from the one sounded for the immigrant children of the early 1900s, and would rest frankly on what one writer has called "the philosophy of the multiethnic society in which all groups are identifiable," a philosophy that "attacks the middle-class value system on many fronts. . . ." Undeniably it was arousing the wrath of tradition-minded teachers, one of whom denounced multiethnicity as a gimmick and declared in a newspaper interview that schools must "organize parents to cooperate, to send their children to school on time, to behave in school." The battle was joined, and it was a long way from being decided.

Again like the Mexicans, the Puerto Ricans appeared to be moving into political office on a slower timetable than the older nationality groups. Inexperience and a certain amount of dispersion through many neighborhoods and districts might explain Puerto Rican political weakness in New York, as might the changing nature of political campaigning in the television era. But it was also possible that Frank Espada, a Puerto Rican who was vice-president of the New York Urban Coalition, had come very near the truth when he stated: "We are in the process of losing our second generation in terms of political involvement. The only Puerto Ricans that can break into the system are those who break into machine politics, which doesn't reflect our aspirations and goals."

Puerto Ricans had to define themselves: to decide what rela-

This 1957 photograph shows Fidel Castro
flanked by three of the five members of the
guerrilla army's top command. The young revo-
lutionist seized control of Cuba in January 1959
from the dictator Fulgencio Batista. Mock trials, executions of his detractors, and escalating
quarrels with the United States ensued. After
Castro declared himself a Communist, the
United States launched the Bay of Pigs debacle.
(UPI/Bettmann)

tionship they would try to create with whites and blacks. They had to consider whether they would look for models in urban American patterns of family life and consumption or in Latin styles. They had to choose between individual and group action, and between militants and traditionalists, if they wished to exert political pressure. Above all, they had to decide upon what emotional and geographic foundations they would build.

That was, paradoxically, both hard and easy, for the Puerto Ricans had never entirely left home. The first generation of Puerto Ricans on the mainland drew comfort from the fact that they could visit the island often and cheaply. Oscar Handlin believes that this may be the key to their failure to create separate institutions such as ethnic churches and private schools, right away, to cushion the shock of separation. Like the French-Canadians of New England as well as the Mexicans of the Southwest, they were "never altogether detached from the lands of their birth" in the fashion of the European immigrant, who knew that each had "decisively severed his ties with his old home . . . and that his future was entirely in the United States."

But the children born to Puerto Ricans in New York did not share their parents' hopes of return. For them, "home isn't a dusty plaza on a tropical island, but a New York block where smells of fried fish and hamburgers mingle with the Latin beat drifting from the corner record store. . . ." Yet they were not ready to disappear entirely into the theoretical melting pot. They might turn out to be both old-countrymen and Americans in a deeper sense than most "hyphenated Americans" of the past. Through such organizations as the Puerto Rican Citizens Committee for Unity (which has a counterpart in MAPA, Mexican-American Political Action, and another in PUMA, Political Unity for Mexican-Americans), they might find a special strength, resting, according to a Fordham University student of Puerto Rican affairs, "not on the continuation of a traditional culture in the form of an immigrant community, but on the solidarity which results from organizing their efforts for the pursuit of group interests in the political arena." *Puertorriqueño* power, as one might say, would be more than a dwindling fortuitous product of their common background. They would use it, too, to perpetuate that identity—to encourage, for example, Spanish-speaking schools and Spanish neighborhoods.

Meanwhile, the Puerto Ricans were leaving their mark, like

those who had gone before—in little *bodegas* selling plantains, in restaurants dishing up *asopao* (a chicken or sea-food stew with rice and vegetables), in papers like *La Prensa* and *El Diario de Nueva York* (which converted Blondie into Pepita and Mickey Mouse into El Ratón Miguelito), in billboards advertising a popular brandy as endowed with *alma española*.

Though Mexicans and Puerto Ricans came from, and settled in, widely different areas—one agricultural, one urban-industrial—there was enough similarity in their American experience to tempt an observer into speculating about the influence of innate Latin qualities. Such a racial theory would collapse into rubble, however, as soon as it was tested against the amazing experience of the Cuban refugees of 1959 to 1969. For the exiles from Castro's revolution seem to epitomize the traditional success story of the foreign boy who makes good.

While the first year's refugee wave, forty thousand strong, was arriving by boat and plane in 1959, United States officials laid plans for the future. Almost from the beginning Washington provided federal temporary assistance funds of up to a hundred dollars a month for refugee families—whom the Cuban revolutionary government allowed to take only five pesos, one watch, one ring, and the clothes on their backs out of Cuba. Washington also allocated special funds to the Miami school system to help handle the influx of Cuban children, whose numbers grew by as many as a thousand a week. In 1965 the federal government started to provide Cubans with air transport to the United States. The Department of Health, Education and Welfare also made grants to experienced social-work agencies, such as the National Catholic Welfare Conference and the International Rescue Committee, to help them maintain Cubans in special resettlement centers and then move them into jobs throughout the country. Under vigorous administration, approximately 109,000 Cubans were placed outside the Miami area, and as far from the Caribbean as Chicago and southern California.

A heavy proportion of the more than 285,000 Cubans who had arrived by early 1967, however, remained in Dade County, which includes Miami. It was a natural debarkation point not far from Havana, and it had a thriving Hispanic colony even before 1959, composed of Puerto Ricans, Cubans, and other Latin-Americans. Miami had long been in the business of welcoming tourists from the southern continent to the United States. By 1969 it was estimated that Cubans made up ten percent of greater Miami's population. As an index to their concentration in certain neighborhoods, by February of 1966 the local Catholic dioceses had to furnish eighty Spanish-speaking priests just for the Cubans; sixteen parishes said the Mass in Spanish; more than five thousand Cuban children were enrolled in parochial schools. Unlike the Mexicans and Puerto Ricans, whose nominal Catholicism did not seem to have a tight hold on them once they were transplanted to America, the Cubans were in the main active church supporters.

They were diligent in their own business as well as the Lord's. The Miami *Herald* referred to them as "the cream of a nation in exile," a somewhat biased judgment, suggesting that everyone who remained within Fidel Castro's jurisdiction was skimmed milk. But it was true that these refugees were endowed with ability, experience, and middle-class concepts of achievement. Most of them were soon off relief and paying back, in taxes, a substantial portion of the hundreds of millions of government dollars spent on the refugee program.

Men like Raul G. Menocal were among the new Cubans of Miami. Menocal had twice been mayor of Havana, and by 1967 he was vice-president in charge of the Latin-American division of a Coral Gables bank. There were also men like Angel Aixala and the Luis Encheniquis, father and son, who began a marine construction company named International Boats that by 1966 had annual gross sales of $1,500,000. And Raul and Jesus Gutierrez, who built a small company into the million-dollar-a-year Calmaquip, selling American products to Latin America. And Manuel Fernandez, who was stripped of his cattle ranch and packing house when he fled at the age of seventy in 1961—but who five years afterward was the contented owner of the Wajay Crackers Company.

Such individuals undoubtedly had head starts in the form of business contacts in the United States. These guaranteed them access to credit, and some had probably found ways to transfer assets out of Cuba despite Castro's laws. But there were also thousands of Cubans like Jose Simon, an attorney. He arrived in Miami so poor that his first, gratefully accepted job was as door-to-door salesman for a milk company. Simon studied English at night, and by early 1967 was a professor of Spanish at Emory

University in Atlanta. At that time 2,500 Cubans were teaching in United States schools and colleges, and 1,900 Cuban physicians were working in United States hospitals.

By the end of Castroism's first decade, the Cuban community in Miami showed a respectable top layer of affluence, demonstrated in the expensive and handsome homes of refugees who owned automobile dealerships and garages, restaurants and hotels, small factories, real-estate agencies, and the like. Many of the Cubans still eagerly awaited the day when the usurper would be overthrown and they would return to their rightful homeland. But thousands were discovering that children born in the house of strangers create blood ties to those strangers and their house. Increasingly Cubans who had children enrolled in American schools—where they were becoming "more American than Cuban"—were applying for citizenship papers and settling in for good. "The Cubans," said one Dade County Chamber of Commerce official, "have put a lot more into this community than they have taken out." As time went by, they were beginning to add their own lives to their investments in America.

The Cubans may have shaken the belief of many native Americans in the laziness and ineptitude of Latin-Americans, long contemptuously referred to as "spicks," "dagos," and "greasers." They may equally have punctured romantic notions that the Latin-American soul is too poetic to be fettered to the office stool. In any event, these particular Cubans represented a picked group of elite immigrants—educated and supremely able to manipulate the machines, the blueprints, the bank figures, and the statutes that add up to power in the modern world.

They had their historical counterparts in many earlier immigrants to America who came well educated or well heeled or both, or who came with skills in metallurgy or glassblowing, for example, comfortably aware that they would be hired by industry as soon as they stepped ashore. They, too, were part of the immigrant procession through America's history.

XIII
The World at Our Doorstep

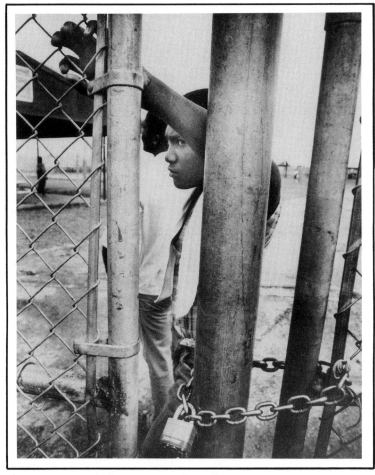

A young Haitian refugee awaits release from a detention center near Miami in 1982. *(Wide World)*

The Immigration and Nationality Act of 1965—actually an amendment of the 1952 McCarran-Walter Act—was a bold reflection of the civil rights revolution that had swept the country in the preceding decade. The toppling of the old national-origins quota system was a historic breakthrough. As he signed the measure, President Johnson declared that it "repair[ed] a deep and painful flaw in the fabric of American justice." Henceforward, he promised, "those who come will come because of what they are—not because of the land from which they sprung." Abandoned was the concept that special consideration should go to people of the same blood as those who had first settled and developed America. North Carolina's conservative Senator Sam Ervin had somewhat plaintively noted, during debate on the measure, that under it the "people of Ethiopia have the same right to come to the United States . . . as the people from England, the people of France, the people of Germany, the people of Holland, and I don't think—with all due respect to Ethiopia—I don't know of any contributions that Ethiopia has made to the making of America." But that was, in fact, the point. No race was to be deemed worthier than any other to become American. It was a sweeping repudiation of a policy less than forty-five years old, a historic turnaround to match the cresting liberal mood of the early 1960s.

But there was another aspect as well. For, as the President also said, "The days of unlimited immigration are past." Immigration would still be regulated in the pursuit of national values and objectives such as the strengthening of immigrant families through reunification; the acquisition of skilled workers, professionals, and other potential contributors to the nation's economic, cultural, or scientific development; and finally, the traditional tender of asylum to victims of persecution. The new preference quotas said, in effect, that systematic management, not chance, would determine the composition of future waves of immigration.

The law aimed to fulfill two goals of mid-century American progressive thought. One was to uproot irrational, though long-standing, ethnic prejudices. The other was to have government compassionately but purposefully manipulate what bureaucratic jargon styled "human resources."

In the two decades after 1965, the first objective was fulfilled almost breathtakingly. As history would have it, the traditionally European dominance of immigration began to dwindle, while the proportion of newcomers from the Western Hemisphere and from Asia shot upward. In the decade from 1900 to 1910, eighty percent of all immigrants had come from Europe. But by the end of the 1970s, the European share had fallen to thirteen percent, and just over eighty percent came from Latin American and Asian countries. Forty percent came from just five nations: China (both mainland and Taiwan), Korea, the Philippines, Cuba, and Mexico. In some parts of major American cities, Spanish was becoming de facto a second official language, but even more astonishing was the mushrooming of Asian neighborhoods, since Orientals had been barred totally by the 1924 law and given a trifling quota as late as 1952. If a heterogeneous population was proof that American democracy was alive and well, then these particular newcomers, who seemed especially foreign to black and white Americans, were evidence that the 1965 law had given the nation a shot of megavitamins.

But with regard to the other target of post-1965 immigration policy—the development and effective application of rational controls to immigration—it was a different story. History was not amenable to tidy planning, and neither were people. In the troubled, crowded, and shrinking world of the 1970s and 1980s, great tides of migration were in motion and surging toward American shores in a modern but vastly magnified repetition of an older story.

The developing nations of the world struggled with economic and natural crises—failed development policies, huge debts, famines, and droughts—that produced uprooting, unemployment, and inflation, and made migration the only promising future for thousands and millions of their citizens, just as it had been for countless Europeans a century earlier. And, as had been the case a century earlier, people went everywhere on the globe in search of opportunities, but the United States was still the primary magnet, taking more than two thirds of all legal immigrants in the world.

Then there was the jet age, the modern counterpart of the revolution that steam had brought to transatlantic travel. From Moscow and Athens—and also from Buenos Aires, Singapore, Bangkok, Manila, Kinshasa, Beirut, Lima, Karachi—it was suddenly possible for any would-be migrant with the price of a ticket to fly to America in less than forty-eight hours, often in less than twenty-four or twelve—to America, whose rich attractions gleamed nightly on television screens the world over, thanks to satellite broadcasts. The promised land was now next door to everyone in the global village.

Still another twentieth-century force propelled migration. Wars, civil wars, revolution, and oppression uprooted people ruthlessly and on a huge scale. Applications for refugee status poured onto the desks of U.S. consuls from residents or escapees of Afghanistan, Cambodia, Laos, and especially Vietnam; from Cuba and Haiti and El Salvador; from the Soviet Union and Ethiopia and the Middle East. The United Nations High Commissioner for Refugees reported in 1980 that as many as twelve million souls were seeking asylum somewhere or other. And in that year alone the United States took in twice as many refugees as the rest of the world combined—some 225,000 Vietnamese, Cambodians, Laotians, Russians, and Europeans who came, as a journalist put it, "at its invitation, and 150,000 who did not."

These converging forces spurred a steady increase in immigration, which not only filled but overflowed the new preference quotas. Post-1965 adjustments to the law merged the Eastern and Western Hemisphere quotas to create an overall annual ceiling of 290,000. But as early as 1971, total legal immigration was 370,478. Two years later it reached 400,063, hovered in that vicinity for a while, then jumped to 462,315 in 1977 and to a refugee-swollen 601,442 in 1978. It settled back to 460,000 the next year, climbed to 596,600 in 1981, and was estimated at around 550,000 for 1982 and 1983. By contrast, during the entire twenty years from 1945 to 1965, annual totals had exceeded 300,000 only three times.

The numbers admitted exceeded the quotas for several reasons. One was the presence in the totals of nonquota immigrants, the spouses, parents, and minor children of U.S. citizens—a number that would grow as each wave of newcomers became naturalized. The other was a series of emergency mass exemptions made for refugees. But the figures on "legals" did not by any means represent a complete count. They excluded a large and often overlooked number of resident aliens who each year chose not to return home. And, much more to the point, they did not reflect a hard-to-measure number of undocumented aliens—people who slipped across America's long land borders without proper clearance, or who checked in correctly at ports of entry with temporary visas and then overstayed their permitted time and vanished in the crowd. Some were "birds of passage" who came and left more than once if their luck in evading inspection held. But others had become firmly, if not officially and visibly, settled into American life. Guesses as to the numbers of these uncounted immigrants present in the United States in the 1980s ranged from a conservative three million to a probably exaggerated twelve million. Adding the number of them who entered each year to the incoming figures could boost annual totals to something like the million-plus of the 1900–1914 period.

Clearly those who led in shaping the 1965 revisions of immigration policy had gotten more than they bargained for. Moreover, the immigration of the 1970s and early 1980s came at a time when the buoyant mood of Lyndon Johnson's first year in office had faded. A lost war in Vietnam, an energy crisis in 1973, runaway inflation followed by recession and unemployment early in the eighties combined to raise doubts and discussion about the wisdom of America's immigration policies and practices, just as cracks in the national confidence had always done. "We have to live within limits," said Senator Alan Simpson of Wyoming in introducing an immigration reform bill in 1982. "The nation wants to be compassionate but we have been compassionate beyond our ability to respond."

The message was not new, but the Senator also uttered a key word that was. The United States, he declared, must be "determined to *control* legal and illegal immigration." What had been troubling Americans since the end of the sixties was a feeling that the country was no longer in unimpeded control of its problems. Nothing demonstrated the fact so well as the complexities of dealing with flaws in the immigration law. Each remedy posed dilemmas as acute as the supposed problem it aimed to solve.

Could we "control legal and illegal immigration" so long as need drove millions from their own impoverished lands? Or would we have to cooperate in some global reallocation of credit and resources to reduce the pressures of migration?

Could we tighten up our immigration controls without creating a huge and costly bureaucracy in the Immigration and Naturalization Service, when the popular political stance was for economy in government? Could we endow the INS withn adequate powers of search and seizure without creating a police state?

If we successfully rounded up and expelled all the undocumented aliens, would it have an adverse effect on the economy? There were employer groups who insisted that it would, and while the point was hotly argued, no one knew the answer for certain.

Most of the undocumented migrants clearly came from Mexico. By dumping them back onto a sagging Mexican economy, we would offend a neighbor and an ally. Could we afford the diplomatic price?

The question of how many refugees we could admit, and from where, was also entangled not only with strong feelings about the American tradition of asylum, but with Cold War politics. From the 1950s onward we had made a point of generously admitting people fleeing from Communist regimes partly as a way of showing our hostility to their rulers. But by the same token, the Reagan administration, early in the eighties, was fighting to exclude Haitian and especially Salvadoran refugees, because by admitting them it would acknowledge that those two anti-Communist allies were also guilty of significant human-rights abuses. Could refugee policy be disentangled from foreign policy? And if some fresh waves of refugees like the Cubans or the Vietnamese knocked and were admitted, would a Congress faced with gigantic budget deficits be willing to spend money to house, feed, train, and relocate them?

All of these riddles melted into an overall question of how well America's constitutional and political system could handle this particular issue as the twentieth century wound down. Immigration law had always been hammered out in the noisy workshop of democratic pluralism, with Congress balancing the claims of employers, unions, ethnic lobbies, budget-cutters, bureaucrats, and organized reformers of left and right. All those voices were now greatly magnified, and in addition the needs of the State and Defense departments and of foreign countries had to be considered. There were times when President Carter's informal characterization of immigration policy as a mess seemed an understatement.

And while the arguments went on, the immigrants continued to arrive and to play their roles in the 380-year-old drama of entry and assimilation into the New World. All over the country, the American people continued their constant process of self-remodeling.

Europe continued to furnish immigrants, though in declining numbers, as families already in America brought in relatives under the new preference system. Italy remained among the top five sending nations through 1973. There was a small but lively Irish migration, but though it produced its share of bartenders and domestics, fully a third of it consisted of professional or technical workers, a far cry from the "Paddies" and "Bridgets" of a century earlier. Especially in New York City, still the greatest immigrant Mecca, an Irish and Italian and Greek presence seemed to sound echoes of the early days of the century, but with a difference. These newcomers were not penniless and unskilled, and though they worked hard and remained loyal to their home-lands (which they could now visit frequently and swiftly), they were quick to acquire the externals, especially the consumer goods, of the American life-style. And, as of olden times, there were Russian Jews arriving, but they were now Soviet émigrés, and not tailors and cutters but more often engineers, teachers, production managers, or dental assistants. Migrants from Carib-bean nations, too, found their way to New York as they had done in the early days of Harlem, but more often with advanced degrees and specialties, even though—like all newcomers—they often had to begin at entry-level jobs for which they were over-qualified. These "new" immigrants from "old" countries said much in themselves about the changing patterns of migration.

But the most visibly novel presence in American life was that of the once-scorned Asians, and the most compelling and dra-matic Asian migration was the tragic ingathering of the Indochi-nese refugees from America's lost war. The first great wave came in the six or eight weeks that followed the fall of Pnom Penh and Saigon in April of 1975. In particular, hundreds of thousands of Vietnamese who had worked with United States forces were in mortal danger of reprisal from the victorious Communists and fled by whatever means were possible. The Americans evacuated nearly 52,000 during the last days before Saigon's capture, though these were only a fraction of those clamoring for space on departing ships, planes, and helicopters. Others were able to buy or charter boats with the last of their savings or possessions and make their dangerous seaborne way to Hong Kong, Malaysia, Thailand, or other temporary stopping places where they huddled in temporary shelters and waited for help. The United States, recognizing its particular obligation to these victims, processed thousands more for emergency admission, and by the middle of May a full 130,000 had been admitted, with 60,000 still languishing in camps. Another 21,000 were taken in during the next twelve months, as quota limits for refugees continued to be brushed aside.

Fortunately there was the 1962 legislation, provoked by earlier refugee crises, that allowed for federal assistance in dealing with this inundation of suffering. Relocation centers were set up at military bases in California, Arkansas, Florida, and Pennsylvania, and workers from voluntary agencies like the International Rescue Committee and the United States Catholic Conference took charge of finding jobs, homes, and individual or church and other organizational sponsors all over the country for these newest and somewhat involuntary Americans. It was not all that difficult a task, since this was a relatively select group of evacuees. Most of the heads of families had worked with the Americans and over two thirds of them spoke English. Many were urban Catholics, educated under the old French system, who had already moved once from North Vietnam to South Vietnam after the partition of 1954 to escape living under Ho Chi Minh. One quarter had even attended college.

By the end of 1975 the last of the 130,000 had moved out of the camps. Even in a hurting economy sixty percent held jobs, though often far below their old pay and status levels. Three years later, however, a survey taken by the Department of Health, Education and Welfare showed that, like earlier refugees with skills, experience of the modern world, and motivation, the Vietnamese were moving up. A full ninety-five percent of those of work-force age were employed, and the number of families with incomes over $800 a month had jumped from fifteen to seventy percent. Very few were using the public assistance services provided by states and municipalities (which Washington reimbursed).

The years 1978 and 1979 brought a second and greater surge of Indochinese migration. In Vietnam, Laos, and Cambodia, forced relocations, expropriations, rationings, and other Draconian economic and political "reeducation" measures taken by the new governments impoverished huge numbers of people, and in

Cambodia, at least, resulted in millions of deaths. Border wars between Cambodia and Vietnam, and Vietnam and China, added to the total of misery. Swarms of farmers, fishermen, and businessmen—especially those of Chinese origin or descent, who were singled out for special discrimination—fled for their lives. Those who escaped by sea had especially horrible experiences. If their overcrowded fishing boats did not drown or shipwreck them, they were often boarded repeatedly by pirates who raped and robbed at will. By the middle of 1979 some 380,000 starving "boat people," whose plight was graphically displayed in the world press, were crowded into already overpopulated neighboring countries in the South China Sea, which could not and did not want to accommodate them and threatened to turn away or sink further incoming boats. Malaysia in particular actually began to do so, and demanded—and got—world action.

An international conference was held in which it was agreed that Western nations and Japan would have to absorb the new refugees. The United States agreed to take by far the largest share. It doubled its already enlarged number of refugee admissions from 7,000 to 14,000 a month, and even in 1981, while handling an exceptional number of Cuban refugees, saved 160,000 places for the Indochinese. As of May 1984 there were nearly 700,000 of the latter living in the United States, slightly over one third of them in California, the next largest number in Texas (just over 56,000), approximately 32,000 in the state of Washington, and some 25,000 each in Illinois, Pennsylvania, and New York. Smaller numbers were scattered throughout the rest of the Union.

The post-1978 Vietnamese migration had more religious and class variety than the earlier one. As one writer puts it, the total Vietnamese populace of America today includes "cosmopolites, bourgeois provincials and dirt-poor peasants . . . gifted intellectuals, street-wise hustlers and unwordly fisherfolk and farmers." Their memories are bitter, and they may have as much ambivalence about the American experience in Vietnam as do the Americans themselves. But as to their expectations in their new homeland, most of them are probably spoken for by a twenty-eight-year-old refugee in New York who told a historian of immigration:

Volunteers from the Cuban exile community
help pull into the dock at Key West, Florida, the
Road Runner, a thirty-nine-foot commercial fishing boat full of refugees, after it arrived from
Cuba in April 1980. U.S. Customs officials
notified the captain, Winston Rourk, of their
intention to fine him for bringing in the fifty-
eight aliens. *(Wide World)*

Tell the people. I am a worthy, proud person. I will do by myself. Give me a chance. I want to work. I want to help my people and to develop your country. This is my desire. I will do everything I can to show that my people are good, worthy people. Not a garbage people, to throw away.

The Indochinese pilgrimage was the most headline-making, but for many American city-dwellers of the 1980s—especially in Los Angeles and New York—the most noticeable of the new Asian immigrants were the Koreans. Like the Vietnamese and the Filipinos, they came from nations that had spent long periods of time garrisoned by American troops; the Philippines had literally as well as metaphorically been an American colony from 1901 to 1946. They were nations, moreover, that were in the path of the global expansion of Western-style industry. So Koreans and Filipinos of the 1980s and their fathers had not merely fought side by side with Americans and worked in their post exchanges, but those who lived in cities had additional tastes of many aspects of the contemporary world. They knew about banks and clinics, in which they worked as both technicians and service personnel; about discos and television sets and polyester suits, which they helped to make; about jetliners, which some of them serviced and some of them flew. Those who migrated were looking for broader opportunities than their crowded, tradition-bound, and politically repressive homelands allowed, and they brought with them a great deal of adaptability and many useful habits.

There were between 300,000 and 400,000 Koreans living permanently in the United States in 1980, and some ninety percent had arrived after 1965. Many of the recent arrivals who could not find satisfactory long-term jobs elsewhere brought, borrowed, or saved enough capital to begin small businesses. In New York City especially, Koreans gradually and almost unnoticeably achieved almost complete dominance of the retail fruit and vegetable business, in part through long, hard hours of work undertaken by family members. This kind of small entrepreneurship was an almost stereotypical success pattern of immigrant history—witness Chinese laundries and Greek restaurants—and one of which the Koreans made special use. A 1980 Census Survey of self-employed workers as a percentage of all employed persons, grouped by national origins, found that people of

Korean background were nearly twice as likely as the national average to be self-employed. Their 11.6 percent in that category compared to 6.8 percent for all persons; 7.9 percent for those of Japanese extraction; 6.9 percent for Italians; and 5.8 percent for Cubans, to name a few competitors. Yet it would be a serious mistake to visualize the "typical" Korean immigrant, adult or child, as someone who spent all his time washing down bins of lettuce and weighing potatoes or attending to the affairs of any kind of store. In one survey of all residents of the United States who had completed at least four years of college, those of Korean background led all the rest with 36.3 percent—as against 11.6 percent for all whites, and 4.5 percent for all blacks. The Koreans were followed by the Chinese at 25.6 percent and the Filipinos at 22.5 percent.

Filipinos were first likely to be seen by many Americans in the course of a hospital stay, because in every year of the eighties, some 6,000 nurses from the Philippines were being recruited to work in the United States. Thousands of Filipino doctors, too, made up part of the average annual migration of 35,000 Filipinos to American cities. Asian-trained doctors, in fact, flocked to American medical life in such numbers in the 1970s that in some states like New York they made up forty percent of the total of all practitioners. American medical organizations, complaining that these newcomers were too inadequately trained to carry major responsibility for national health care, convinced Congress to pass a Health Professions Act in 1976, limiting and geographically scattering the number of residencies in U.S. hospitals open to foreign graduates.

Other Filipinos came with or pursued advanced degrees in all the burgeoning fields of science and business, as well as in the arts. They blended, along with the Koreans and Vietnamese, into a stream of Chinese, Japanese, Pakistani, Indian, and other Asian arrivals (including Israelis, Palestinians, and others from the Middle East, which was once known as Asia Minor), who could be found at work behind counters, at drawing boards and computer terminals, or in clinics and laboratories. All were part of an explosion that saw Asian and Asian-descended people become the fastest-growing ethnic group in the population between 1970 and 1980 by more than doubling their number, to a total of some 3.5 million.

The picture could, of course, be painted in colors too rosy.

311

There were Asian immigrants who did not move beyond entry-level jobs, including such traditional occupations as cooks, gardeners, and waiters. There were many in the shrinking ranks of blue-collar labor. There were undoubtedly some who contributed to statistics of crime, addiction, mental illness, and chronic dependency. They were, after all, human.

But the general trend was toward rapid advance and assimilation. While many Asian-Americans remained in ethnic neighborhoods, their newly arrived relatives and their grown children showed an inclination to move away from the strong ethnic self-assertiveness common in the 1960s (even when this might sometimes allow them to profit by anti-discrimination legislation). They did not, as a rule, organize around the principles of "minority rights," and if anything, their political and social attitudes supported the conservative call for a return to church, work, and family values that was becoming mainstream thinking in the 1980s.

This clearly increased their acceptability. Most Americans remained unfamiliar with East Asian history, languages, and culture, and some, exposed to Vietnamese or other Asian immigrants for the first time, were undoubtedly surprised to find how many of them were educated Christians. But there was almost no *overt* showing of the poisonous anti-Oriental movements of a half century and more earlier; the "Yellow Peril" seemed to be safely buried in the past.

Not that the millennium had arrived. It was possible to hear mutterings that all Koreans were besotted followers of the Reverend Sun Myung Moon's Reunification Chruch, and that the "Moonies" were the well-heeled advance guard of a takeover. There was also a current of resentment against the Indochinese. Public opinion tended to lag behind official policy; a May 1975 poll showed only a third of the American people willing to take in the refugees—their attitude possibly reflecting the statement of California Congressman Burt Talcott: "Damn it, we have too many Orientals!" In the following year, in the Gulf port of Seadrift, Texas, there was an ugly affair. A group of Vietnamese refugee shrimp fishermen incurred the wrath of local competitors in the same waters. The Ku Klux Klan entered the picture. A local fisherman was shot in a dispute, whereupon the townsmen accused two Vietnamese of the deed and set fire to three of the refugees' boats and one of their homes, causing the Vietnamese families to leave the town.

Yet the Seadrift episode was newsmaking because of its rarity, and the root cause seemed as much economic as racial. And there were plenty of Americans to echo the sentiment of a letter writer to a national newsmagazine who declared: "I am sick, sick, sick of Vietnam [and] the boat people. . . . How many Americans who are poor, elderly or disabled and living in our ghettos can buy their way out?" Yet despite this, the fact remained that the United States took in more refugees than any other nation and extended to these "outsiders," regardless of race, all the privileges of citizenship, a record matched by no other society.

The Indochinese migration was one more aftershock of the war that refused to go away. But it also had an effect on the future. As it tore through the "roof" of 17,400 refugee admissions a year set by the 1965 law, it was a reminder of how hard it was to guarantee such ceilings in a world where human-rights "emergencies" had almost become routine, and it also focused American thinking about immigration on a number of special issues that required new legislation.

For one thing, the coordinated federal and local efforts needed to resettle the Indochinese were a strong reminder that the day had passed when thousands of uprooted newcomers could be thrown into society to sink or swim with only the help of the political boss, the employer, or the settlement-house worker. To avoid massive problems, future immigrants would require at least some public assistance with such chores as job-seeking, language training, and health care. They needed the network of social services that Americans now took for granted. So immigration policy could not be set without some consideration of the country's willingness and ability to spend large quantities of public money.

Secondly, the ad hoc international conference that had dealt with the boat people demonstrated that many countries were involved, willingly or not, in dealing with refugees. American immigration programs could not be worked out in a diplomatic vacuum. Foreign policy officials and their considerations would have to play a part.

As a corollary, the question of asylum would need rethinking. Some Americans were troubled with guilt over the revelation that more could have been done to save victims of Hitler during

World War II. Many had a sense of obligation to fleeing anti-Communists the world over, since the United States gave them such robust verbal encouragement. But where did responsibility end? How much room in the annual quotas did refugees deserve as against members of divided families? What, precisely, *was* a refugee in contrast to any other immigrant? And once refugees were admitted, how would the burden of caring for them be fairly shared? And who should have the power to make the needed decisions?

Congress tried to cut some pathways through this thicket in the Refugee Act of 1980. It tried to unify the various relief enactments of the preceding thirty-odd years that had dealt with Poles, Russians, Hungarians, Cubans, Chinese, and Indochinese (with Afghanistanis, Ethiopians, Ugandans, Libyans, and others waiting in the wings). It set up a permanent Office of Refugee Resettlement to work with states in providing refugees with a list of spelled-out entitlements to assistance. (The states contracted for the services; the Federal government picked up the bill for a specified time.) It also created another permanent office, Coordinator of Refugee Affairs. That official's job was to deal with officials in the State Department handling human-rights affairs and to represent the United States before international bodies considering refugee issues.

In addition to making these improvements in administrative machinery, the new law abolished the "seventh preference" quota and set instead a special, separate quota of up to 50,000 refugees annually, which could be exceeded for "grave, humanitarian reasons" by the President in consultation with Congress. (As a tradeoff, the worldwide ceiling was dropped to 270,000, so that in effect the new total ceiling became 320,000 with the possibility of emergency stretching.) Most significantly for future political debate, it accepted as an official definition of a refugee a person who could not return home "because of a well-founded fear of persecution on account of race, religion, nationality, membership in a particular social group, or political opinion."

The law was signed by President Carter, who had strongly supported it, on March 17, 1980. And as if some malign force aimed to show how hard it was to play King Canute and order the waves to reverse themselves, within weeks a new inrush of refugees from Cuba suddenly took place. In mid-April the United States confronted the Mariel boatlift.

It began on an April day when some ten thousand Cubans, unhappy with Castro's new order, swarmed into the grounds of the Peruvian embassy in Havana, demanding asylum and safe conduct out of Cuba. Momentarily outraged and embarrassed, Castro executed a sudden, surprising turnabout. He announced that the dissidents were free to leave if anyone from America wished to bring them out. In fact he would open the port of Mariel, a short distance from the capital, for just that purpose. The news electrified the Cuban-American community. Within days hundreds, even thousands of chartered boats of every size and degree of seaworthiness were making their way across the Florida Strait. Once there, Castro had a surprise for them. They could not take back the friends and relatives awaiting them without agreeing to evacuate other Cubans, picked by Havana, as well. As it turned out, many of these were convicted criminals. The Cuban dictator was not merely ridding himself of dissidents and the discontented, but relieving overcrowding in his jails. As many as 16,000—perhaps more—of those who came had prison records for nonpolitical offenses.

But this was not known in early April, and so the Mariel boatlift went on, overwhelming the U.S. Coast Guard and the newly enacted refugee act. The traffic was illegal and the boat owners subject to heavy fines—which made no difference. By the time Castro closed the exit down at the end of May, a full 125,000 "Marielitos" had poured ashore at Key West and other Florida points, and were being housed (often tumultuously) in temporary camps, while overworked INS officials tried to screen out and recommit the felons.

The Carter administration was caught in a dilemma. Already bedeviled by its inability to free the hostages seized at the embassy in Teheran the preceding November, it risked looking even more inept if it could not control how many Cubans, and of what kind, could land on American soil. And yet . . . to cut off the flow by a naval blockade would mean turning America's back on 125,000 people running away from communism, a clear propaganda triumph for the other side. So the President chose to extend a welcome to the refugees, in his words, with open heart and open arms, and to invoke his executive discretion to admit all 125,000 as lawful resident aliens. The decision carried some political advantage in South Florida's Cuban community, but that was offset by the bitter resentment of other Floridians and

Americans generally, convinced that they would bear the main burden of providing additional social workers and policemen to handle Castro's wretched refuse. The perception was scarcely fair. The majority of Marielitos quickly joined their thriving compatriots in Miami and other heavily Cuban-American cities, but so indeed did some of the criminals who escaped the hasty screening of U.S. authorities.

Scarcely had the furor over Mariel died down when a new Caribbean refugee problem claimed public attention. As many as several hundred Haitians a week were coming ashore on Florida beaches after hazardous small-boat journeys. They claimed the same refugee status as the Cubans, but were decidedly not welcomed with open arms and hearts. Haiti, under the rule of Jean-Claude "Baby Doc" Duvalier, was not only desperately impoverished—four out of five residents earning under $500 a year and unemployment rates of fifty percent in its capital city— it was indubitably a police state. Yet it was not Communist, and therefore, by the canons of American foreign policy, it was part of the "free world." The INS position, in consequence, was that the Haitians did not merit *political* asylum. They were "economic refugees," and, however pitiable their plight, if they came ashore without proper papers, they must be sent back. Vainly the Haitians insisted that the mere act of departure made them lawbreakers in Duvalier's eyes and that they would be terribly punished on their return.

Knowledgeable or lucky Haitians learned that they could apply for hearings on their asylum petitions, and during the waiting period many of them, released on parole, simply disappeared into Miami's Haitian community. As many as fifty thousand of them were there, fighting for such bottom-rung jobs as were open to the illiterate and unskilled. The INS countered thereafter by keeping Haitian asylum applicants in detention camps. Haitian and civil liberties organizations charged that the INS likewise put unfair and dishonest pressures on the would-be asylees to return "voluntarily." Twice Federal judges investigated these complaints and forced the INS to rehear thousands of cases in which there had been civil rights abuses. They also forced the INS to release its unwilling "guests."

The whole episode foreshadowed another conflict of the early 1980s involving asylum claimants from El Salvador. The army-backed government there had a long track record of intimidat-

316

ing, kidnapping, and killing its suspected opponents. But the Reagan administration, supporting the regime against a left-wing insurrection, insisted that there was a "new" El Salvador making substantial progress in democracy and human rights. So the INS denied asylum to the Salvadorans as well, using the same arguments as against the Haitians: it was economic hardship, not terror, that drove them out, and as one INS official put it: "If we're going to let the Haitians in because they're hungry, then how can we stop the people from India and China from coming in?"

A number of Americans, especially in the liberal churches, were so outraged that the United States was forcing Salvadorans back to what they saw as certain punishment that they invoked the age-old tradition of the church as sanctuary. They organized an underground railroad for smuggling Salvadoran refugees to safety in American cities. Late in 1985 several workers in the sanctuary movement were unearthed by police, tried, and sentenced to jail. It was a sign of rising national passions over the asylum issue, brewed in Southeast Asia and then heated further by events in Central America.

M ost of the strong feelings, however, did not run in favor of admitting more refugees. The refugee crises of 1980 actually turned attention to another tangle, popularly assumed to be the worst of all—illegal immigration. The heaviest immigrant inflow was coming from America's next-door neighbor, Mexico, and much of it was unauthorized.

There was ample reason for Mexicans to migrate, as there had been for a century past. Despite substantial progress (some from an oil boom in the seventies, but much on borrowed capital), Mexico was still impoverished. In the countryside, malnutrition, disease, and illiteracy still cut deep into life expectancy and hopes of improvement. And a swelling population—from under twenty million in 1945 to seventy-two million in 1980 and rising—far outstripped the ability of the cities to provide jobs. Even those lucky enough to find work in a place like overcrowded Mexico City could earn only the equivalent of four U.S. dollars a day. In America, that much could be earned in an hour, picking crops, keeping house, or working in a processing plant.

Legal migration was almost impossible, because the 20,000-per-country annual limit had Mexican visa applicants backed up

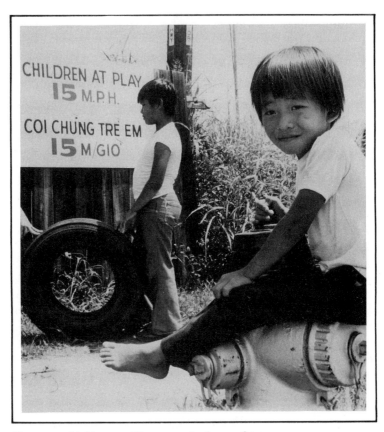

Five-year-old Nguyen Giang, perched on a fire hydrant, poses for the camera in 1977 outside the largest Vietnamese settlement in the United States, located in East New Orleans. The CHILDREN AT PLAY sign warns motorists in two languages, English and Vietnamese. *(Wide World)*

on waiting lists years long. But illegal entry remained temptingly easy. Temporary entry permits, so-called "green cards," could be forged or duplicated or one could slip across unpatrolled roads at night. There were even specialists, known as coyotes who would take whole parties across and provide American documents and job leads for fees of as much as $10,000. They "serviced" both Mexicans and other entry-seeking Latin American nationals who could meet their price.

The overworked INS and its border patrol of only about 3,500 agents could not run serious document inspections on thousands of vacationers, shoppers, and visitors who crossed daily at every legitimate checkpoint. Nor could it patrol every mile of unfenced boundary. INS agents could and did make constant sweeps in Mexican-American neighborhoods and in the kinds of places where illegal aliens (or, to use a less prejudicial term that liberals perferred, undocumented aliens) might be working. But when they did flush out unauthorized entrants, they could do nothing but ship them back across the border, knowing that many would return again and again.

Awareness of growth in the number of the undocumented came when the statistics of INS "apprehensions" began to rise. In the whole decade from 1961 to 1970 there were 1.6 million of them. It was 8.3 million for 1971–80, with a high of 1.07 million in 1979. In 1983, a record was set with 1,248,000. Many of those seized and reported might be repeaters. Or, alternatively, they might be only a fraction of those who got through the barricades.

That was the most maddening aspect of the problem. No one knew or could know the exact figures. While most of the undocumented aliens in the country were correctly presumed to be poor Mexicans, a large number were "visa-abusers." These were people from anywhere in the world, fluent and affluent enough to convince American consuls abroad that they were coming to the United States only temporarily to study or do business, who would then overstay their temporary visas and never return home. It was impossible to keep track of them; in 1980 alone, twelve million such temporary visas were issued. The INS was embarrassed in that year when President Carter ordered the deportation of Iranians in the U.S., only to learn that they could be neither counted nor located accurately.

What was the total number of illegal aliens in the United States in the early 1980s? To answer was like trying to estimate the number of drops in a flowing stream. Educated guesses ranged between three million and six million, with something on the order of another 250,000 to 500,000 arriving annually. The figure was inflated or diminished in political debates, depending on whether the speaker wanted to see a large problem or a small one.

Whatever the actual number of undocumented aliens, there was a widespread—or at least widely encouraged—anxiety about something that critics of immigration policy were calling a "silent invasion." The term had an appeal to many groups. In a sputtering U.S. economy that was losing ground in manufacturing to foreign competitors, organized labor was on the defensive. Idled union members, faced with disadvantageous contracts and with plant closings, were readily persuaded that they were victims of a labor surplus caused by "cheap" immigrant workers, and all the more so when the U.S. unemployment rate briefly rose to nearly 11 percent during a 1983–84 recession before settling back to 7.5 percent.

There was likewise a conviction among taxpaying Americans that the "illegals" were heavy users of welfare, food stamps, clinics, unemployment benefits, and other costly social services. Like the "coolie labor" theme, this was an updated refrain from the turn of the century. In the 1980s, however, it had added appeal, for some localities did bear a heavy service load. The new immigrants tended to concentrate heavily in a few metropolitan areas like Miami, Los Angeles, Houston, or New York. Furthermore, if even legal Mexican immigrants were on the whole poorer than other new arrivals, as the statistics showed they were, then presumably the "illegal" Mexicans were more so, and more of a public burden.

Venerable nativist stereotypes also got renewed currency from the special circumstances of the 1980s. For one thing, consciousness of the world's population explosion and finite resources bred a general sense that we were all living on a crowded planet and there was less to share with strangers. For another, the failure of the swiftly increasing number of Hispanics—whether poor Mexicans and Puerto Ricans or well-off Cubans, Colombians, Peruvians, and Venezuelans—to adopt English as quickly as other immigrants was a growing irritant

:, black and white, but especially
..nore often in direct competition with

..5, the *first* language of eight million Amer-
..argest single non-English-speaking bloc. The
..obably even larger, for it was based on census
..that undocumented Hispanics rarely answered for
..overy. In a city like Miami (which elected its first
..Cuba mayor in 1985) it had become difficult to find
..yment in many retail establishments unless one could
..k Spanish with the customers. Most large American cities
..d a Spanish-language newspaper, which was an old immigrant
custom—but a new wrinkle was provided by 120 Spanish radio
stations around the nation and seventeen Spanish TV channels
linked in a network that also beamed news and other programs
from Mexico into millions of homes. On public transit lines in
major cities one could see advertisements in Spanish lining the
walls, touting fast-food chains, beer, wine, soft drinks, cold
remedies, and whatever was deemed marketable to Hispanics. This Spanish-language "explosion" was something new
in America's experience with newcomers and proved a long-run
irritant and focus of debate. In the 1970s, when civil rights cultural pluralism and the celebration of ethnicity were temporarily
in high favor, courts and legislatures had interpreted anti-
discrimination statutes in such a way as to require public agencies to print ballots, voting instructions, application forms, information brochures, and other such materials in the most
common minority language, which, in most cases, was Spanish.
So Hispanic immigrants had fewer incentives to learn English
than did earlier arrivals.

In addition, in 1968 Congress had passed a Bilingual Education Act to assist immigrant schoolchildren in their adjustment
to American life by offering them instruction in their own
tongue until they could catch up with native-born children. In an
even more hospitable accommodation to cultural diversity, in
1974 the act was broadened to offer instruction in many advanced subjects in the students' native tongue rather than clearly
identifying English as a primary language of instruction, to be
mastered as quickly as possible and thereafter used exclusively.
There was even talk of self-consciously promoting the use of
two languages (primarily Spanish and English) by all school-

children, Hispanic and "Anglo" alike—a totally novel co
most Americans.

The purpose of the legislation was to smooth the pa
assimilation, and it was possible to argue that Hispanics
actually learning to pursue the American life-style in their o
tongue. But by the eighties many Americans began to belie
that since a common language was indispensable to a healthy an
unified culture, the adoption of English was *the* fundamental test
of adaptation, and Hispanics alone were unwilling or unable to
pass it. "If the Mexican language [sic] and Mexican customs are
so important to these people," wrote one woman to a Corpus
Christi newspaper after local Chicano refinery workers protested
a rule against speaking Spanish on the job, "perhaps if they lived
in Mexico they would be happier." The message was: Anglicize
or exit!

The concern with illegal immigration therefore became the
carrier for a number of anxious and nativistic—particularly anti-
Hispanic—feelings, although each contention of the critics was
disputable:

—Was America becoming overcrowded? Not necessarily; in
fact, some experts claimed, the American birthrate was in decline after the baby boom of the 1940s and 1950s, and since a
certain amount of population growth was necessary to keep the
economy from stagnating, immigration should be moderately
encouraged. Actually, immigration accounted for less than one
quarter of the total American population growth from 1970 to
1980, as against forty percent in the 1900–1910 period. America
might, some said, easily accept half a million immigrants a year
and, if the national fertility rate stayed the same, reach a manageable population of only 274 million by 2050.

—Not enough jobs to go around? Again, some demographers
asserted that by the early twenty-first century, when the baby-
boom generation had retired, there would not be enough
American-born children to fill their places in the work force.
Moreover, both legal and illegal immigrants spent money in
America and thereby created jobs. And finally, there was evidence that the "illegals," bred to a work-or-starve ethic, took
primarily low-level jobs (busboys, kitchen help, laundry work,
fish cleaning, chicken plucking) that Americans simply would
not fill when welfare or other alternatives were available. Said
one employer: "American citizens don't want to work for the

minimum wage. . . . They simply can't get by on three dollars and thirty-five cents an hour." Said another: "I'd like to hire Americans, but when you're in a bind, you hire who you can."

—Did the illegals drain the public treasury? It was widely asserted so, especially after a Supreme Court decision in 1982 that required Texas to furnish free public education to all alien children, stating that to do otherwise would deny their rights and create a "sub-class of illiterates within our boundaries." But a closer look at the facts revealed ambiguities. Thousands of the undocumented paid state and local excise taxes on the food and drink and clothing that they bought; paid real estate taxes in the rents they handed over to landlords; paid income taxes in the form of payroll deductions. Yet few dared to claim refunds for fear of attracting the attention of the authorities. For the same reason, except in dire medical emergencies, they were reluctant to go anywhere in search of help or benefits if it meant answering questions about themselves. All in all, according to some analysts, the undocumented immigrants, living essentially an underground existence, probably took less out of the economy than they paid in. And because they were often illiterate and fearful of asserting their rights, they were subject to exploitation by unscrupulous employers and merchants, and occasional brutality by overzealous Border Patrol officers. In all, more sinned against than sinning.

D espite such arguments, the widespread perception of an immigration policy in disarray spurred Congress and two successive Presidents to action. Immigration bills were passed by the House but defeated in the Senate in 1972 and 1973. In 1977 President Carter offered proposals for reform, which Congress buried. But in 1978 Congress itself sponsored the most professional and far-reaching study of the entire problem in years by appointing a joint, bipartisan Select Commission on Immigration and Refugee Policy. It was chaired by Notre Dame's respected president, the Reverend Father Theodore Hesburgh, and its staff director, Lawrence Fuchs, was a recognized authority on immigration history who taught at Brandeis. The Select Commission had money to spend on travel and hearings, and it collated all the existing information and issued its own recommendations early in 1981. By that time the Reagan administration was just settling in, and soon thereafter it submitted yet another reform plan of its own.

All of these proposals were knit by common threads. Uniformly, they faced two intractable questions. First, how could the millions of undocumented aliens already present possibly be located and expelled? And second, how could the door be closed effectively on future unauthorized entrants? All of them emerged with a twofold compromise answer.

With regard to the "illegals" who had already established themselves in American life, the best thing to do was to accept reality and give them a chance to emerge from the shadows and apply to be legalized. As Doris Meissner, the acting INS Commissioner in 1982, would put it in testimony before Congress, the United States had "neither the resources, the capability nor the desire to uproot and deport millions of illegal aliens, many of whom have become integral members of their communities."

And as for preventing future violations, the various plans all recognized that so long as illegals could find jobs in America, they would go on challenging and evading U.S. border guards. The answer was not to seal the entire border but to cut off the jobs at the source by forbidding employers, under threat of significant penalties, to hire workers who could not prove that they were in the country legally.

These were the twin pillars of the gathering immigration-reform consensus—legalization without penalties of the undocumented already long on the scene if they applied (popularly known as amnesty) and employer sanctions. Beyond that there were some other points of agreement. A large backlog of legal visa applicants had to be cleared up, and the country could afford to be more generous and raise legal ceilings, at least modestly. Refugees should continue to be dealt with outside the normal ceilings, as the 1980 act provided. Some provision should be made for the temporary sojourn, each year, of workers who were needed to fill short-term labor vacuums, particularly in crop harvesting. Finally, the INS and the Border Patrol should be better funded and managed. The Select Commission had bluntly described the INS as "an inbred, mismanaged and sometimes corrupt agency."

In all, there was agreement that limits on total immigration would always remain in place. In the words of the Select Commission's report, "As important as immigration has been and remains to our country, it is no longer possible to say as George

A group of 269 immigrants takes an oath of citizenship aboard the battleship *USS Massachusetts* at Fall River in 1976. The countries from which they emigrated include Portugal, Canada, Great Britain, Poland, Ireland, Japan, China, and Korea. *(Wide World)*

Washington did that we welcome all of the oppressed of the world. . . . The United States of America—no matter how powerful and idealistic—cannot by itself solve the problems of world migration." But compassion, tradition, and self-interest dictated that the front door to legal immigration should always remain at least partly ajar, while the back door to illegal entry must be firmly shut.

In the 97th Congress (1982–83), immigration reform was brought to the floor by Senator Alan Simpson (R) of Wyoming and Representative Roman Mazzoli (D) of Kentucky. The bill they introduced early in 1982 contained provisions for amnesty to aliens who had been continuously in residence since the end of 1977; for employer sanctions; for an overall annual legal ceiling of 425,000 (not including refugees); for an expansion of an already existing guest-worker program called H-2 to a maximum of 50,000 per year; and for various other provisions including a commitment to develop, within the short-run future, some kind of tamper-proof identifying document for lawful aliens to show to employers.

In the hearings and the voting on the Simpson-Mazzoli bill as it moved through the legislative process, the shape of the alliances for and against it clearly emerged. They were fascinatingly complex and contradictory, revealing that the immigration problem was enmeshed with many other issues and cut across traditional political lines.

Supporters included organized labor, environmental groups anxious to control population growth, liberals who liked the practical humanitarianism of the amnesty provision—and, incongruously side-by-side with them, conservatives and nativists eager to halt the presumed inundation of non-English-speaking welfare cheats.

Opponents were equally diversified. Chief among them were spokesmen for organized Hispanic groups like the Mexican American Legal Defense Fund. MALDEF believed that employers would play it safe under the proposed law and automatically reject any Hispanic-looking or Hispanic-sounding job applicant. Then there were employers' associations and business groups that were equally unhappy with Simpson-Mazzoli, some because they liked having a constant supply of cheap, hardworking, and tractable immigrant labor, but some legitimately worried that employers taken in by false identification papers could be unfairly penalized. The State Department was troubled because the Mexican government made clear its extreme unhappiness with the bill. (Mexico preferred a negotiated solution of some kind, such as a joint effort to match unemployed Mexican nationals with labor-seeking American bosses.) The INS was appalled at the job it would face in processing millions of new applications for legal status from those receiving amnesty. Civil libertarians were cool to the idea of requiring anyone living in America to carry and produce an I.D. card in order to demonstrate his or her right to a job; it smacked of authoritarianism. And some conservatives, like North Carolina's Senator Jesse Helms, were outraged at the very idea of amnesty to "lawbreakers." They called it one more assault by permissiveness on the fabric of American values.

Finally, there were numerous critics who simply felt that if the INS could not enforce existing immigration laws, it could not possibly administer new ones. How would it find and prosecute the guilty violators among bosses and workers except through the same sweeps and raids that had already proved ineffective? They wanted a stronger law or none at all.

The opposing forces were so well balanced that an effective consensus for legislation was almost impossible to achieve. The Simpson-Mazzoli measure passed the Senate in 1982, but did not reach the House floor before the 97th Congress expired. In 1984 it was approved by both Senate and House in slightly differing versions, but died in conference. Then, in the waning days of 1986 and of the 99th Congress, after a long period of quiescence, there was a sudden renewal of the sense that some kind of action on immigration was urgent. An immigration law was passed and signed that embodied the two major elements of the original Simpson-Mazzoli proposal— an amnesty for all undocumented aliens who could prove continuous residence in the U.S. from January 1, 1982 onward, and a set of escalating fines for employers who knowingly hired "illegals." As 1987 began, the country waited to see how the new measure would be implemented and what its impact would be.

In a sense, the battle over Simpson-Mazzoli was a prolongation of a debate that had gone on from America's beginnings. What was partly at stake was America's self-image, its proclaimed national purpose. How many "new Americans" should we welcome from abroad, and who should they be? The case for being the world's asylum was a powerful one. But so was the argument that as a people we also had responsibilities to those who came before and struggled to create a patrimony for their descendants that should not be squandered. At some point, this line of thinking ran, those of us already on the American scene would have to learn to protect our own.

But at what point? When should we close the door on people whose needs and whose potential contributions are as great as those of our own forefathers? The question was not asked with any urgency when our frontiers were wide open and there was land, bread, and work for all. Only in the 1920s, when there was a perception that the good old days had passed, did restrictionism enjoy a real triumph. Happily, the racist aspects of the 1924 law were overthrown after only four decades, but the principle of restriction remained, and the old fears were kindled anew in the 1970s, when Americans lost their conviction of global omnipotence and some of their faith in the total superiority of their way of life. Our sense of the urgency of the "immigration problem" waxes and wanes with our general self-confidence as a people.

What we do about immigration may actually be less than we collectively desire. The number of would-be new Americans is partly dependent on the global economy. The Great Depression reduced immigration even below the quotas of the 1924 act. When there are no jobs in America, even the oppressed of other lands stay home or look elsewhere for escape. But when, in piping times, America's standard of living gleams before the eyes of the wretched of the earth, millions will try to enter the gates, legally if they can, but by stealth or fraud if they must. The amount of control that can be exerted in this nation of free traditions is limited. Some suggest that if we want to keep immigrants out, we must work with their governments to give them incentives to stay home.

And meanwhile, through all the changes of policy, the historic leaven of immigration will continue to work. The natural increase of those who make it to America, plus the nation's pluralist politics, guarantee eventual assimilation. The grandchildren and great-grandchildren of yesterday's despised Southern and Eastern Europeans are hard to distinguish from the grandchildren and great-grandchildren of 1924's restrictionists. In major American cities everywhere today, Asians and Hispanics, whatever language they speak or traditions they preserve at home, melt along with "Anglos" into a global culture, a service economy, an urban landscape, a welfare state.

It cannot be otherwise. The young see to that. A Laotian refugee tells a writer in the 1980s:

> The Afghan remembers his beautiful mountains, and the Lao remembers his green rice fields, and at night they dream of them, and they hear the shepherd's flute and the boatman's song and they see their kinfolk and their friends that they left behind. With the children, of course, it is different. They will become Americans very quickly. Once they start to school, you can almost see it happening before your eyes.

It is happening all the time. And when those children are grown, they, as Americans, may wonder about how wide to open the door to other applicants from who knows where. But they are unlikely ever to shut it totally, for then America would not be America. The debate over whom we should welcome and how many goes on through the generations, and so long as it goes on with civility, it is a good thing, for it is life-giving. Immigration is one of those perennial questions like civil rights or the limits of government, through which, by answering them over and over again, we Americans define ourselves.

About the Author

Bernard A. Weisberger, born in 1922 in Hudson, New York, and educated at Columbia University and the University of Chicago, is a professor, writer, editor, and consultant for radio and television programs. He has written some fourteen books, including *Reporters for the Union, They Gathered at the River, The American Newspaperman, Pathways to the Present, Cold War, Cold Peace,* and most recently, the English language version of *Statue of Liberty: The First Hundred Years.* He has taught at many colleges and universities, including Vassar, the University of Chicago, New York University, and the University of Rochester. From 1981–1983, he served as a historical consultant and writer for Bill Moyers' *A Walk Through the 20th Century,* an award-winning PBS television series.

Bernard A. Weisberger now lives in Elizaville, New York.

Index

Evarts, William M., 190

Fairchild, Henry Pratt, 210
Federalists, 105–7, 151
Fermi, Enrico, 264–65
Fermi, Laura, 257, 265
Fernandez, Manuel, 298
Fifteenth Amendment, 187, 199, 202
Filipinos, 310, 311
Fillmore, Millard, 156
Fisk (black academy), 202
Fiske, John, 214
Fitzgerald, F. Scott, 7
Flexner, Abraham, 259
Follen, Paul, 122
Foran Act (1885), 187
Force Bill (1890), 203
Ford, Gerald, 287
Foreign Policy Association, 259
Fortune, T. Thomas, 204
Fourteenth Amendment, 199, 203
Francesco (brig), 166
Franklin, Benjamin, 85, 100, 250
Frank Steele (steamer), 124
Franz Josef, Emperor, 163, 167
Frazier, E. Franklin, 247
Freedmen's Bureau, 200
French, 137, 141, 142, 157
French and Indian War, 88, 92, 94
French Revolution, 131
Freud, Sigmund, 233
Fronde, War of the, 16
Fry, Varian, 259–60
Fuchs, Lawrence, 323
Furcolo, Foster, 243

Galbraith, John Kenneth, 216
Galileo, 15
Gamow, George, 264
Gansevoort, Peter, 93
Garibaldi, Giuseppe, 157, 217
Garvey, Marcus, 250–52
Gates, Sir Thomas, 50
Gay Nineties, 211
Geary Act (1892), 191
Gentleman's Agreement (1908), 193
George, James Z., 203
George III, King, 86, 89, 98
George V, King, 229
Georgia, 35, 47–48, 57
German(s), 60, 112, 137, 174; and
   Catholic Church, 141, 142, 144–45;
   in Civil War, 157; contributions of,
   to American life, 130–31; emigra-
   tion of, to America, 121–24;

hostility toward, 228–29; and in-
   dentured servants, 101;
   Lutheranism, 138–39; merging of,
   into American society, 235; in
   Minnesota, 124; in nonfarm labor,
   176; in Pennsylvania, 61–67, 89–90;
   in politics, 145; in Texas, 123; treat-
   ment of, during WWII, 267;
   urbanization of, 116; in War for
   Independence, 88–94; well-known,
   in America, 125–30, 132
Germania Orchestra, 130
German Land Association of Chi-
   cago, 124
German Reformed Church, 63
Gerry, Elbridge, 100, 104
Gibbons, James, 144
Gilded Age, 195
Giovannitti, Arturo, 236
Glorious Revolution (1688), 37, 38,
   68
Goebbels, Joseph Paul, 257
Goldman, Eric, 216
Gomez, Mordecai, 74
Gompers, Samuel, 219
Grady, Henry W., 202
Grant, Madison, *The Passing of the
   Great Race,* 228
Grant, Percy Stickney, 210
Grant, Ulysses, 128, 197
Great Depression, 231, 248–50, 261,
   282, 287, 328
Great Northern Railroad, 173
Greeks, 216, 277, 306
"Green cards," 319
Gropius, Walter, 264
Grosz, George, 264
Guerra, Manuel, 286
Gustavus Adolphus, King (Sweden),
   28
Gutierrez, Jesus, 298
Gutierrez, Raul, 298

Haber, Fritz, 257
Haitians, 305, 316, 317
Halle, Hiram, 258
Hamburg Company, 15
Hamilton, Alexander, 90, 105
Hampton Institute (Virginia), 202,
   204–5
Hancock, John, 98
Handlin, Oscar, 120, 253, 296
Hanna, Edward J., 282
Hanna, Marcus A., 174

Locke, Alain, 247
Locke, John, 15
Lodge, Henry Cabot, 203, 214, 225
Logan, James, 71
London Company, 48, 49, 50, 51
Louis XIV, 15, 37, 75, 94, 98
Louis Napoleon, 127
Louis Philippe, King, 127
Lubell, Samuel, 240–41
Lucena, Abraham de, 74
Lutherans, 63, 89, 138–39

Macaulay, Thomas Babington, 127
McCarran, Pat, 271, 273
McCarran-Walter Immigration and
    Nationality Act (1952), 269–71,
    273, 283, 301
McCloskey, George, 143
McCloskey, John, 143, 144, 150
McCloskey, Patrick, 143
McGrath, J. Howard, 243
McKay, Claude, 247
McKinley, William, 128, 224
MacLeish, Archibald, 7
Madison, James, 99–100, 106
Magnuson, Warren G., 267
Mainzer, Adelsverein, 123
Malanescu, Yolanda, 276
Malthus, Thomas R., *Essay on the
    Principle of Population,* 112
Manchester Guardian Weekly, 257
Manhattan Island, purchase of, 29
Mann, Heinrich, 264
Mann, Thomas, 264
Mansa Kankan Musa, 76, 78
Marcus, Jacob R., 72
Mariel boatlift, 314–16
Marranos, 73
Marshall, Thurgood, 253
Maryland, 81, 141
Mary II, Queen, 37
Mason, George, 99
Massachusetts Bay, 47
Massasoit, 56
Matthews, Captain, 82
Mayflower, 45, 55–56, 61
Mayo-Smith, Richmond, 214, 221
Mazzoli, Roman, 326, 327
Meissner, Doris, 324
Meitner, Lise, 264
"Melting-Pot," 102, 181, 221–22, 235,
    286
Mennonites, 63, 172–73
Menocal, Raul G., 298
Mercury (brigantine), 97

Methodists, 138, 197
Metropolitan Museum of Art (New
    York), 157
Metternich, Prince, 122
Mexican(s), 272, 296, 297, 298, 305;
    immigration, 279–89; and Simp-
    son-Mazzoli bill, 327; undocu-
    mented aliens, 305, 317–20
Mexican American Legal Defense
    Fund (MALDEF), 326
Mexican-American Political Action
    (MAPA), 296
Miami Herald, 298
Mies van der Rohe, Ludwig, 264
Milhaud, Darius, 262
Milton, John, 15
Minnesota, Germans in, 124
Minuit, Peter, 28–29
Missouri Synod, 138
Mittelberger, Gottlieb, 63, 66
Modoc Indians, 196
Molek, Peter, 167, 177
Molière, 15
Monk, Maria: *Awful Disclosures of the
    Hôtel Dieu Nunnery of Montreal,*
    152; *Further Disclosures,* 152
Monroe, James, 142
Montcalm, Louis Joseph de, 59
Montezuma, 12
Moon, Sun Myung, 312
Moravians, 63
Moreau de Saint-Méry, Médéric, 107
Morgenthau, Hans J., 264
Morris, Gouverneur, 100–101
Morse, Jedidiah, 106
Mühlenberg, Frederick, 89, 90
Mühlenberg, Heinrich (Henry)
    Melchior, 89, 90–92
Mühlenberg, Peter, 89–90
Mühlenberg family, 88–92, 138
Münch, Friedrich, 122, 125
Murphy, Charles, 150
Museum of Natural History (New
    York), 228
Muskie, Edmund Sixtus, 243, 244
Mussolini, Benito, 257

National Association for the Ad-
    vancement of Colored People, 206,
    246
National Catholic Welfare Con-
    ference, 297, 307; War Relief
    Services of, 259
National Coordinating Committee,
    259

339